Survival

GLOBAL POLITICS AND STRATEGY

Volume 63 Number 3 | June–July ~~~~

T0275248

'The Taliban has fought against the US and the Kabul state for two decades in the face of casualties that would have shattered the morale and recruitment of almost any other army. The Vietnamese communists are the only parallel I can think of.'

Anatol Lieven, An Afghan Tragedy: The Pashtuns, the Taliban and the State, p. 28.

'I must admit to ambivalence about the US withdrawal, knowing that intensified violence will likely follow in its wake. At the same time, the United States' staying would not have alleviated the terrible toll the war already is taking on Afghans, and over the years the US role in the war has been a factor perpetuating the violence, particularly in rural areas.'

Laurel Miller, Biden's Afghanistan Withdrawal: A Verdict on the Limits of American Power, p. 42.

'Younger staffers believed that the president had to embrace the forces of change. Their argument about being on the "right side of history" prevailed … Unfortunately, history has neither a right nor a wrong side, a point reinforced by the subsequent events in Libya and Syria.'

Lawrence Freedman, The Trouble with Regime Change, p. 177.

Survival

GLOBAL POLITICS AND STRATEGY

Volume 63 Number 3 | June–July 2021

Contents

Cover: Brendan Smialowski/AFP via Getty

On the cover
On 14 April 2021, the day he announced the withdrawal of US troops from Afghanistan, US President Joe Biden places a wreath in Arlington National Cemetery in memory of the Americans killed in that country.

On the web
Visit www.iiss.org/publications/survival for brief notices on new books on Europe, Culture and Society, and Latin America.

Survival **editors' blog**
For ideas and commentary from *Survival* editors and contributors, visit www.iiss.org/blogs/survival-blog.

Review Essays

Book Reviews

Closing Argument

Survival
GLOBAL POLITICS AND STRATEGY

The International Institute for Strategic Studies

2121 K Street, NW | Suite 600 | Washington DC 20037 | USA
Tel +1 202 659 1490   Fax +1 202 659 1499   E-mail survival@iiss.org   Web www.iiss.org

Arundel House | 6 Temple Place | London | WC2R 2PG | UK
Tel +44 (0)20 7379 7676   Fax +44 (0)20 7836 3108   E-mail iiss@iiss.org

14th Floor, GBCorp Tower | Bahrain Financial Harbour | Manama | Kingdom of Bahrain
Tel +973 1718 1155   Fax +973 1710 0155   E-mail iiss-middleeast@iiss.org

9 Raffles Place | #49-01 Republic Plaza | Singapore 048619
Tel +65 6499 0055   Fax +65 6499 0059   E-mail iiss-asia@iiss.org

Pariser Platz 6A | 10117 Berlin | Germany
E-mail iiss-europe@iiss.org

Survival Online www.tandfonline.com/survival and www.iiss.org/publications/survival

Aims and Scope *Survival* is one of the world's leading forums for analysis and debate of international and strategic affairs. Shaped by its editors to be both timely and forward thinking, the journal encourages writers to challenge conventional wisdom and bring fresh, often controversial, perspectives to bear on the strategic issues of the moment. With a diverse range of authors, *Survival* aims to be scholarly in depth while vivid, well written and policy-relevant in approach. Through commentary, analytical articles, case studies, forums, review essays, reviews and letters to the editor, the journal promotes lively, critical debate on issues of international politics and strategy.

Editor **Dana Allin**
Managing Editor **Jonathan Stevenson**
Associate Editor **Carolyn West**
Assistant Editor **Jessica Watson**
Production and Cartography **John Buck, Kelly Verity**

Contributing Editors

Ian Bremmer	Toby Dodge	Melissa Griffith	Hanns W. Maull	Steven Simon
Rosa Brooks	Bill Emmott	John L. Harper	Jeffrey Mazo	Angela Stent
David P. Calleo	Mark Fitzpatrick	Matthew Harries	'Funmi Olonisakin	Ray Takeyh
Russell Crandall	John A. Gans, Jr	Erik Jones	Teresita C. Schaffer	David C. Unger
				Lanxin Xiang

Published for the IISS by
Routledge Journals, an imprint of Taylor & Francis, an Informa business.

About the IISS The IISS, a registered charity with offices in Washington, London, Manama and Singapore, is the world's leading authority on political–military conflict. It is the primary independent source of accurate, objective information on international strategic issues. Publications include *The Military Balance*, an annual reference work on each nation's defence capabilities; *Strategic Survey*, an annual review of world affairs; *Survival*, a bimonthly journal on international affairs; *Strategic Comments*, an online analysis of topical issues in international affairs; and the *Adelphi* series of books on issues of international security.

SUBMISSIONS

To submit an article, authors are advised to follow these guidelines:

- *Survival* articles are around 4,000–10,000 words long including endnotes. A word count should be included with a draft.
- All text, including endnotes, should be double-spaced with wide margins.
- Any tables or artwork should be supplied in separate files, ideally not embedded in the document or linked to text around it.
- All *Survival* articles are expected to include endnote references. These should be complete and include first and last names of authors, titles of articles (even from newspapers), place of publication, publisher, exact publication dates, volume and issue number (if from a journal) and page numbers. Web sources should include complete URLs and DOIs if available.
- A summary of up to 150 words should be included with the article. The summary should state the main argument clearly and concisely, not simply say what the article is about.

- A short author's biography of one or two lines should also be included. This information will appear at the foot of the first page of the article.

Please note that *Survival* has a strict policy of listing multiple authors in alphabetical order.

Submissions should be made by email, in Microsoft Word format, to survival@iiss.org. Alternatively, hard copies may be sent to *Survival*, IISS–US, 2121 K Street NW, Suite 801, Washington, DC 20037, USA.

The editorial review process can take up to three months. *Survival*'s acceptance rate for unsolicited manuscripts is less than 20%. *Survival* does not normally provide referees' comments in the event of rejection. Authors are permitted to submit simultaneously elsewhere so long as this is consistent with the policy of the other publication and the Editors of *Survival* are informed of the dual submission.

Readers are encouraged to comment on articles from the previous issue. Letters should be concise, no longer than 750 words and relate directly to the argument or points made in the original article.

ADVERTISING AND PERMISSIONS

For advertising rates and schedules

USA/Canada: The Advertising Manager, Taylor & Francis Inc., 530 Walnut Street, Suite 850, Philadelphia, PA 19106, USA Tel +1 (800) 354 1420 Fax +1 (215) 207 0050.

UK/Europe/Rest of World: The Advertising Manager, Routledge Journals, Taylor & Francis, 4 Park Square, Milton Park, Abingdon, Oxfordshire OX14 4RN, UK Tel +44 (0) 207 017 6000 Fax +44 (0) 207 017 6336.

SUBSCRIPTIONS

Survival is published bimonthly in February, April, June, August, October and December by Routledge Journals, an imprint of Taylor & Francis, an Informa Business.

Annual Subscription 2021

	UK, RoI	US, Canada Mexico	Europe	Rest of world
Individual	£172	$290	€ 233	$290
Institution (print and online)	£620	$1,085	€ 909	$1,142
Institution (online only)	£527	$922	€ 773	$971

Taylor & Francis has a flexible approach to subscriptions, enabling us to match individual libraries' requirements. This journal is available via a traditional institutional subscription (either print with online access, or online only at a discount) or as part of our libraries, subject collections or archives. For more information on our sales packages please visit http://www.tandfonline.com/page/librarians.

All current institutional subscriptions include online access for any number of concurrent users across a local area network to the currently available backfile and articles posted online ahead of publication.

Subscriptions purchased at the personal rate are strictly for personal, non-commercial use only. The reselling of personal subscriptions is prohibited. Personal subscriptions must be purchased with a personal cheque or credit card. Proof of personal status may be requested.

Dollar rates apply to all subscribers outside Europe. Euro rates apply to all subscribers in Europe, except the UK and the Republic of Ireland where the pound sterling rate applies. If you are unsure which rate applies to you please contact Customer Services in the UK. All subscriptions are payable in advance and all rates include postage. Journals are sent by air to the USA, Canada, Mexico, India, Japan and Australasia. Subscriptions are entered on an annual basis, i.e. January to December. Payment may be made by sterling cheque, dollar cheque, euro cheque, international money order, National Giro or credit cards (Amex, Visa and Mastercard).

Survival (USPS 013095) is published bimonthly (in Feb, Apr, Jun, Aug, Oct and Dec) by Routledge Journals, Taylor & Francis, 4 Park Square, Milton Park, Abingdon, OX14 4RN, United Kingdom.

The US annual subscription price is $1,023. Airfreight and mailing in the USA by agent named WN Shipping USA, 156-15, 146th Avenue, 2nd Floor, Jamaica, NY 11434, USA. Periodicals postage paid at Jamaica NY 11431.

US Postmaster: Send address changes to Survival, C/O Air Business Ltd / 156-15 146th Avenue, Jamaica, New York, NY11434.

Subscription records are maintained at Taylor & Francis Group, 4 Park Square, Milton Park, Abingdon, OX14 4RN, United Kingdom.

ORDERING INFORMATION

Please contact your local Customer Service Department to take out a subscription to the Journal: **USA, Canada:** Taylor & Francis, Inc., 530 Walnut Street, Suite 850, Philadelphia, PA 19106, USA. Tel: +1 800 354 1420; Fax: +1 215 207 0050. **UK/Europe/Rest of World:** T&F Customer Services, Informa UK Ltd, Sheepen Place, Colchester, Essex, CO3 3LP, United Kingdom. Tel: +44 (0) 20 7017 5544; Fax: +44 (0) 20 7017 5198; Email: subscriptions@tandf.co.uk.

Back issues: Taylor & Francis retains a two-year back issue stock of journals. Older volumes are held by our official stockists: Periodicals Service Company, 351 Fairview Ave., Suite 300, Hudson, New York 12534, USA to whom all orders and enquiries should be addressed. *Tel* +1 518 537 4700 *Fax* +1 518 537 5899 *e-mail* psc@periodicals.com *web* http://www.periodicals.com/tandf.html.

The International Institute for Strategic Studies (IISS) and our publisher Taylor & Francis make every effort to ensure the accuracy of all the information (the "Content") contained in our publications. However, the IISS and our publisher Taylor & Francis, our agents, and our licensors make no representations or warranties whatsoever as to the accuracy, completeness, or suitability for any purpose of the Content. Any opinions and views expressed in this publication are the opinions and views of the authors, and are not the views of or endorsed by the IISS and our publisher Taylor & Francis. The accuracy of the Content should not be relied upon and should be independently verified with primary sources of information. The IISS and our publisher Taylor & Francis shall not be liable for any losses, actions, claims, proceedings, demands, costs, expenses, damages, and other liabilities whatsoever or howsoever caused arising directly or indirectly in connection with, in relation to or arising out of the use of the Content. Terms & Conditions of access and use can be found at http://www.tandfonline.com/page/terms-and-conditions.

The issue date is June–July 2021.

The print edition of this journal is printed on ANSI-conforming acid-free paper.

An Afghan Tragedy: The Pashtuns, the Taliban and the State

Anatol Lieven

It is an old cliché that the Pashtun highlands of Afghanistan and Pakistan are highly resistant to state authority, and old masters of 'the art of not being governed' (to use James Scott's phrase).[1] Like so many clichés, this has a real basis in historical fact. The old name 'Yaghistan' (the land of lawlessness, rebellion or dissent)[2] was given to them by the people of the region, not by Western observers. This name, and what it indicates, also corresponds very closely to patterns in other Muslim tribal regions, first systematically analysed by Ibn Khaldun in the fourteenth century CE in the Maghreb.

As an index of the Afghan state's failure to make its society 'legible' (in another phrase of Scott's), it may be noted that in the whole of modern Afghan history there has never been a census that could be regarded as remotely reliable. As for Max Weber's classic definition of a state as 'a human community that (successfully) claims the monopoly of the legitimate use of physical force within a given territory',[3] that has never been true of Afghanistan. Even when the Afghan state was at its strongest, local communities insisted, usually successfully, on keeping rifles, on conducting limited armed disputes with other kinship groups, and on executing their own members who violated traditional community norms.

Only in the late 1940s, as a result of the import of modern tanks and aircraft, did the Afghan state army become strong enough to defeat a general

Anatol Lieven is a professor at Georgetown University in Qatar and a senior fellow of the Quincy Institute for Responsible Statecraft in Washington DC. His most recent book is *Climate Change and the Nation State: The Realist Case* (Penguin Books, updated 2021).

Survival | vol. 63 no. 3 | June–July 2021 | pp. 7–36   https://doi.org/10.1080/00396338.2021.1930403

tribal uprising – and that superiority lasted a bare 30 years. It collapsed with the anti-communist revolts and army mutinies of the late 1970s, and since then, no Afghan state – not even the Taliban, which came closest – has successfully possessed a monopoly of organised armed force across the whole of Afghanistan.[4]

This basic truth obscures an important nuance, however. The Pashtun tribes have not been categorically hostile to state authority as such; after all, Pashtun tribes created the kingdom of Afghanistan in the first place, and most rural Pashtuns accepted Taliban rule in the 1990s willingly enough. Rather, they have been hostile to three kinds of government: those lacking traditional or religious legitimacy; those which force them to pay too many taxes; and those which try rapidly to change their lives, their society and their traditions. In the traditional Pashtun tribal view, the legitimate role of the state, though essential, is also highly limited. Apart from leading the people against invaders, it is to judge tribal disputes, and thereby prevent these disputes from creating a state of permanent warfare.[5] Given the traditional omnipresence of weapons in Pashtun society, and the cultural obsession with honour and prestige, journalist Anand Gopal has observed that 'the role of dispute resolution in Pashtun society cannot be emphasised enough … In post-2001 Kandahar, the Taliban's judicial services became one of the key advantages that the movement had over the state.'[6]

The Pashtun tragedy lies in the fact that in practice, this rejection of state interference has usually amounted to a rejection of the modernising state as such, since modernising states need to raise taxes to pay for development, find it very hard to base themselves on tradition, and by definition have to set out to change society.

Scott, as an anarchist, sympathises unconditionally with the hill peoples of Southeast Asia in their flight from and resistance to local states. The melancholy history of Afghanistan, by contrast, would suggest that the only thing worse than having a state is not having a state; and indeed, this tragic dilemma is summed up in a very old Pashtun proverb: 'feuding ate up the mountains, and taxes ate up the plains'.[7]

The great value of Scott's approach is that it reminds us of something that Western societies have long forgotten, and that the vast majority of the

Western 'experts' who tried (or pretended) to develop Afghanistan after 2001 simply could not comprehend (as was probably true also of their Soviet equivalents 20 years earlier): the intense nastiness of most states in history, especially in their formative stages. As a famous nineteenth-century British-Indian policeman wrote of the history of South Asia in general:

> There has seldom been any idea of reciprocity, of duties and rights, between the governor and the governed ... For in India, the difference between the army of a prince and the gang of a robber was, in the general estimation of the people, only in degree – they were both driving an 'imperial trade', a *padshahi kam*.[8]

In other words, if Pashtuns have often revolted against the Afghan state (whether foreign-backed or purely indigenous), they have often had good reasons to.

There is, however, a reciprocal relationship between state nastiness and tribal resistance. It takes a great deal of nastiness (or at least the threat of it) to persuade tribes to pay taxes, but without taxes, what is the state? Either an impotent shadow, or a dependency of some foreign state and its subsidies. Both of these fates have befallen Afghanistan repeatedly over the past 200 years.

Key to the West's failure successfully to build a new order in Afghanistan after 2001 was not just an inability to understand the historic alienation of ordinary Afghans in general, and Pashtuns in particular, from 'their' state, but also a refusal to recognise that, given the miserable history and eventual collapse of Afghan states, the Taliban may have been the best state-building option left, at least as far as rural Pashtuns were concerned. Not by any means a good option – just better than all the others.

The weakness of Pashtun nationalism

The standard way in which modernising states in conservative societies have been able to legitimise their authority to conduct radical reforms has been through nationalism (this has also been true in many communist societies, albeit in a somewhat veiled way) – by arguing that the reforms are essential to strengthen the nation against its enemies. The radical reforms of the Meiji era in Japan and of Mustafa Kemal Ataturk in Turkey are classic examples of this. Given that Afghanistan was founded by a Pashtun dynasty and named after the Persian word for Pashtuns – and embodies Pashtun national hopes, elements of Pashtun identity and traditions of Pashtun resistance to British imperial conquest – Pashtun nationalism would seem a natural course for modern Afghan states to have pursued; and indeed, under the government of Sardar Daud Khan (prime minister, 1953–63; president, 1973–78), the Afghan state did attempt to do this.

The strategy foundered, however, on several local realities. In the first place, the conquests of the Sikhs and the British meant that for almost 200 years, a majority of ethnic Pashtuns have not lived in Afghanistan – much longer, in fact, than Afghanistan has existed as a state. Today, as few as one in three may do so, and thanks to massive population movements, both from Afghanistan and from the Pashtun areas of Pakistan, Karachi (not Kabul, Kandahar or Peshawar) may be the largest Pashtun city in the world.

Karachi may be the largest Pashtun city

In Afghanistan itself, Pashtuns, though representing the largest share of the population (the general estimate is about 40%, though nobody can say for sure), are not a majority, whatever they may like to believe. A strong espousal of Pashtun ethnic nationalism by the state inevitably frightens and infuriates the other large ethnic minorities of Afghanistan, and any rebel movement seeking to rule the whole of Afghanistan has to make at least some concessions to their feelings. The failure of the Pashtun-based Taliban to do so in the 1990s was a key reason for the speed with which they collapsed in the face of US attack in 2001.

A rather striking example of the way in which even educated and liberal Pashtuns tend completely to ignore the role and views of other ethnicities in Afghanistan can be found in a book by Abubakar Siddique, tellingly entitled *The Pashtun Question: The Unresolved Key to the Future of Pakistan and Afghanistan*. In 271 pages, the word 'Tajiks' (a people who represent around a quarter of Afghanistan's population) appears precisely three times.[9] In the real world, the Tajiks of Afghanistan cannot be ignored.

State-promoted Afghan-Pashtun nationalism has also broken on the obstacle of local geopolitical reality. Any programme of Pashtun national mobilisation in Afghanistan inevitably requires as a chief goal the abolition of the 'Durand Line': the frontier drawn by the British Raj that in 1947 became the frontier between Afghanistan and Pakistan, and that cuts through the middle of the Pashtun ethnicity. In the 1950s and early 1960s, Sardar Daud did launch an abolition campaign in Afghanistan. While this mobilised the country's tiny Pashtun intelligentsia, the weakness of the state machine meant that the campaign could not be spread effectively among the masses, and it was regarded by the non-Pashtuns of Afghanistan with indifference or outright hostility.

The result for Afghan–Pakistan relations was disastrous. Pakistan is not merely far larger and more powerful than Afghanistan, it sits squarely across Afghanistan's chief route to the sea. The result of Sardar Daud's strategy was to bring about a Pakistani blockade of Afghan trade and a dire economic crisis for Afghanistan. This led to Sardar Daud's removal from office by his cousin, King Mohammed Zahir Shah. Sardar Daud's return in a coup ten years later undermined dynastic legitimacy and paved the way for the catastrophic communist coup five years later. Moreover, fear of Afghan- (and Indian-) backed irredentism among the Pashtuns of Pakistan has led successive Pakistani governments to intervene in Afghanistan by backing various proxies, ending with the Taliban.

On the other hand, the residual strength of Pashtun nationalism in Afghanistan is shown by the fact that no Afghan government (even the Taliban, which enjoyed massive backing from Pakistan) has officially recognised the Durand Line, despite the obvious benefits that would flow from doing so.

Appeals by the Pashtun-led Afghan state to the Pashtuns of Pakistan, while provoking disastrous hostility on the part of the Pakistani state and military, have also overwhelmingly failed. Pakistani Pashtun activists such as the Pashtun Tahafuz Movement may chant 'Lar ao Bar, Yaw Afghan' (roughly speaking, 'Pashtuns on both sides of the border are Afghans'), but the realities of Pakistani Pashtun politics are very different. The reason was pithily summed up for me by an activist of the moderate Pashtun-nationalist Awami National Party:

> Our old programme of union with Afghanistan is dead and everyone
> knows it, because no-one in their senses wants to become part of
> Afghanistan, today or for all the future that we can see. Pakistan is bad,
> but Afghanistan is a nightmare, and has been for a generation.[10]

Even before the start of the Afghan catastrophe of the past four decades, the economic centre of the Pashtun world had shifted decisively to Pakistan. The Pakistani-Pashtun political and business elites, and especially the Pashtun transport companies that link northern Pakistan with the port of Karachi (with its huge and growing Pashtun population), have very strong motives indeed not to join any Afghanistan-based effort to destroy Pakistan.

Equally importantly, Afghan-Pashtun national identity itself, while a powerful force, has never been able to claim the undivided loyalty of Pashtuns in a way characteristic of stronger nationalisms. Tribal and religious allegiances have been, and remain, of great importance. Both the poverty of the state and the indifference or hostility of the rural Pashtun population to education have meant that the Afghan state could not imitate successful national-modernising states elsewhere and instil unequivocal Pashtun nationalism through a widespread rural state-school system.

Accompanying all this is the alienation of many Pashtuns from the Afghan state going back to its very foundation. The kingdom of Afghanistan was created in the 1740s in what had been Iran's eastern borderlands by a chieftain who had become a general in the service of an Iranian monarch. Ahmed Shah Abdali came from a leading aristocratic lineage of one of the two main Pashtun tribal confederations, the Abdali (whom he renamed the Durrani, after his own new title 'Dur-e-Durran', or 'Pearl of Pearls'). This created an enduring rift with the other great confederation, the Ghilzai, with its more democratic and egalitarian traditions.[11] It is striking that every radical Pashtun movement revolting against Afghan governments – all the way down to the Taliban – has been mainly Ghilzai in composition. As Thomas Barfield writes in *Afghanistan: A Cultural and Political History*:

> while Afghanistan's Durrani rulers (1747–1978) may have originated in
> an egalitarian Pashtun tribal system, they employed a classic hierarchical

model of governance to maintain power exclusively within their own dynastic lines. They abandoned the democratic and federal political institutions commonly used among the Pashtun tribes at the local level, and replaced them with autocracy. Because of this, the relationship between the Pashtun tribes and their putative dynastic leaders was always a troubled one, in which co-operation (or conflict) depended on the issues involved.[12]

The Durrani kings, their courts and later the bureaucracy that they created naturally adopted the ancient, dominant, regional culture of royal authority, that of the Iranian–Turkic rulers of Iran, Central Asia and northern India. This included adopting the Persian language (the local Afghan form of which was later given the official Afghan name of 'Dari' by way of trying to make it sound more national) as the language of government, higher culture, trade and communication. Not just the Pashtuns of the royal court and government, but much of the established Pashtun population of Kabul adopted Persian as their language. There was therefore little reason for a purely Pashtu-speaking rural Pashtun to identify with the royal state. Pashtun ethnic alienation from the Afghan state grew after the fall of the Taliban in 2001, due to the new ascendancy of the Tajiks and the (hitherto despised and oppressed) Hazara in the Afghan government, but the phenomenon has much older and deeper roots.[13]

Hostility to the reforming state

A failure to understand the instinctive rejection of effective state power by rural Pashtuns lay at the heart of Western fantasies of rapid democratic state-building in Afghanistan after 2001 – a project that has inevitably failed, where a modest approach attuned to Afghan traditions and realities might have established at least a provisional and limited form of state order.

I had a rather striking personal experience of this when I took part in an Italian conference on law and order in Afghanistan in 2002. Almost none of the Italian officials and experts present understood this point – although it should have been obvious enough to any Italian who had read Carlo Levi's

Christ Stopped at Eboli, or other classic accounts of the traditional relationship between southern Italian peasants and the state. As Levi wrote of returning to Basilicata (where he had been exiled by Benito Mussolini) after a brief permitted return to northern Italy:

> I thought of my feelings of strangeness, and of the complete lack of understanding among those of my friends who concerned themselves with political questions, of the country to which I was now hurrying back. They had all asked about conditions in the south, and I had told them what I knew. But although they listened with apparent interest, very few of them seemed really to follow what I was saying. They were men of various temperaments and shades of opinion, from stiff-necked conservatives to fiery radicals. Many of them were very able, and they all claimed to have meditated upon the 'problem of the South' and to have formulated plans for its solution. But just as their schemes and the very language in which they were couched would have been incomprehensible to the peasants, so were the life and needs of the peasants a closed book to them … At bottom, as I now perceived, they were all *unconscious worshippers of the state*.[14]

In words that are equally applicable to the traditional tribal Pashtuns, Robert Montagne, the French colonial officer and ethnographer of the Berbers, argued for the complete incompatibility of their traditional tribal system with regular administration and development: 'There is no place for the ordered anarchy of the Berber cantons in a modern state.' He immediately added, however, that, having imposed (colonial) state domination on the Berber tribes,

> one will witness the growth of what is the greatest problem of all in the administration of Berber areas; the fact that, in the eyes of the population, and of the chiefs, during the period before our arrival, law and order was synonymous with boundless tyranny and ruin for the majority, while anarchy appeared, as did general lack of law and order, as a form of justice and a precondition of individual prosperity.[15]

A majority of Western works analysing the failure of the Western state-building project in Afghanistan after 2001, while they may be incisive enough in criticising Western plans and their implementation (or not) by the Afghan state, are hampered by their lack of understanding that rejection of state law and authority by rural Pashtuns is rooted not just in the contemporary failings and Western sources of these institutions, but also in long and bitter memories of state oppression, and in the fundamental incompatibility of modern state authority and Pashtun tribal tradition. 'Democracy' does not necessarily make any difference at all to these patterns – least of all democracy as practised in Afghanistan since 2001, with elections managed by local warlords and bosses, seats shared out by prior agreement and formal power concentrated in the central government.[16]

In the specific area of the rule of law, standard Western analysis is undermined still further by the authors' instinctive hostility to sharia law as (in their view) a regressive code opposed to modern law and state authority, and underpinning the negative aspects of customary law, including the Pashtunwali (the 'Pashtun way'); whereas a more accurate and historically grounded analysis would see sharia as a key source of state order, and the only legal code other than customary law that enjoys instinctive legitimacy among ordinary Afghans.

On the other hand, Western observers inclined to romanticise the tribes (as all too many have tended to do) should heed the words of Ibn Khaldun, who established the classic and enduring model of analysis of the relationship between tribes and government seven centuries ago (an analysis which also largely underlies the best overall study of Afghan tradition, that of Barfield):

> The very nature of their [the Bedouins'] existence is the negation of building, which is the basis of civilization … Furthermore, it is in their nature to plunder whatever other people possess. Their sustenance lies wherever the shadow of their lances falls … When they acquire superiority and royal authority, they have complete power to plunder as they please. There no longer exists any political power to protect property, and civilisation is ruined … Furthermore, every Bedouin is anxious to be the

leader … There are numerous authorities and amirs among them. Their subjects have to pay taxes to many different masters. Civilisation decays and is wiped out.[17]

As a British journalist covering the mujahideen war against the Soviets and Afghan communists in the late 1980s, I witnessed and even shared the intense romanticisation of many Western journalists of Pashtun tribal traditions as reflected in the mujahideen – a romanticisation driven partly by Western Cold War allegiances, partly by inherited British affection dating back to Rudyard Kipling and British officials on the frontier, and partly by admiration for their genuinely impressive courage and resilience in the face of heavy odds.[18]

When, in 1992, the communist state fell and the mujahideen took over, the enduring truth of Ibn Khaldun's vision became apparent. This was reflected not so much in the destruction of Kabul in fighting between the mujahideen parties, as this was largely along ethnic lines and could have occurred in many ethnically divided societies. Rather, it was the complete collapse of the state across the Pashtun areas of eastern and southern Afghanistan, the epidemic of plunder and extortion, and the inability of local society to generate the most rudimentary new state institutions and services.

This complete absence of the most basic state institutions and services had already struck me during my visits to the 'liberated' areas of Pashtun Afghanistan.[19] I instinctively compared this with the marked tendency of other twentieth-century insurgent movements – the IRA, almost all the communist movements, Algeria's FLN and the Tamil Tigers (and later the Taliban in Afghanistan) – to set up parallel and alternative institutions of governance to replace the existing state that they were fighting against. That the squabbling mujahideen parties could not agree on this was not so surprising, but local Pashtun society as such also seemed quite uninterested in spontaneously generating local institutions and services.

Then again, given their past experience of the Afghan state, the people of the area had no special reason to wish to re-establish it. The point is that state services in rural Pashtun areas could not be 'restored', because in most places they had never existed: neither schools, nor clinics, nor electricity, nor clean water. To the people of these areas, the traditional face of the state – when it had appeared to them at all – was that of the conscripting officer, the brutal and corrupt policeman, and the even more corrupt tax collector.[20] Why indeed would anyone have wanted them back?[21]

And when the police did come back, after the overthrow of the Taliban and the creation of a 'democratic' state by the West, they wore very much the same corrupt and oppressive face as before.[22] This was not just due to the specific failings of individual policemen, or even of the post-2001 Kabul state; the problem was rooted in the very old predatory traditions of state forces in the region.[23]

It is interesting that Antonio Giustozzi's brilliant work on Afghan warlords serving as early local state-builders in the past 40 years, *Empires of Mud*, is about Ismail Khan of Herat and the Uzbek and Turkmen warlords (with some reference to the Tajiks and Hazaras). No tribally based Pashtun warlord appears to have qualified in Giustozzi's eyes as even the most embryonic of state-builders.[24] The suffering caused to ordinary people by predatory local warlords after 1992 led to the rise of the Taliban and their version of Islamic state authority, and the acceptance of this by a large majority of Pashtuns.[25]

On the other hand, Montagne, like many other French officials in the Maghreb and British officials on the Afghan frontier, also noted the striking contrast between the tribes' lack of overall authority (and constant feuding among themselves), and their capacity for spontaneous military cooperation in the name of common identity and values when faced with an outside enemy:

> Our military officers in the Middle Atlas have recognised this for a long time past. 'When you wish to pacify them', Maurice Le Glay makes one of his heroes say in a novel, 'you will find before you only a scatter of humanity. You have to chase after each tent in order to talk to the head of each small family, and to establish any sort of control over them at all takes years. If you face them in battle though they fall upon you all at once and in vast numbers, and you wonder how you can possibly extricate yourself.'[26]

Like the tribes of the Maghreb, and many of the peoples of Scott's 'Zomia', the Pashtun highlands have also long been an area of religiously inspired revolt, culminating in the Taliban. Pashtun history can therefore also be viewed through the prism of Ibn Khaldun's analysis of enduring patterns of political revolution (in the older, literal sense) in the medieval Maghreb; of mountain and desert tribes who, relying on their superior solidarity (*asabiya*) and fighting skills, and inspired by puritanical and reformist religion, overthrow and replace a decadent ruling dynasty in the cities of the plains, only to become decadent and corrupt in turn, and to be overthrown by a new wave of religiously inspired tribal revolt.

State power vs ordered anarchy

The old distinction in the Pashtun lands between the 'settled areas' or 'areas of government' (*Hukumat*) and Yaghistan has been equated with the extremely evocative distinction between the areas dominated by honour (*Nang*) and those dominated by rent or tax (*Qalang*).[27] This corresponds very closely indeed to the old Maghrebi distinction between the 'Bled-el-Makhzen' (Land of Government, or Rule) and 'Bled-es-Siba' (Land of Anarchy, Freedom or Disorder). Or, as the Prophet Muhammad said in a Hadith cited by Ibn Khaldun: 'submission follows the plough'.

On the other hand, the traditional world of the Pashtun tribes was not one of unrestrained chaos. It was in fact an almost paradigmatic example of 'ordered anarchy' (in the phrase coined by E.E. Evans-Pritchard for the Nuer of southern Sudan),[28] with the traditional Pashtun ethnic code of the Pashtunwali providing the rules of order, underpinned by the moral code laying down what it is to 'do Pashto', or live a correct Pashtun life.

This was, however, very definitely an anarchic order. The legitimate role of the monarch (or his immediate representative) was mostly to mediate and judge in major tribal disputes that could not be resolved by local *jirgas* (councils) of elders and religious figures. To this day, it is such community councils (or extended families themselves, in the case of an internal dispute or offence) that decide on the great majority of disputes and offences in rural Pashtun society in Afghanistan, with no reference whatsoever to the state and its law. Mike Martin, a British officer who served in Helmand and has written a brilliant work of political sociology on the province, predicts that in the future as in the past,

> the villages will govern themselves, as they have always done. If they require anything of the government, they will go to it in the district centre (not for nothing is the district centre literally known as the *hukomat* or 'government' in Helmand). *They do not want the government to come to them.* As before, the main service that they require of government is fair, impartial dispute resolution.[29]

The purpose of the Pashtunwali is to manage, limit and when possible resolve particular conflicts between kinship groups, not to end conflict in Pashtun society or to punish criminals. It also by nature works far better at the local level, where everyone's prestige (or 'name', in the Pashtun phrase), power and character is well known, than at an impersonal national or regional level. Hence the need for the ruler's mediation in larger disputes – which are also very often exacerbated by the obsession in Pashtun traditional culture with 'name' (*Nom*), honour (*Nang*) and revenge (*Badal*).

The idea of individual citizenship, or indeed of individual rights (especially for women), is absent. The role of relative power is always present below the surface, though veiled and to some extent softened by common values. In this sense, such traditional tribal codes are closer to traditions of customary international law (which also operate in an anarchic global system and under the permanent influence of the relative power of states) than they are to domestic state legal codes, whether Western or Asian.

Of course, these patterns of Pashtun history and culture are not unchanging. From the mid-nineteenth century to the 1970s they were greatly affected by the development and extension of the modern state (however flawed and partial), as well as by the irruption of the British Empire into the region. Over the past two generations they have been shaped by terrible wars, which have now extended over more than four decades; by huge movements of refugees; by the heroin trade; by massive urbanisation; and by aid flows and ideological influences from outside Afghanistan.

The two finest studies of rural Pashtun Afghanistan (both focusing on Helmand) since 2001, by Martin and an American political officer, Carter Malkasian, bring out both the continued power and the fragility of tribal allegiances.[30] On the one hand, almost every former mujahideen commander and warlord turned state 'official' they mention based his power in part on tribal affiliation and loyalty, even though this support was gained with the help of heroin money, international aid and/or an official position given by Kabul.

On the other hand, the fragility of these tribal power bases was demonstrated by two sweeping Taliban local victories over the warlords in the province of Helmand, in 1995 and 2006 (admittedly, these exploited the resentment of tribal groups that had lost out in the division of the spoils). According to both Martin and Malkasian, the key reason for their defeat, in addition to corruption and oppression by the local Afghan state forces serving these warlords, and the presence of a disenfranchised 'immigrant' minority of Pashtuns from elsewhere who settled in new irrigation zones in the 1970s, was that their deep-seated rivalries made them incapable of allying effectively against the disciplined and united Taliban.[31]

If the greatest and most legitimate role of the state in rural Afghan society is the resolution of local disputes between tribes and warlords (which can only be achieved with the recognised ability to bring armed force to bear if necessary), then the divisions innate to democracy may be the greatest obstacle to its creation in Afghanistan. For such decisions can only be reached and enforced by a strong united power, whether of an individual ruler or a disciplined and united movement – not by a 'fluid franchise construct', in Martin's accurate description.

Pashtuns like to talk of the old 'democratic' tradition of the Loya Jirga, or 'great council' (like the one that acclaimed Ahmed Shah as emir). In fact, the decisions of Loya Jirgas have almost always been reached in advance by a strong ruler, albeit in consultation with chieftains and elders. The Loya Jirga then puts a public stamp of approval on them. A weak ruler is ill-advised to summon such an assembly – as King Mohammed Zahir Shah found when he introduced an elected parliament in the 1960s. The result was a complete inability to pass laws, and an explosion of quarrels and feuds among the representatives, accompanied and fuelled by their rival attempts to extract patronage from the state by every means at their disposal.

A state like that of Afghanistan since 2001, which is forced to seek support by granting patronage and positions to local warlord and tribal factions without being strong enough to impose its will on them, negates its basic traditional *raison d'être* in the eyes of ordinary people. As for parliamentary elections since 2001, at best these are consensual but fraudulent (in Western terms), with the seats apportioned in advance between the different warlords and factions. At worst, every election tears open the old disputes and leads to a new round of factional conflict.

Nasty, illegitimate, impoverished: Afghanistan's modern history

At the heart of the interrelated ineffectiveness and nastiness of the Afghan state has been a lack of revenue. A devastating blow was dealt to the economic base of the region by the European seizure and development of the Indian Ocean trade routes from the end of the fifteenth century CE. Previously, the territory of what is now Afghanistan had been the chief route for the trade of South Asia, and much of Southeast Asia, through the Middle East to Europe.

The loss of this trade impoverished Afghanistan's cities, and also largely destroyed the tax base of states attempting to rule the area.[32] Raising taxes from the tribes, by contrast, was always an extremely challenging proposition, given that, in addition to their poverty and natural aversion to paying taxes, the heavily armed Pashtun tribes possessed the ability to kill the tax collectors. The armies necessary to collect taxes from the tribes would devastate and impoverish the countryside, provoke lasting bitterness and future revolt, and eat up so much of the revenue collected that very often this kind of revenue collection was simply not a paying proposition.[33] As Ibn Khaldun wrote:

> A tribe paying imposts did not do so until it became resigned to meek submission with respect to paying. Imposts and taxes are a sign of oppression and meekness that proud souls do not tolerate.[34]

Any ruling body attempting to build up state power in the Afghan region has therefore been chronically short of revenue. Ahmed Shah, founder of the Afghan state, conquered huge areas of northwest India, Central Asia and Iran, but his was a purely military and tributary empire, with its original seed in the contents of an expropriated Iranian treasure chest.[35] It was based on a confederation of Pashtun tribes, on the personal submission to Ahmed Shah of local rulers and tribes, and on the irregular payment of tribute when this could be enforced. It did not involve either regular administration or systematic tax collection – something that would certainly not have been accepted by Ahmed Shah's own Durrani tribesmen. It depended on military force, and this force was maintained not by regular salaries dependent on taxation, but by plunder (for example, the sack of Delhi in 1757 CE).[36] As Barfield writes, 'the Durrani Empire's greatest sources of revenue were derived from territories that it never directly controlled. And that revenue would only continue to flow as long as the Durranis remained militarily dominant.'[37]

Following Ahmed Shah's death, the ability of the Pashtuns to plunder surrounding territories dried up as state power was restored (to an extent) by the Qajars in Iran, and by first the Sikhs and then the British in northwestern India. Relying on the vastly greater resources of Punjab, the Sikh kingdom of Ranjit Singh conquered the Peshawar Valley (the greatest single Pashtun-populated area) from the Durranis and extracted tribute – intermittently – from many of the Pashtun tribes who had previously paid it – intermittently – to Ahmed Shah.

The true founder of the modern Afghan state was the 'Iron Emir', Abdur Rahman Khan (ruled 1880–1901). He did so on the basis of four combined features that might be called the essential mixture of successful Afghan statecraft: traditional (in this case dynastic and religiously confirmed) legitimacy; outside subsidies; effective dispute resolution; and extreme ruthlessness. His non-interference in the lives of his subjects, as long as they did not revolt against him, also helped.

The subsidies came from Britain's Indian Empire, after it had abandoned its disastrous attempts to conquer Afghanistan and embarked instead on building up Abdur Rahman's rule as a buffer against the

Russian Empire. These subsidies allowed Abdur Rahman to build up the rudiments of a regular army and bureaucracy without having to increase taxes on the tribes.

As to his exceptional ruthlessness, the more colourful aspects of this may have been exaggerated by British observers – but there is abundant evidence of its basic truth, including in the emir's own memoir.[38] Abdur Rahman himself claimed to have killed 120,000 of his subjects – a very large proportion of the Afghan population at that time.[39]

A rather vivid illustration of the nature of the Pashtun tragedy under Abdur Rahman is to be found in David B. Edwards's study of traditions of morality and moral conflict among the Pashtuns, *Heroes of the Age*.[40] Chapter three is a study of the ethical culture of Abdur Rahman, emphasising his ruthless ferocity, and ending with the words, 'for in the end, the subjects he addressed so grandly … wanted nothing so much as to tear him limb from limb'. Edwards also gives due weight to Abdur Rahman's claims that the nature of Afghanistan made such ruthlessness necessary if a ruler was to maintain order and justice.

An obsession with honour had ghastly results

Chapter two tells the story of the youth of Sultan Muhammad Khan, a leading figure among the Safi tribe of the Ghilzai, who took part in the last great purely tribal rebellions in Afghan history, the Ghilzai revolts in the second half of the 1940s. If Abdur Rahman's story is one of ruthless oppression exceptional even for an Afghan ruler, Sultan Muhammad's is one of an obsession with honour and merciless revenge that was pathological even by the standards of Pashtun tribal tradition, and had ghastly results not just for his neighbours, but for some of his own family: 'feuding ate up the mountains, and taxes ate up the plains'. This dreadful story is a perfect evocation of a famous anthropologist's blistering characterisation of systems like the Pashtunwali: 'honour divorced from virtue'.[41]

The perils of attempting a programme of state modernisation on the basis of Afghan revenue alone was most vividly illustrated by the fate of Abdur Rahman's successor, King Amanullah Khan, in the 1920s. The Afghan–British war of 1919 and the end of the British protectorate also meant the end of most British subsidies. Amanullah's radical modernising programme therefore required considerable increases in Afghan taxation.

The resistance this caused among the tribes fused with the reaction of the Muslim clerical classes against Amanullah's westernising reforms, and the reaction of both clerics and tribal elites against the increase in the power of state officials and judges. The result was a mass revolt that overthrew Amanullah in 1929, after he was deserted by his unpaid soldiers. Following a brief period of chaos and rule in Kabul by Habibullah Kalakani (known by his nickname Bacha-ye-Saqao, 'the son of the water carrier'), a Tajik ex-soldier who, in a combination of roles familiar to readers of historian Eric Hobsbawm, became a brigand and then a rebel, the Durrani monarchy was re-established by Pashtun tribal militias under a different branch of the royal family.

The resumption of state modernisation in the late 1940s was made possible by new outside subsidies, now offered by both the US and the USSR as part of the Cold War and their competition for influence in Afghanistan. This programme was to land Afghanistan in the same trap that has afflicted many developing societies.[42] It gave great influence to outside states with their own ideological and geopolitical agendas; it raised expectations of progress and prosperity that it could not fulfil; it created a large class of junior officers and officials who could not be adequately paid; and, although its effects were very limited, they were sufficient to raise conservative religious resistance, now expressed not just by traditional clerics but by new groups of radical Islamist students.

The final result was the communist coup of 1978, the anti-communist revolts (replicating in certain respects those against King Amanullah 50 years earlier) and Soviet military intervention. Thus began the civil wars that have plagued Afghanistan for more than four decades. Since then, the Afghan 'communist' state of 1978–92 and the 'democratic' state from 2002 to the present have maintained a precarious balance between the Pashtuns and other ethnicities, but have lacked legitimacy as clients of the infidel Soviets and Americans respectively.

Both were (are) totally dependent for their state budgets on subsidies by their superpower backers. Both also alienated religious conservatives with their reform programmes, without being able to win over the rural population by either providing effective state services or performing the traditional state role of ending local disputes. Neither exerted real control over most of the country.

The Taliban and Islamic order

The course of Afghan history in the 1990s – and very likely after the US withdrawal as well – was set out for me by a Qazi (Islamic judge) with whom I spoke in a 'liberated' area of Paktika province in 1989.[43] I mentioned the lack of any institutions of authority in the area, and my fear that this would lead to chaos when the communist government eventually fell. He began by replying that this would be prevented by the Pashtunwali: 'It doesn't stop all feuds, but it prevents them going too far.'

I questioned this, pointing out how the traditional tribal order had been weakened by the colossal disruptions of the war, and the growing power of the mujahideen parties, of foreign money, of local warlords and of the heroin trade. 'Yes, you may be right', he replied. 'But if the Pashtunwali fails, then we have the sharia, Islamic law, which everyone respects and which it is my job to implement.'[44] Chaos did indeed follow the fall of the communist state three years later, and order was indeed restored by the Taliban on the basis of their interpretation of sharia.

The importance, and acceptance, of sharia in a tribal context, its difference from state law, and its ability to discipline tribesmen without reducing their fighting spirit were noted by Ibn Khaldun seven centuries ago:

> Clearly ... governmental and educational laws destroy fortitude, because their restraining influence is something that comes from outside. The religious laws, on the other hand, do not destroy fortitude, because their restraining influence is something inherent.[45]

In extending their version of sharia order, the Taliban built on two old traditions among the Pashtun tribes. The first was the practice whereby local religious figures (often Sayyids, claiming non-Pashtun descent from the Prophet Muhammad, and thereby outside tribal allegiances) would mediate in tribal disputes.[46] The second was the tendency of prestigious religious leaders to preach the need to reform local behaviour in the name of a 'return' to strict Koranic and puritanical rules of behaviour. After the arrival of the British in the region, this was very often linked with the mobilisation of the tribes for jihad against the infidel – and sometimes against allegedly irreligious and westernising rulers in Kabul.[47]

In one sense, these influences were outside the Pashtun tribal tradition, and even ran directly contrary to it. They often explicitly demanded changes to Pashtun social traditions. Moreover, from the first, Arabian puritanical influence was directly or indirectly present. Thus, Sayyid Ahmad Barelvi, who sought to reform Pashtun custom and mobilise the tribes for jihad against the Sikhs and British, had studied in Arabia and was influenced by Wahhabism. As with the Taliban, the combination of religious prestige, hatred of the infidel enemy and puritanical attempts to change Pashtun custom accounted for the combination of respect and aversion with which these preachers were regarded among the tribes. As Ernest Gellner has written:

> The manner in which demanding, puritan Unitarianism enters tribal life, and the manner in which the tribes are induced on special occasions to accept overall leadership, are the *same*. The exceptional crisis in the tribal world provides the opening, the opportunity, for that 'purer' form of faith which normally remains latent, respected but not observed.[48]

The point is that puritanical Islamic reforms, though they have involved tension with tribal custom, are a very old tradition among the Pashtuns. Indeed, it could be called as old as Islam, since sharia has played some of the same reforming and civilising roles among the Pashtun tribes – up to the present day – as it did among the pagan tribes of Arabia 1,400 years ago. It is very striking that women, when they are given the chance to speak, usually, and by huge majorities, prefer sharia to the Pashtunwali.[49]

The appeal of puritanical religion to the tribes (in which hatred and contempt for the luxurious and decadent city was mixed with a desire to plunder it) was highlighted by Ibn Khaldun.[50] This puritanism was funded and encouraged by Saudi Wahhabi preachers in the Afghan refugee camps in Pakistan in the 1980s. It was not created by them.

As for the Taliban's attitudes to women, this alas was squarely in line with conservative Pashtun rural tradition. As Malkasian observed, 'overall … Taliban oppression was just a gradation in the general Pashtun oppression of women'.[51] The impression that these attitudes were something radically new and external came from the Taliban's arrival in the more sophisticated and modern urban world of Kabul (or what was left of it after four years of civil war).[52]

To understand the power of the Taliban's appeal to sharia and religious puritanism among Pashtuns (and some members of other ethnicities) in the 1990s, it is necessary to recognise that the chaos, oppression and internecine conflict after the fall of the communist state were seen by ordinary Afghans not just as dreadful, but as a deep moral and cultural disgrace, following as it did the anti-Soviet jihad, which had been widely seen as a great, religiously ordained moral effort.

Moreover, in the Pashtun areas the collapse of the modern state, and the failure of the Pashtunwali to restrain the conflict and oppression that followed, left sharia as the last code standing. There was probably no other moral foundation on which state order could realistically have been reconstructed. It must also be admitted that any authority trying to restore order in the circumstances of Afghanistan in the mid-1990s would have had to use some pretty ruthless measures.

After the US invasion of 2001, the Taliban was able to seize control of one master narrative of the Pashtun tradition, and two that combined the Pashtun tradition with Islam. The first was that Pashtuns should always hold supreme power in Afghanistan, though a respected place would be allocated for other (Sunni) ethnicities.[53] The second was the absolute religious duty of 'defensive jihad', or the notion that the duty of every Muslim was to fight against the occupation of Muslim lands by infidels.[54]

The third narrative was summed up for me by a friend in Peshawar, who explained why the Afghan Taliban had gained so much sympathy even from secular Pashtuns: 'One main reason for sympathy for the Taliban is that every Pashtun has been taught from the cradle that to resist foreign domination is part of what it is to do Pashto' – that is, to follow the Pashtun way.[55] The passionate belief of the Taliban themselves in these narratives, and their own embodiment of them, has been demonstrated in their poetry.[56]

In one respect, the Taliban are a significantly new force – albeit one that also has specific roots in the Ghilzai egalitarian tradition. Unlike most of the great saints of the past, their leaders are not famous clerics from Sayyid lineages. They came from very poor, very ordinary Pashtun villages in southern Afghanistan. This seems to have contributed to their internal discipline – compared to the great Sayyid saints, who, being saints, found it very difficult to submit to each other's orders.

This was not an entirely new pattern in Pashtun history. As Fredrik Barth has written, there was a long tradition that in moments of crisis, 'persons of less established sanctity might emerge' as local leaders of jihad.[57] Nonetheless, the Taliban leadership's deep-rootedness in the poor, rural Pashtun society of southern Afghanistan does seem to have contributed to its astonishing ability – quite unprecedented in Pashtun history – to create and maintain a united, disciplined (at least by traditional Pashtun standards) and extraordinarily resilient movement.

Since every village has a mullah, this also gives the Taliban an ability to systematically reach into every Pashtun village to make sure that its orders are obeyed – something that no other Afghan (or Pakistani, or even Indian) state has ever achieved. This must be set against the known splits within the Taliban, for example, the past rivalry between the Quetta and Peshawar leadership councils.[58] The radical and systematic increase in the status and power of the previously lowly and often despised village mullah is in Pashtun terms the most truly revolutionary element in Taliban history.[59]

The Taliban has fought against the US and the Kabul state for two decades in the face of casualties that would have shattered the morale and recruitment of almost any other army. The Vietnamese communists are the only parallel I can think of – and indeed, the Taliban may have learned the importance of discipline and organisation indirectly from communism.[60] There are provinces in Afghanistan where five Taliban governors in a row have been killed – and yet a new volunteer for the position has always stepped forward. This marks a striking contrast with all previous religiously inspired Pashtun tribal uprisings, which grew rapidly but also collapsed quickly after the first major defeat.[61]

Together with deep religious belief, hatred of the infidel invader and sheer grit, it is above all this unity and discipline that have given the Taliban the edge over the factionalised and corrupt forces of the Kabul state, and have allowed it, both in government and in rebellion, to play the traditional and essential role of judging local disputes that the Kabul state has been unable to fulfil. The Taliban, like communist and nationalist insurgencies elsewhere in the world, has done this through an elaborate structure of alternative governors and judges in all the rural districts of the south and east, as well as its informal religious and kinship networks.[62] As Malkasian writes, 'for those today who claim that Afghanistan is ungovernable, Taliban rule offers a striking counter-example'.[63] One might say that the Taliban is only organised and united compared to the existing Kabul state; but then, in the long run it only has to be better than the Kabul state – and stay that way – in order to win.[64]

The Taliban is united and disciplined

In Malkasian's view (and that of other observers), this unity and discipline more than compensated for the Taliban cadres' lack of education and experience – not that most local Afghan government officials are known for their education either. It accounted not just for their success as insurgents, but for a couple of truly remarkable achievements in power before 2001 (at least by the standards of Afghanistan): the suppression of heroin cultivation, and the successful and universal implementation of the World Health Organization's polio-vaccination programme.

As this last case indicates, it would be wrong to see Taliban fighters simply as religiously inspired, unusually disciplined tribal rebels. In their own way, they also see themselves as inheritors of the Pashtun royal state-building tradition in Afghanistan (much though they despise the memory of the decadent and westernised monarchy). This, as well as sheer opportunism, helped them in the past to gain some surprising recruits even among former Pashtun-communist officers and officials.

These patterns, together with the constant contacts and conversations taking place between members of the government and Taliban fighters who, though ostensibly on opposite sides, belong to the same Pashtun tribes, suggest that after the US withdrawal, the collapse of the Afghan state in the Pashtun areas may at some point happen not just very quickly, but also quite peacefully, as Pashtun soldiers and police simply go home, while their commanders flee or make their own deals with the Taliban. This, after all, is very much what happened both when the communist state collapsed in 1992 and the mujahideen took over, and as the Taliban swept through the Pashtun areas in 1994–96 and displaced the mujahideen warlords.

To reconcile rural Pashtuns to the state would be a great achievement in itself, but to achieve a stable and lasting hegemony over Afghanistan as a whole, the Taliban would have to do three things. The first would be to gain sufficient international subsidies, or aid. This it might be able to get (from China, Russia and the European Union, if not from America) in return for suppressing heroin production and fighting against the Islamic State and its international terrorist allies in Afghanistan – as it is indeed already doing.

The second task would be to make sufficient concessions to cultural modernity, at least in the city of Kabul, to retain enough modern technocrats to make the Afghan state work and to administer international aid. Can the Taliban compromise in this way? The former Taliban leader Mullah Mansour – who was very foolishly and pointlessly killed by the US – could have done so; but as for the present leadership – who can say? Not even themselves, perhaps, before they actually take power.

Finally, and most importantly of all, the Taliban would have to reach an accommodation with Afghanistan's other main ethnic groups – Tajiks, Hazaras and Uzbeks – guaranteeing them autonomy and safety in their own areas. Without this, Afghanistan will be doomed to a future of unending civil war fuelled by outside backers; for while China and Russia might abandon these minorities, Iran cannot abandon the Shia Hazara without a serious loss of prestige as leader of the Shia world.

The Taliban is not a monolithically Pashtun force. It has gathered a good deal of support among other ethnicities by appealing to religious conservatism,[65] but its leadership is still overwhelmingly Pashtun, and seen as such by most of the other peoples. Moreover, the Taliban's record towards the other ethnicities when in power before 2001 was sometimes atrocious (though the atrocities were pretty evenly divided among all sides).

Perhaps united pressure from China, Iran, Pakistan and Russia – and from the US, assuming that Washington retains any interest in Afghanistan after US troops withdraw – might bring the Taliban to concede such autonomy.

These questions cannot be answered before the US withdraws and the existing Kabul state enters its final death throes. Some things do, however, feel certain on the basis of the experience of the past generation. Whatever happens in Kabul, the Taliban will remain the most powerful military and political force among the Pashtuns of Afghanistan; whatever limited compromises it may make, it will remain loyal to its version of conservative, rural, Islamic Pashtun culture; and it will never surrender. Anyone trying to shape the future of Afghanistan will have to shape it in accordance with these facts.

Notes

1   James C. Scott, *The Art of Not Being Governed: An Anarchist History of Upland Southeast Asia* (New Haven, CT: Yale University Press, 2009).

2   Or, in Michael Barry's felicitous translation into French, *Le Royaume de l'Insolence* (Paris: Flammarion, 1984).

3   Max Weber, 'Politics as a Vocation', in H.H. Gerth and C. Wright Mills (trans and eds), *From Max Weber: Essays in Sociology* (New York: Oxford University Press, 1946), pp. 77–128, available at http://fs2.american.edu/dfagel/www/class%20readings/weber/politicsasavocation.pdf. Originally published as Max Weber, 'Politik als Beruf', *Gesammelte Politische Schriften*, 1921.

4   See Antonio Giustozzi, *The Army of Afghanistan: The Political History of a Fragile Institution* (London: C. Hurst & Co., 2016), pp. 7, 124–31.

5   A vivid and amusing anecdote depicting the traditional role of the state in mediating local disputes (though in this case between Uzbeks in northern Afghanistan) is to be found in G. Whitney Azoy's classic work on the game of *buzkashi* under president Sardar Daud Khan in the 1970s. A match in Kunduz, in which the rival teams represented local 'big men' and their factions, was getting seriously out of hand, leading to the risk of wider violence. The local governor took over the job of referee. One of his aides 'handed the Wali a sawed-off shotgun, whose snub-nosed barrel was shrouded in a green velvet cloth. With no fanfare whatsoever, the Wali placed it on the table in front of him. There it remained all afternoon, neither handled nor even mentioned but unquestionably real. Both a symbol of government power and an instrument of self-defense in case matters got worse, the shotgun with its green cloth [green for Islam, presumably] served as the perfect veiled threat. There were no more disputes over

decisions.' G. Whitney Azoy, *Buzkashi: Game and Power in Afghanistan* (Philadelphia, PA: University of Pennsylvania Press, 1982), p. 103.

6   Anand Gopal, 'The Taliban in Kandahar', in Peter Bergen (ed.), *Talibanistan: Negotiating the Borders Between Terror, Politics and Religion* (New York: Oxford University Press, 2013), pp. 23–4.

7   Akbar S. Ahmed (trans.), *Mataloona: Pukhto Proverbs* (Karachi: Oxford University Press, 1975), p. 47.

8   W.H. Sleeman, *Rambles and Recollections of an Indian Official* (Karachi: Oxford University Press, 1980 [1844]), pp. 394–6.

9   Abubakar Siddique, *The Pashtun Question: The Unresolved Key to the Future of Pakistan and Afghanistan* (London: C. Hurst & Co., 2014).

10   Quoted in Anatol Lieven, *Pakistan: A Hard Country* (London: Penguin, 2011), p. 379.

11   For the classic study of Swat political society, see Fredrik Barth, *Political Leadership Among Swat Pathans* (London: Athlone Press, 1959). See also Sultan-i-Rome, *Swat State, 1915–1969: From Genesis to Merger* (Karachi: Oxford University Press, 2008). For the standard British imperial account, see Henry Walter Bellew, *A General Report on the Yusufzais* (Lahore: Sang-e-Meel Publications, 2013 [1864]).

12   Thomas Barfield, *Afghanistan: A Cultural and Political History* (Princeton, NJ: Princeton University Press, 2010), p. 4.

13   See International Crisis Group, 'Afghanistan: The Problem of Pashtun Alienation', ICG Asia report no. 62, 5 August 2003.

14   Frances Frenaye, Carlo Levi (trans.), *Christ Stopped at Eboli* (London: Penguin, 2000 [1947]), pp. 236–7. Emphasis added.

15   David Seddon, Robert Montagne (trans.), *The Berbers: Their Social and Political Organisation* (London: Frank Cass, 1973 [1931]), pp. 69–70.

16   See Noah Coburn and Anna Larson, *Derailing Afghan Democracy: Elections in an Unstable Political Landscape* (New York: Columbia University Press, 2014); and Barfield, *Afghanistan*, p. 7.

17   Ibn Khaldun, N.J. Dawood (ed.), Franz Rosenthal (trans.), *The Muqaddimah: An Introduction to History* (London: Routledge and Kegan Paul, 1967), pp. 118–19. For discussion of a similar attitude to leadership among the Ghilzai Pashtuns, see Barfield, *Afghanistan*, p. 79. For the importance of Ibn Khaldun's dichotomy to Afghan history, see Barfield, *Afghanistan*, pp. 56, 63–5.

18   See, for example, Radek Sikorski (then a journalist with the mujahideen, later to become Poland's foreign minister), *Dust of the Saints: A Journey Through War-torn Afghanistan* (New York: Paragon Publishers, 1990).

19   See Robert Johnson, *The Afghan Way of War* (New York: Oxford University Press, 2011), p. 235.

20   For a vivid and erudite traveller's account of what ordinary Afghan society outside Kabul was like in the 1970s (in this case, northern and northwestern Afghanistan), see David Chaffetz, *A Journey Through Afghanistan: A Memorial* (Chicago, IL: University of Chicago Press, 1981).

21   Sleeman also records the following Indian saying about the police:

'Regarding witches there is a proverb: "Hik dain bait arak charhe" (An ugly witch to start with and then she rides a hyena) of persons who add to their innate repulsiveness by additional horrors – a saying which used to be applied to the police constable and his uniform.' Sleeman, *Rambles and Recollections of an Indian Official*, p. 44.

22 On the corruption, brutality and incompetence of the Afghan National Police, see Antonio Giustozzi and Mohammed Isaqzadeh, *Policing Afghanistan* (London: C. Hurst & Co., 2013), pp. 21, 78–96, 153–63; and Graeme Smith, 'No Justice, No Peace: Kandahar 2005–2009', in Whit Mason (ed.), *The Rule of Law in Afghanistan: Missing in Inaction* (Cambridge: Cambridge University Press, 2011), pp. 301–7. On the Afghan Local Police, see Human Rights Watch, '"Just Don't Call It a Militia": Impunity, Militias, and the "Afghan Local Police"', 2011, https://www.hrw.org/sites/default/files/reports/afghanistan0911webwcover_0.pdf.

23 See Mike Martin, *An Intimate War: An Oral History of the Helmand Conflict* (London: C. Hurst & Co., 2014), p. 239.

24 See Antonio Giustozzi, *Empires of Mud: Wars and Warlords in Afghanistan* (London: C. Hurst & Co., 2009).

25 See Alex Strick van Linschoten and Felix Kuehn, *An Enemy We Created: The Myth of the Taliban/Al Qaeda Merger in Afghanistan, 1970–2010* (London: C. Hurst & Co., 2012), pp. 113–24; Sayyed Mohammad Akbar Agha, *Memories of the Afghan Jihad and the Taliban* (Berlin: First Draft Publishing, 2014), pp. 87–94; and Abdul Salam Zaeef, Alex Strick van Linschoten and Felix Kuehn

(eds), *My Life with the Taliban* (London: C. Hurst & Co., 2010), pp. 57–77.

26 Barfield, *Afghanistan*, p. 35.

27 See Akbar S. Ahmed, *Millennium and Charisma Among Pathans: A Critical Essay in Social Anthropology* (London: Routledge and Kegan Paul, 1978), pp. 75–83.

28 E.E. Evans-Pritchard, *The Nuer: A Description of the Modes of Livelihood and Political Institutions of a Nilotic People* (Oxford: Oxford University Press, 1940), pp. 139–91. Emphasis added.

29 Martin, *An Intimate War*, p. 252. Emphasis added.

30 Martin, *An Intimate War*; and Carter Malkasian, *War Comes to Garmser: Thirty Years of Conflict on the Afghan Frontier* (London: C. Hurst & Co., 2013).

31 Malkasian, *War Comes to Garmser*, pp. 72–101, 254–6 and *passim*; and Martin, *An Intimate War*, pp. 115–25, 132–8, 247–9. The continued fighting between mujahideen factions and commanders, even when they were all on the point of being overthrown by the Taliban, is also emphasised by Giustozzi, *Empires of Mud*, pp. 80–4.

32 See B.D. Hopkins, *The Making of Modern Afghanistan* (London: Palgrave Macmillan, 2008), pp. 110–16.

33 For the experiences of a British official in the 1840s attempting to gather taxes from the tribes of Bannu, see Lt H.B. Edwardes, *Political Diaries 1847–1849* (Lahore: Sang-e-Meel Publications, 2006 [1911]).

34 Ibn Khaldun, *The Muqaddimah*, p. 111.

35 For the antecedents, background and rise of Ahmed Shah Abdali, see Henry Priestley, Muhammad Hayat Khan (trans.), *Afghanistan and Its Inhabitants* (Lahore: Sang-e-Meel Publications,

1999 [1874]), pp. 57–64.

36 See Hopkins, *The Making of Modern Afghanistan*, p. 87.

37 Barfield, *Afghanistan*, p. 100.

38 For Abdur Rahman's autobiography, see Sultan Muhammad Khan (ed.), *The Life of Abdur Rahman, Amir of Afghanistan* (Whitefish, MT: Kessinger Publishing, 2009 [1900]). See also Hasan Kawun Kakar, *Government and Society in Afghanistan: The Reign of Emir Abd al-Rahman Khan* (Austin, TX: University of Texas Press, 1979); and Vartan Gregorian, *The Emergence of Modern Afghanistan: Politics of Reform and Modernisation* (Stanford, CA: Stanford University Press, 1969), pp. 129–62. For a highly coloured account by a British engineer who worked for Abdur Rahman, see Frank A. Martin, *Under the Absolute Amir of Afghanistan* (Lahore: Vanguard Books, 1998 [1912]). For a fascinating fictionalised account of Abdur Rahman's reign by a British doctor who treated his harem, see Lillias Hamilton, *A Vizier's Daughter: A Tale of the Hazara War* (Kabul: Shah M. Books, 2004 [1900]).

39 See Khan, *The Life of Abdur Rahman, Amir of Afghanistan*, pp. 218–19.

40 David B. Edwards, *Heroes of the Age: Moral Faultlines on the Afghan Frontier* (Berkeley, CA: University of California Press, 1996), pp. 33–126.

41 Christoph von Fuerer-Haimendorf, *Morals and Merit: A Study of Values and Social Controls in South Asian Societies* (London: Weidenfeld and Nicolson, 1967), pp. 218–19. The force of this condemnation is all the greater because Fuerer-Haimendorf was a pretty comprehensive moral relativist.

42 See Timothy Nunan, *Humanitarian Invasion: Global Development in Cold War Afghanistan* (Cambridge: Cambridge University Press, 2016).

43 For an earlier version of this analysis with particular regard to the Pakistani Pashtuns, see Lieven, *Pakistan*, chapters ten and eleven, pp. 371–41.

44 *Ibid.*, p. 118.

45 Ibn Khaldun, *The Muqaddimah*, pp. 96–7.

46 See Barth, *Political Leadership Among Swat Pathans*, pp. 98–9; and W.R.H. Merk, *The Mohmands* (Lahore: Vanguard Books, 1984 [1898]), p. 12.

47 See Sana Haroon, *Frontier of Faith: Islam in the Indo-Afghan Borderland* (London: C. Hurst & Co., 2007).

48 Ernest Gellner, 'Flux and Reflux in the Faith of Men', in Ernest Gellner, *Muslim Society* (Cambridge: Cambridge University Press, 1981), p. 53. Emphasis in original.

49 See Lieven, *Pakistan*, pp. 118–21.

50 See Ibn Khaldun, *The Muqaddimah*, pp. 125–8. See also Barfield, *Afghanistan*, pp. 1–85.

51 Malkasian, *War Comes to Garmser*, p. 62.

52 For a memoir of that time by a member of the old Kabuli merchant class (Pashtun, but Dari-speaking), see Qaid Akbar Omar, *A Fort of Nine Towers* (London: Picador, 2013).

53 See Robert D. Crews and Amin Tarzi, 'Introduction', in Robert D. Crews and Amin Tarzi (eds), *The Taliban and the Crisis of Afghanistan* (Cambridge, MA: Harvard University Press, 2008), pp. 21–36; and Abdulkader Sinno, 'Explaining the Taliban's Ability to Mobilise the Pashtuns', in *ibid.*, pp. 59–89.

54 See Lieven, *Pakistan*, pp. 47–8.

55 Lieven, *Pakistan*, p. 390.

56 See Alex Strick van Linschoten and Felix Kuehn (eds), Mirwais Rahmany and Hamid Stanikzai (trans), *Poetry of the Taliban* (London: C. Hurst & Co., 2012).

57 Barth, *Political Leadership Among Swat Pathans*, pp. 61–2.

58 See Antonio Giustozzi, *The Taliban at War: 2001–2018* (Oxford: Oxford University Press, 2019), pp. 77–121.

59 On the previous lowly status of the Pashtun village mullah, see Ahmed, *Millennium and Charisma Among Pathans*, pp. 53–4. Ahmed's description, written in the 1970s, makes clear how radical a transformation the Taliban has brought about.

60 See Giustozzi, *The Taliban at War*, pp. 1–2, 239–40.

61 See Olaf Caroe, *The Pathans* (Oxford: Oxford University Press, 1976), pp. 300–6.

62 See Gopal, 'The Taliban in Kandahar', p. 3.

63 Malkasian, *War Comes to Garmser*, pp. 57–60.

64 On the systematisation of Taliban recruitment, command structures, logistics, medical services and intelligence after 2009, see Giustozzi, *The Taliban at War*, pp. 159–95.

65 See Thomas Ruttig, 'Negotiations with the Taliban', in Bergen, *Talibanistan*, pp. 435–6.

Biden's Afghanistan Withdrawal: A Verdict on the Limits of American Power

Laurel Miller

US President Joe Biden and other American officials do not appear to have illusions about the troubles that lie ahead in Afghanistan. In announcing his troop-withdrawal decision on 14 April, Biden said nothing about what the war would look like after the American departure this summer, and made no promises that the social and political gains many Afghans have enjoyed in the last 20 years would be preserved.[1] Pentagon leaders have only gone so far as to express 'hope' that Kabul's forces will be able to stymie Taliban advances.[2] The conflict in Afghanistan is as deadly as ever, and most observers expect it to worsen as the Taliban – in a triumphalist mood, having apparently outlasted the US and NATO – press for a battlefield win against the Afghan government in the next phase of the war.

The Biden administration has framed the decision to leave as recognition that the United States' original military objectives were achieved a decade ago, when Osama bin Laden was killed in his Pakistan hideout and al-Qaeda's capabilities in Afghanistan were substantially degraded, and that wars are not supposed to be 'endless'. These are only partial explanations. The 'ending forever war' slogan may be in vogue among American critics of involvement in Afghanistan, but it is hard to imagine that, had Biden believed that truly crucial goals were at stake, he would have declared that time was up simply because it was taking too long to achieve them. More

Laurel Miller is Director of the Asia Program at the International Crisis Group. From 2013 to 2017, she was deputy and then acting Special Representative for Afghanistan and Pakistan at the US State Department.

Survival | vol. 63 no. 3 | June–July 2021 | pp. 37–44   https://doi.org/10.1080/00396338.2021.1930404

fundamentally, the decision expresses Biden's judgement that America's ability to impose its will in Afghanistan is limited, and his redefinition of how intent the US needs to be on trying to do so.

Biden's realism

Biden seems to have reached that judgement years ago, as reflected in these lines from his 14 April remarks about a visit to Afghanistan at the end of 2008: 'What I saw on that trip reinforced my conviction that only the Afghans have the right and responsibility to lead their country, and that more and endless American military force could not create or sustain a durable Afghan government.'[3] His view that the war's outcome, either through military or political means, could not be shaped by American hands was evident in the three-part test he laid out in explaining how he made his decision. For the United States to tie its exit to improved conditions in Afghanistan, those conditions would have to be practically achievable, within a reasonable period and at an affordable cost. Not having received good answers as to whether these requirements could be met, he couldn't justify keeping troops in the country.

Notably, Biden did not say that he asked how important it was for US security or other interests to improve conditions in Afghanistan, nor what the downsides of failure would be. He framed his inquiry as 'can we' rather than 'should we', and concluded that the US should not aim to do things it cannot plausibly achieve. The problem, in other words, was not that American involvement in the war was endless; it was that the US found itself unable to end its involvement on the terms that it preferred – either extinguishing the insurgents militarily, or getting them to lay down their arms through negotiation – and that American leaders had for too long resisted acknowledging as much.

Implicitly, the decision also represents a significant revision of what is important for the US to achieve. When the George W. Bush administration went to war in Afghanistan, Bush decided that it was necessary for the US not only to pursue the terrorists directly responsible for the 9/11 attacks but also to eliminate the Taliban regime that had hosted al-Qaeda leaders, preventing the Taliban from enabling the terrorists and setting an example that would deter other potential terrorist abettors around the world. From the decision that Taliban governance in Afghanistan was intolerable flowed most of what the US did in Afghanistan over the next two decades. Having toppled the government, it had to be replaced with something, and when the Taliban regrouped as an insurgency, the US was compelled to prevent the situation it had deemed intolerable from re-emerging.

Assessing US interests

Much has been said about the expansion of American aims in Afghanistan from going after the 9/11 perpetrators to nation-building and counter-insurgency, suggesting this was mission creep. But the root of the expansion was planted at the very start. The logic behind removing the Taliban regime dictated commitment to the project of constructing and sustaining a replacement regime. And because such a project was exceedingly difficult in a country as poorly resourced, minimally institutionalised and under-developed as Afghanistan, even 20 years was not much time for completion.

In the alternative history in which the US does not go down the road of nation-building, it would have had to eschew regime change, leaving the Taliban in place and instead battling it only so far as necessary to protect expeditionary US forces engaged in counter-terrorism. Had the US taken this course, it probably would have become much less enmeshed. But whether continued Taliban rule would have been better for most Afghans, and how conflict within the country would have evolved without the Americans, are imponderables.

Biden has now effectively decided that it no longer matters greatly to US interests – if it ever did – whether the Taliban is in power in Afghanistan. It is not certain that the Taliban will regain national power, as its likely military push will be contested by other Afghans. But it is a possible outcome, as senior US military leaders have acknowledged.[4] The US is still on the Afghan government's side, of course, and has said that American financial and diplomatic support will continue. But even if the most powerful military in the world could not vanquish the Taliban insurgency at any sensible cost, it could have prevented the Afghan government's defeat had its active presence in Afghanistan continued. Deciding to end that presence is tantamount to admitting that, for the US, defeat is an undesirable but tolerable outcome.

Not unexpectedly, this aspect of the withdrawal decision has been left unarticulated. Somewhat surprising, though, is how little has been disclosed so far about the risk assessment that inevitably played a part in the decision-making process. Biden said on 14 April that the US had 'accomplished' the original objective of ensuring that 'Afghanistan would not be used as a base from which to attack our homeland again'. But that statement raises the question of precisely what it means to 'ensure' that such prevention endures into the future. After al-Qaeda had been weakened, and after US leaders stopped talking about winning the war, many US officials considered an ongoing military presence to be an insurance policy against a resurgence of the terrorist threat. They saw the derisively termed 'whack-a-mole' approach to suppressing that threat as at least effective in containing the moles, and the cost of maintaining a few thousand troops as worth it for this purpose.

In dispensing with the insurance-policy rationale for staying, Biden said that the US would 'prevent re-emergence of terrorists' through other means, from bases and with resources elsewhere. These alternatives may well prove sufficient, and they will certainly free the US from the entanglement in counter-insurgency in Afghanistan that a continued presence there would require.

Strategic recalibration

Whether or not the United States' security interests in Afghanistan will be served after its withdrawal, following a 20-year investment in combatting the terrorist threat from bases there, it is jarring that the pull-out has gotten under way before the US has put alternative means in place.[5] During the presidential campaign, Biden had said that a small but persistent military presence would be needed in Afghanistan for counter-terrorism purposes.[6] No doubt, in more closely examining that option, he appreciated its infeasibility.[7] If US troops stayed, the Taliban would once again contest their presence, having put kinetic resistance on pause only in exchange for a US promise, in the February 2020 US–Taliban agreement, to withdraw completely by 1 May 2021.[8] Moreover, the US could not, as a matter of political reality, park its forces in Afghanistan only for its own purposes while declining to actively support the Afghan government in its existential fight with the Taliban.

The withdrawal decision was also an explicit rejection of the idea that the United States' military presence gave the US necessary leverage to promote a negotiated settlement of the conflict. Biden asserted that US troops should not be used as a 'bargaining chip' in another country's war, and that the US gave 'a decade' to the argument that troops were needed as leverage for diplomacy. This is an odd characterisation of what American forces were doing in Afghanistan over the last ten years, particularly because peace initiatives have been central to US policy only for the last two. A decade ago, the US declared a policy of seeking a negotiated return of the Taliban to a share of power through compromises with other Afghans on how the country would be governed.[9] But, until midway through the last administration, White House enthusiasm was tepid on such diplomacy, the Pentagon was generally resistant to it and the intelligence community was deeply sceptical about it, so the US proceeded in fits and starts. The troops were there mainly for US security purposes, not to promote peace.

In any case, it's fair to say that the leverage argument no longer has any salience, if it ever did. It was the promise of leaving, not the threat of staying, that served as negotiating leverage against the Taliban, and the US exhausted that leverage in the 2020 deal that set a timetable for withdrawal. The US had brought the Taliban to the table by giving it the enormous concession of a separate deal with the US up front, before even starting peace talks. There is no evidence that US military pressure forced the Taliban to negotiate with Washington, nor to begin, last September, a halting process of negotiations with the Afghan government, and little reason to believe that with a few thousand troops on the ground the US could force the Taliban to make compromises. Even more to the point, once the US signed a deal that did not link the withdrawal timeline to any requirement of progress in an Afghan peace process, there was no credible path for halting the withdrawal while also keeping the peace process going.

The US has said that it will continue to practise peace diplomacy and that it will support United Nations facilitation of the peace process. This, of course, it should do, as any chance of success, however slim, is worth chasing. But the clear downgrading of Afghanistan's importance, which the withdrawal decision represents, does not furnish reason for great confidence that the US will robustly sustain its diplomacy. Perhaps the regional powers will be motivated to pick up the slack, though based on past performance this eventuality seems doubtful.

From the perspective of working in an organisation dedicated to mitigating and resolving deadly conflict, I must admit to ambivalence about the US withdrawal, knowing that intensified violence will likely follow in its wake. At the same time, the United States' staying would not have alleviated the terrible toll the war already is taking on Afghans, and over the years the US role in the war has been a factor perpetuating the violence, particularly in rural areas. Moreover, it is not difficult to appreciate why a US president would decide that American security interests do not justify the indefinite deployment of troops in Afghanistan. The terrorist threat to the American homeland emanating from the region is diminished, and is comparable to threats sourced elsewhere in the world.

Biden's decision shows that he has judged the American expenditure of blood and treasure in Afghanistan as only partly 'worth it'. The US achieved the strategic marginalisation, though not the complete elimination, of al-Qaeda in Afghanistan. But by deciding that the Taliban's potential return to power other than through a negotiated settlement is tolerable, Biden has determined that the counter-terrorism achievement did not require the much larger war effort against the Taliban, or at least not the last ten years of it. Whether that assessment turns out to be correct depends on whether the Taliban itself will keep a lid on al-Qaeda and other groups, as it has promised; whether the US will do so from afar, regardless of who governs the country; or whether that lid matters so much after all.

*　　　　*　　　　*

Any plausible future looks bleak for many Afghans – the people for whom the war really does seem to be endless. A US decision to abrogate the US–Taliban agreement and keep troops in the country probably would not have brought diplomatic initiatives to negotiate the war's end, always a long shot, closer to success. Yet the American departure puts political solutions even farther out of reach by incentivising the Taliban to go all out in testing its relative strength against government forces that now have no US backup. Arguably one measure of whether the 20-year American effort in Afghanistan was worth it will be whether the US left Afghanistan, if not at peace, at least better off than it found it. That depends on which results of the American effort last through the trying times ahead.

Notes

1   See White House, 'Remarks by President Biden on the Way Forward in Afghanistan', 14 April 2021, https://www.whitehouse.gov/briefing-room/speeches-remarks/2021/04/14/remarks-by-president-biden-on-the-way-forward-in-afghanistan/.

2   Thomas Gibbons-Neff, Helene Cooper and Eric Schmitt, 'Pentagon Struggles to Wean Afghan Military Off American Air Support', *New York Times*, 6 May 2021, https://www.nytimes.com/2021/05/06/us/politics/afghanistan-withdrawal-biden-milley-austin.html.

3   White House, 'Remarks by President Biden on the Way Forward in Afghanistan'. See also Steven Simon and Jonathan Stevenson, 'How Much Is Enough in Afghanistan?', *Survival*, vol. 51, no. 5, October–November 2009, pp. 47–67.

4   See, for example, Dan De Luce and Mosheh Gains, 'Top U.S. General Says Afghan Forces Could Struggle to Hold Off Taliban Without Washington's Help', NBC News, 22 April 2021, https://www.nbcnews.com/politics/national-security/top-u-s-general-says-afghan-forces-could-struggle-hold-n1265017.

5   See, for instance, Vivian Salama and Gordon Lubold, 'Afghan Pullout Leaves U.S. Looking for Other Places to Station Its Troops', *Wall Street Journal*, 8 May 2021, https://www.wsj.com/articles/afghan-pullout-leaves-u-s-looking-for-other-places-to-station-its-troops-11620482659.

6   See, for instance, 'Transcript: Joe Biden on "Face the Nation"', CBS News, 23 February 2020, https://www.cbsnews.com/news/transcript-joe-biden-on-face-the-nation-february-23-2020/.

7   See Laurel Miller, 'The Myth of a Responsible Withdrawal From Afghanistan', *Foreign Affairs*, 22 January 2021, https://www.foreignaffairs.com/articles/afghanistan/2021-01-22/myth-responsible-withdrawal-afghanistan.

8   See US Department of State, 'Agreement for Bringing Peace to Afghanistan Between the Islamic Emirate of Afghanistan Which Is Not Recognized by the United States as a State and Is Known as the Taliban and the United States of America',

29 February 2020, https://www.state.gov/wp-content/uploads/2020/02/Agreement-For-Bringing-Peace-to-Afghanistan-02.29.20.pdf.

9   See Hillary Rodham Clinton, 'Remarks at the Launch of the Asia Society's Series of Richard C. Holbrooke Memorial Addresses', US Department of State, 18 February 2011, https://2009-2017.state.gov/secretary/20092013clinton/rm/2011/02/156815.htm.

US–China Relations in the Shadow of Spengler

Lanxin Xiang

The Trumpism that inflamed fierce racial tensions at home has also racialised US policy abroad. Donald Trump both exposed and celebrated the racism at America's core – the legacy of slavery and Jim Crow – further polarising US politics and destroying much of what little domestic political cohesion he had inherited. He extended his white nativism to foreign policy in casting China as not merely a great-power rival but an implacable alien foe. Although the Biden administration rightly blames the disunity of America on Trumpism, it also frames Trump's China policy as the one thing he got mainly right. This is hugely problematic. Trump's late-term China policy was openly racist. While Joe Biden is not by any means a racist, the China policy *he* inherited still carries dangerous undertones of racial animus.

The political elite in Washington still harbour a 'unipolar fantasy', remain preoccupied with the question of decline and are horrified by the prospect that the world order they built will crumble.[1] Now, however, they also face a national crisis of Trump-induced domestic instability, and may feel compelled to try to defuse it by casting China as an alien threat. This would be a grave political and strategic mistake. Not only will it fail, but it may also provoke strong anti-Western backlash among Chinese both at home and abroad.

Lanxin Xiang is Director of the Institute of Security Policy, China National Institute for SCO International Exchange and Judicial Cooperation (CNISCO) and Director of Strategic Compass Dialogues based in Washington, London and Geneva. He is retiring from a professorship in Geneva.

Survival | vol. 63 no. 3 | June–July 2021 | pp. 45–53   https://doi.org/10.1080/00396338.2021.1930405

The ghost of Spengler

Racism in Western strategic thought is nothing new. Over a century ago, Oswald Spengler prophesied a declining West and left its white leaders with a terrible proposition: if the rise of the non-white peoples is causing the West's demise, the white world should either eliminate them or retard their advancement. The worst solution, according to Spengler, was integration. While Nazi Germany decided to eliminate an entire ethno-religious group, today's West at times seems to be returning to the idea of economic retardation and military intimidation against the most advanced non-white country – namely, China.

At the end of the nineteenth century, to justify the Western conquest of the East, German Kaiser Wilhelm II popularised the notion of the Yellow Peril. Then it was a metaphor that presented East Asians as a psycho-cultural menace and an existential racial threat to the West. Its twenty-first-century incarnation is more dangerous, for it has become almost exclusively national, and directed against a single nation-state. The comparably racist Japan-bashing of the 1970s and 1980s now seems quaintly historical, as Japan is generally recognised as the 'Western' country that it effectively has become, starting in the nineteenth century, and most obviously with the American occupation of 1945. China has not become 'Western'. Still more ominously, the new Yellow Peril theme has substantial political cover, since it is embedded in a moral crusade of good versus evil, and democracy over authoritarianism, to defend and advance 'universal values' that in fact originated in the West. This stance is threatening to fuel a new Spenglerian cold war.

The contemporary United States, however, lacks a strategic thinker like George Kennan. Nobody is available to craft a 'Long Telegram' explaining modern Chinese history or the endogenous cultural roots of China's rapid rise. By default, Washington is resorting to declinism, in line with the theme of Spengler's *The Decline of the West*, and reviving the Yellow Peril trope to cast racial aspersions – a weapon it avoided using during the original Cold War, in which the chief adversary was a Caucasian power.

Declinism is a morbid fear that never declines. It has the same fascination for historians that love has for romantic poets, and is most useful to politicians when blaming others for one's own internal problems. Blending anxieties about the West's downfall, fears of the alien Other and the Spenglerian worry that the East will outnumber and enslave the West, the American position is, in effect, that the Chinese as a race do not deserve economic and technological advances. This view is more revisionist than any outlook that can reasonably be ascribed to China.

Amid rising global racism, hostility towards people of Chinese descent has gained momentum, especially since the coronavirus outbreak. At the onset of the pandemic, Walter Russell Mead called China the 'real sick man of Asia'.[2] Many in the West and elsewhere objected to the racist tone of the remark. But when American politicians and government officials began repeatedly and baselessly referring to the 'bat-eating Chinese', 'Confu Virus' and Xinjiang 'genocide', and Trump himself called COVID-19 'the Chinese virus' and 'Kung flu', the Western media eventually became numb. Trump and his followers normalised such racist language. It provoked strong emotional reactions in China and rekindled a nationalistic sentiment within the Chinese population of an intensity unseen since the era of Mao Zedong.

Not so grand strategy

The US-sponsored security scheme in Asia also has an air of Yellow Peril. According to a recently declassified Indo-Pacific strategy document, the purpose is to create an Asian NATO to contain China and stop the decline of the West.[3] But the geopolitical concept of the 'Indo-Pacific', newly established by the United States to achieve this goal, is too clever by half. It is designed to make it look as though the US still takes allies seriously, while also giving the appearance of racial inclusiveness. The core of the strategy is the Quadrilateral Security Dialogue – known as the Quad – which consists of two white powers (the US and Australia) and two honorary white powers (Japan and India). Japan has long enjoyed this status, being the only non-white member of the G7. India, always more palatable to the West because of its democratic system and British imperial lineage, has long been considered to have a racial make-up that further qualifies it for this honorary status. The 'Aryan origins' of the Indians have historically been accepted in the West, and were promoted enthusiastically by prominent figures such as Richard Wagner, Houston Stewart Chamberlain and Spengler himself.

Not surprisingly, Hindu nationalists have adopted 'Indigenous Aryanism' as part of their ideology.

Perhaps because of the new branding and old presumptions, many US policymakers and analysts seem convinced that US allies support its treating China as its main rival, reinforcing a tough US stance. But if any such global democratic consensus exists, it is very fragile. The Trump administration adopted a comprehensive containment strategy against China on military, political and economic fronts, with the unabashed objective of undermining the rule of the Chinese Communist Party. However, mainstream American foreign-policy leaders and European and Asian allies of the United States do not support regime change in China.[4]

Furthermore, the United States' Indo-Pacific strategy is arguably more talk than action. Countries in the Asia-Pacific will strongly resist choosing between China and the US.[5] The US has focused on the regional military balance, with the aim of building a 'mini-NATO' in the region. As of now, however, there is neither a serious military organisation nor a clear military strategy. The only notable development in that direction is the reinvigoration of the Quad. But it is far from becoming a coordinated military command centre.[6] While the Quad may hold summit meetings and conduct joint military exercises, its cooperative capabilities do not seem to improve much, and it seems unlikely to seriously enhance deterrence against China, especially given the Biden administration's downgrading of the military dimension of the US strategy and upgrading of the diplomatic one.

The fatal flaw of the Indo-Pacific strategy, though, is economic. The two major powers of the so-called Indo-Pacific theatre – the US at the eastern-most point of the Pacific Ocean and India at the westernmost point of the Indian Ocean – are not parties to the trade and investment agreements of this key geo-economic belt. The US withdrew from the Trans-Pacific Partnership, which eventually became the Comprehensive and Progressive Agreement for Trans-Pacific Partnership (CPTPP), while India pulled out of the Regional Comprehensive Economic Partnership (RCEP) negotiations. The RCEP covers 30% of the global population and 30% of global GDP, and is the largest trading bloc in history. China is a member of the RCEP, and has made clear its willingness to join the CPTPP. Thus, to make the

Indo-Pacific strategy cohere, the Biden administration is bound to face strong pressure either to join the CPTPP or to persuade India to join the RCEP. Both options are fraught. The US Congress, not to mention the progressive wing of the Democratic Party, would almost certainly block US membership of the CPTPP, while Indian Prime Minister Narendra Modi would not assent to India's membership in the RCEP. Other regional players would be reluctant to support an actively confrontational strategy in light of their economic dependence on China. From this perspective, the US Indo-Pacific strategy appears very thin both militarily and politically.

Despite these strategic weaknesses, the Biden administration has emphasised multilateral diplomacy to keep China in check and intends to count on its allies to deal with challenges from Beijing.[7] But it will take a major effort to rejuvenate America's reputation as a serious multilateral player. Trump repeatedly withdrew from multilateral systems and attacked multilateral institutions. While former US secretary of state Mike Pompeo was diplomatically active, his performance in the Indo-Pacific region had an adverse effect. When he visited countries in the region, Pompeo would attack China in a hysterical way, and threaten his hosts that they would have to choose between the US and China, making himself a nuisance to many regional leaders. This kind of behaviour led most Asia-Pacific countries, including Japan and South Korea, to conclude that their only value and importance to the US lay in whether they picked a side, and that otherwise the US did not pay much attention to bilateral relations. Overall, the substance and style of Pompeo's diplomacy has greatly diminished the United States' reputation and credibility in the Indo-Pacific region.

Pompeo attacked China hysterically

Granted, the Biden administration has improved the tone of US diplomacy and created a position for an Indo-Pacific coordinator. But given the United States' decreased credibility as an ally and a multilateral actor, it is unlikely that the Indo-Pacific strategy can continue being a key element of the United States' China policy. It might instead become what the Chinese call a 'chicken rib': a comforting thing that someone is reluctant to give up although it is of little value.

Towards more nuanced US policy

Despite the apparent continuity in China policy between the Trump and Biden administrations, the so-called bipartisan consensus rests on shaky domestic as well as strategic ground. The United States' internal crisis stems from demographic change, as the white population is about to lose its dominant position. As the old political elite tries to maintain national unity by holding onto democratic values, populist leaders like Trump attack not only those values but also the procedural rules of the game, including the electoral process itself. With a once stable and relatively civil two-party system thrown into vicious chaos, the notion of authentic bipartisanship is wishful thinking. When the Biden administration realises this grim reality, and stops trying to forge consensus where it cannot exist, it may be better able to formulate an equitable and effective China policy, based not on wistfulness for the old days of American politics but frank and candid analysis of the facts.

Here are a few relevant ones. Firstly, the Chinese government, unlike the Russian one, did not interfere in American domestic politics. Secondly, the persistent political gridlock in Washington does make China's governing system look better, as its record in addressing the pandemic shows. Thirdly, the overreaching claim of some members of China's elite that authoritarianism is superior to democracy has no substantial popular support, as a majority of the Chinese people know the defects and weaknesses of the Chinese system.[8] Fourthly, ethnic Chinese have not been a major factor in the racial unrest and economic decline of the West. On the contrary, Chinese immigrants tend to constitute highly assimilative and productive 'model minorities'.

More broadly, improving the lot of the middle class is a key policy pledge that helped Biden defeat Trump's populist presidency. Based on Biden's political calculations, foreign affairs in the next four years will be closely linked to US domestic affairs. But according to a Democratic Party research report released in September last year, most of America's middle class are not interested in fighting a new cold war against China.[9] They could welcome manufacturing jobs created as a result of Chinese investment. Thus, the cold-war rationale implied in the Indo-Pacific strategy will not help Biden's 'middle-class foreign policy' at all. Nor will China-bashing help Biden win back the middle class and defeat right-wing populism in coming congressional and presidential elections. Rather, the decline of the middle class, which Trump has exploited skilfully, could be slowed or arrested through engagement with China. Certainly, economic decoupling makes little sense, even if domestic political considerations may make it hard for Biden to take that position.

In areas like technology, the message conveyed to the Chinese remains unabashedly racist: China does not deserve technological advancement because the country's internal system is not Westernised. Such attitudes echo the racialist disposition for technology development promoted by Spengler 90 years ago. He vehemently argued against technological advancement because it could arm the 'colored races' against white civilisation. In his words: 'The exploited world is beginning to take its revenge on its lords. The innumerous hands of the colored races – at least as clever, and far less exigent – will shatter the economic organization of the whites at its foundations.'[10] The argument against technological advancement in China is based on a terrible scenario of a future world ruled by China. Yet China has never voiced or developed a historical ambition to dominate the world, and is willing to participate in international rule-setting for technological development. For Washington to continue to intimate that it harbours such an ambition merely to prop up the United States' investment in a misguided strategy only fans Chinese ultra-nationalism, and potentially amounts to a self-fulfilling prophecy of a racial clash.

Of course, there remains a fundamental dispute between China and the West on the question of political legitimacy. The prevailing Western assumption is that any political problem in China comes from the absence of true democracy. This is a gross oversimplification. In Western tradition, legitimacy means the popular acceptance of an authority, which in turn means a specific position of power in an established government. In the Western democratic context, therefore, political legitimacy depends on the structural arrangement of power along democratic lines.

Chinese civilisation, however, has never developed an appreciable structural dimension in politics. The Confucian conception of politics is entirely temporal, based on the idea that legitimacy is determined by a ruler's moral behaviour. The essence of any political legitimacy is that the population at large has confidence in its government's actions and considers them morally appropriate and legally executed. On this criterion, the Chinese population considers the Chinese communist government legitimate. It is only Western liberal-democratic orthodoxy that prevents serious dialogue between China and the West on this fundamental disagreement.

* * *

Henry Kissinger recently raised the spectre of a Sino-American war.[11] Indeed, the most worrying aspect of US–China relations is that both powers have adopted assertive and uncompromising postures. The US sees China as the primary strategic challenger to its pre-eminent position, and China is vigorously asserting what it considers to be its rightful place in the world. On both sides, domestic pressures to harden their external positions are considerable, and moderate voices have largely been marginalised. On the eve of the First World War too, each great power assumed a teleologically offensive frame of mind, thinking in terms of a war to end all wars. A single spark can start a prairie fire in today's world. The US and China must take care not to sleepwalk into another 1914.

Despite conspicuous Western impulses towards the racial tribalism of the last century, countervailing factors suggest that a unified Western strategy against China is not morally and practically sustainable. Accordingly, China should not overreact to hostile Western rhetoric. At a delicate moment when the West – and in particular the United States – is in a genuine state of alarm about its decline, as white supremacy crumbles in as many Western countries as it has resurfaced, China should adhere to Deng Xiaoping's admonition to control its hubris and tone down its 'wolf-warrior' language. There is no reason for it to risk war by panicking over a white-dominated democratic alliance or an Asian version of NATO, because neither appears likely to materialise.

Notes

1   See David Calleo, *Follies of Power: America's Unipolar Fantasy* (Cambridge: Cambridge University Press, 2009).

2   Walter Russell Mead, 'China Is the Real Sick Man of Asia', *Wall Street Journal*, 3 February 2020, https://www.wsj.com/articles/china-is-the-real-sick-man-of-asia-11580773677.

3   'United States Strategic Framework for the Indo-Pacific', https://trumpwhitehouse.archives.gov/wp-content/uploads/2021/01/IPS-Final-Declass.pdf.

4   See, for example, Kurt M. Campbell and Ely Ratner, 'The China Reckoning', *Foreign Affairs*, vol. 97, no. 2, March/April 2018, pp. 60–70.

5   See Feng Zhang, 'China's Curious Nonchalance Towards the Indo-Pacific', *Survival*, vol. 61, no. 3, June–July 2019, pp. 187–212.

6   On this general point, see Stephan Frühling, 'Is ANZUS Really an Alliance? Aligning the US and Australia', *Survival*, vol. 60, no. 5, October–November 2018, pp. 199–218.

7   See Peter Rudolf, 'The Sino-American World Conflict', *Survival*, vol. 63, no. 2, April–May 2021, pp. 87–114.

8   For a detailed analysis of the Chinese political system, see Lanxin Xiang, *The Quest for Legitimacy in Chinese Politics: A New Interpretation* (Abingdon: Routledge, 2019).

9   See Salman Ahmed et al. (eds), 'Making U.S. Foreign Policy Work Better for the Middle Class', Carnegie Endowment for International Peace, 2020, https://carnegieendowment.org/files/USFP_FinalReport_final1.pdf.

10 Oswald Spengler, *Man and Technics: A Contribution to a Philosophy of Life* (Abingdon: Routledge Revivals, 2018 [1931]), p. 51.

11 See, for example, Guy Faulconbridge, 'U.S. Needs New Understanding with China or It Risks Conflict, Kissinger Says', Reuters, 26 March 2021, https://www.reuters.com/article/us-usa-china-kissinger-idUSKBN2BI2MK.

Noteworthy

India's cruel second wave

'After successfully combating the first wave, the country was filled with confidence, but this storm has shaken the nation.'

Indian Prime Minister Narendra Modi comments on surging COVID-19 cases in India during a radio address on 25 April 2021.[1]

'How did it all go so horribly wrong in three short months? … The virus was forgotten for we had already declared ourselves the victors. And then the second wave struck, as any thinking person knew it would, and struck with the ferocity of a tidal wave, making the events of 2020 seem like a ripple in a bathtub … India has emerged as the epicentre of the global pandemic, a country brought to its knees by a tiny virus barely 100 nanometres in diameter. And we are paying the price of our complacency, mute spectators to this danse macabre.'

Zarir Udwadia, a consultant physician and researcher in Mumbai, comments on the situation in India in a Financial Times op-ed dated 29 April 2021.[2]

'India shut down too abruptly when the virus arrived, and then was too quick to reopen. In March 2020, the country was locked down at four hours' notice though it did not yet have many cases. Millions of people, many of them migrant workers, were left stranded without food and shelter. Facing economic disaster, the government reopened the country before the pandemic really took hold.'

Nobel laureates Abhijit V. Banerjee and Esther Duflo analyse the situation for the New York Times.[3]

'We are just burning bodies as they arrive. It is as if we are in the middle of a war.'

Mamtesh Sharma, an official at Bhadbhada Vishram Ghat crematorium in New Delhi, comments on the surge in demand for the crematorium's services.[4]

'It's like one of those movies in which the world has been attacked, and there are bodies everywhere. You wait for the superhero to come and save everyone. Only in this case, there is no superhero.'

Malvika Parakh comments on the scene at Ghazipur crematorium in New Delhi as she awaits the cremation of her father, who died from COVID-19 on 28 April 2021.[5]

China and America's tense summit

'China urges the US side to fully abandon the hegemonic practice of willfully interfering in China's internal affairs. This has been a long-standing issue and it should be changed. It is time for it to change. And in particular, on the 17th of March, the United States escalated its so-called sanctions on China regarding Hong Kong, and the Chinese people are outraged by this gross interference in China's internal affairs and the Chinese side is firmly opposed to it.

Anchorage is a midpoint between China and the United States, but after all, it's still the United States territory, and I accept that the Chinese delegation has come here at the invitation of the United States. However, just the other day, before our departure, the United States passed these new sanctions. This is not supposed to be the way one should welcome his guests, and we wonder if this is a decision made by the United States to try to gain some advantage in dealing with China, but certainly this is miscalculated and only reflects the vulnerability and weakness inside the United States. And this will not shake China's position or resolve on those issues.'

Chinese State Councilor Wang Yi speaks at a meeting with US Secretary of State Antony Blinken in Anchorage, Alaska, on 18 March 2021.[6]

'I have to tell you, in my short time as Secretary of State, I have spoken to I think nearly a hundred counterparts from around the world, and I just made my first trip, as I noted, to Japan and South Korea. I have to tell you, what I'm hearing is very different from what you described. I'm hearing deep satisfaction that the United States is back, that we're re-engaged with our allies and partners. I'm also hearing deep concern about some of the actions your government has taken, and we'll have an opportunity to discuss those when we get down to work.

A hallmark of our leadership, of our engagement in the world is our alliances and our partnerships that have been built on a totally voluntary basis. And it is something that President Biden is committed to reinvigorating.

And there's one more hallmark of our leadership here at home, and that's a constant quest to, as we say, form a more perfect union. And that quest, by definition, acknowledges our imperfections, acknowledges that we're not perfect, we make mistakes, we have reversals, we take steps back. But what we've done throughout our history is to confront those challenges openly, publicly, transparently, not trying to ignore them, not trying to pretend they don't exist, not trying to sweep them under a rug. And sometimes it's painful, sometimes it's ugly, but each and every time, we have come out stronger, better, more united as a country.'

Blinken responds to remarks by Wang and Yang Jiechi, director of the Chinese Central Commission for Foreign Affairs.[7]

Russia in Ukraine

'If Russia wanted to do it in secret, they would do it in secret. They're doing everything they can for us to see them, and to show us how cool [Russian President Vladimir] Putin is.'

Dmytro Kotsyubaylo, commander of a volunteer unit of the ultranationalist Ukrainian militia Right Sector, comments on Russia's military build-up near Ukraine in April 2021.[8]

'These ships are, concretely, a threat from the Russian state.'

Captain Mykola Levytskyi of Ukraine's coastguard comments on a build-up of Russian vessels in the Azov Sea.[9]

'We are not afraid, because we have an incredible army and incredible defenders … Our citizens need clear signals that in the seventh year of the war, a country that is a shield for Europe at the cost of lives of our people will receive support not just as partners from the stands, but as players of one team, directly on the field, shoulder to shoulder.'

Ukrainian President Volodymyr Zelensky speaks to the nation in an address broadcast on 21 April 2021.[10]

'When I was a child, when we argued in the courtyard, we said the following: "If you call someone names, that's really your name." When we characterise other people, or even when we characterise other states, other people, it is always as though we are looking in the mirror.'

Russian President Vladimir Putin responds to remarks by US President Joe Biden, who agreed with an interviewer's characterisation of Putin as a 'killer'.[11]

'I believe that the objectives of the surprise check have been fully achieved. The troops have demonstrated the ability to provide a reliable defence of the country. In this regard, I made a decision to complete [the exercises].'

Russian Defence Minister Sergei Shoigu announces the withdrawal of Russian troops from the Ukrainian border, claiming that they had been in the area to conduct exercises.[12]

'Armenian genocide': Biden's call

'Each year on this day, we remember the lives of all those who died in the Ottoman-era Armenian genocide and recommit ourselves to preventing such an atrocity from ever again occurring. Beginning on April 24, 1915, with the arrest of Armenian intellectuals and community leaders in Constantinople by Ottoman authorities, one and a half million Armenians were deported, massacred, or marched to their deaths in a campaign of extermination. We honor the victims of the Meds Yeghern so that the horrors of what happened are never lost to history. And we remember so that we remain ever-vigilant against the corrosive influence of hate in all its forms.'

Joe Biden becomes the first US president to refer to the deportation and killing of Armenians beginning in 1915 in what is now Turkey as a 'genocide', in a statement released on 24 April 2021.[13]

'The statement lacks a legal basis in terms of international law, has deeply injured the Turkish people and has opened a wound in our relationship that will be difficult to repair.'

Turkey's Ministry of Foreign Affairs responds to the statement.[14]

Sources

1 Benjamin Parkin, 'India Airlifts Medical Supplies from Abroad as Covid "Shakes Nation", *Financial Times*, 25 April 2021, https://www.ft.com/content/4f2ffa2c-b8bf-4d6d-9c25-13c0063604d2.

2 Zarir Udwadia, 'India's Covid Wards Are Like Scenes from Dante's "Inferno", *Financial Times*, 29 April 2021, https://www.ft.com/content/ad200d93-3247-409a-8afb-482234b4655c.

3 Abhijit Banerjee and Esther Duflo, 'India Is Now the World's Problem', *New York Times*, 6 May 2021, https://www.nytimes.com/2021/05/06/opinion/covid-india-crisis.html?action=click&module=Opinion&pgtype=Homepage.

4 Sheikh Saaliq and Aijaz Hussain, 'As COVID-19 Surge Continues in India, Hospitals and Crematoriums Are Overwhelmed', *TIME*, 25 April 2021, https://time.com/5958329/india-covid-19-surge/.

5 Aman Sethi, "Death Is the Only Truth." Watching India's Funeral Pyres Burn', *New York Times*, 30 April 2021, https://www.nytimes.com/2021/04/30/opinion/india-covid-crematorium.html.

6 US Department of State, 'Secretary Antony J. Blinken, National Security Advisor Jake Sullivan, Director Yang and State Councilor Wang at the Top of Their Meeting', press release, 18 March 2021, https://www.state.gov/secretary-antony-j-blinken-national-security-advisor-jake-sullivan-chinese-director-of-the-office-of-the-central-commission-for-foreign-affairs-yang-jiechi-and-chinese-state-councilor-wang-yi-at-th/.

7 *Ibid.*

8 Anton Troianovski, "A Threat from the Russian State": Ukrainians Alarmed as Troops Mass on Their Doorstep', *New York Times*, 22 April 2021, https://www.nytimes.com/2021/04/20/world/europe/-ukraine-russia-putin-invasion.html?action=click&module=In%20Other%20News&pgtype=Homepage.

9 *Ibid.*

10 'Ukraine's President Warns of Possible War with Russia', *New York Times*, 21 April 2021, https://www.nytimes.com/video/world/europe/100000007722441/zelensky-ukraine-russia-war.html.

11 Anton Troianovski, 'Russia Erupts in Fury over Biden's Calling Putin a Killer', *New York Times*, 18 March 2021, https://www.nytimes.com/2021/03/18/world/europe/russia-biden-putin-killer.html.

12 Henry Foy and Roman Olearchyk, 'Russia Orders Troops to Pull Back from Ukraine Border', *Financial Times*, 22 April 2021, https://www.ft.com/content/eb18eb9e-a2bd-47d6-b5cc-338ca2095d4f?emailId=6082504845b88d00042a8369&segmentId=22011ee7-896a-8c4c-22a0-7603348b7f22.

13 White House, 'Statement by President Joe Biden on Armenian Remembrance Day', 24 April 2021, https://www.whitehouse.gov/briefing-room/statements-releases/2021/04/24/statement-by-president-joe-biden-on-armenian-remembrance-day/.

14 Ayla Jean Yackley and Aime Williams, 'Turkey Rejects Biden's Recognition of Armenian Genocide', *Financial Times*, 24 April 2021, https://www.ft.com/content/c928c4b4-3c79-4589-97be-d6e1af04c4b0?emailId=608645a740986e0004dbd24c&segmentId=22011ee7-896a-8c4c-22a0-7603348b7f22.

The Fleet in Being: An Alternative US Strategy

Kenneth Weisbrode

While American global leadership has been far from perfect, to many Americans and others throughout the world it does appear preferable to the strategic alternative of ceding direction to illiberal, authoritarian regimes – in particular, China and, to a limited extent, Russia. Designing and implementing a new and appropriately assertive American foreign policy should start with a view of the United States as a power with enduring responsibilities in multiple regions with the goal of making the world safe for democracy. A successful policy must also align aims and resources, including human resources.

American responsibilities can be fulfilled only in cooperation with other nations and with an understanding of their interests, views and vulnerabilities vis-à-vis their own neighbours and other powers. A consensus is forming around a strategy of constructive US disengagement from international commitments, especially those that anticipate the use of force. This understanding does not include many specific plans to implement policies, or to consider many consequences, one of which is likely to be a more contested and possibly diminished US influence in certain regions, chiefly Central Europe, Southeast Asia and Southwest Asia.

One possible, promising approach would be a strategy inspired by the early-modern concept of a 'fleet in being' to advance US interests

Kenneth Weisbrode is assistant professor of history at Bilkent University and author of *The Year of Indecision, 1946* (Viking, 2016).

Survival | vol. 63 no. 3 | June–July 2021 | pp. 57–70   https://doi.org/10.1080/00396338.2021.1930407

by promoting regional security communities and cooperative security within and among those communities, which include the United States. A strategy based on this concept could reconcile a preference for military disengagement and the enduring need for political engagement. The 'fleet' – a force held in reserve in order to influence others' strategic choices – would substitute multilateral institutions in which the US preserves and augments its important role for more direct projections of its power.

The fleet in being would make for a more coherent and effective strategy than the three putative alternatives: unipolar hegemony, spheres of influence and offshore balancing. Greater political engagement would reduce the demand and the temptation to use force and therefore could allow for the reduction of the defence and security infrastructure designed for projecting military power with the potential use of force in mind. The deliberate combination of such engagement with gradual military disengagement would also help mitigate the uncertainty and possible conflicts that the latter might entail.

Conceptual and historical underpinnings

The fleet in being is originally a naval concept, nominally dating from the turn of the eighteenth century. It involves a naval force that exerts influence by being held in port or otherwise away from a main theatre of battle rather than being deployed directly against an enemy, thus compelling the enemy to redirect its own force. In other words, it operates indirectly by diversion. It can do this in several ways, the most common one being by posing an implicit threat that 'causes or necessitates counter-concentrations and so reduces the number of opposing units available for operations elsewhere'.[1] It also may be used to harass and evade, or to protect a weaker set of assets against a more formidable force in a naval facsimile of guerrilla warfare.[2] As such, the fleet in being operates to stage holding actions – that is, to buy time. In practice, however, it is not a purely defensive device, but rather an 'offensive–defensive' one requiring active operations to be credible. It is so designed to thwart an adversary's strengths by directing them away from one's most vulnerable positions, to preserve an element of unpredictability and therefore to improve the capacity to shape overall conditions to one's advantage.

The term was reportedly coined by the Earl of Torrington, the English admiral, in 1690.[3] Commanding his nation's fleet in the English Channel during the War of the League of Augsburg, Torrington resisted fighting against a superior French force until his own could be reinforced. He proposed keeping his fleet 'in being' in order to affect the positioning of the French fleet without drawing it fully into battle. This did not work as hoped, mainly because Torrington was ordered to attack the French fleet anyway.[4] Whether or not he actually invented the term, the concept was not new. The Roman navy employed something like a fleet in being, although the rationale had to do with the political needs of its allies, who manned many of its ships.[5] Torrington's Dutch allies also made use of a similar force posture and strategy.

Traditional American naval strategy has not looked favourably upon the concept. Alfred Thayer Mahan emphasised direct action. Although he conceded the importance of psychological effects in wartime, which may include peripheral raids, Mahanian strategy generally abjures indirect approaches. For him, the fleet in being would have utility only as a temporary measure to keep rivals 'on edge'.[6]

Other strategists have been more sympathetic. For example, while Julian Corbett shared Mahan's view that the ultimate aim of any naval force is command of the sea, he recognised that the fleet in being could advance this aim so long as it is kept *actively* in being – not merely in existence, but in active and vigorous life'. Thus it 'avoid[s] decisive action … till the situation develops in our favour'.[7] It is, in other words, both a way of hovering in order to keep the enemy in check and also an element of strategic depth, or part of a containment strategy in multiple theatres. It served this function for Britain during the eighteenth century, when the navy could not maintain a large presence at once in the Mediterranean and the West Indies, and blockades of important routes in both areas were not feasible.[8]

Fleets in being have generally been deployed to compensate for weakness or vulnerability. It should follow that stronger powers could make use of the fleet in being in reverse, that is, as a deterrent.[9] N.A.M. Rodger has written that 'arguably', in some instances, 'the Navy was a more effective deterrent when it did not often fight, for real battles … might expose the limitations as well as the strengths of sea power'.[10] A fleet in being has never been the decisive factor in defeating an enemy, or in gaining mastery of the ocean. But at the right places and at the right times, it has paid off well.

In peacetime, the navy's main objective was to keep important trading routes open and secure, but it could not do so everywhere at once. A mobile fleet in being thus constituted a deterrent in the sense that it redirected the resources and attention of adversaries. In wartime, when fleets in being may be combined with more active operations, as in William Pitt's 'amphibious' policy in the Seven Years' War – which was meant as 'a strategic lever to multiply the value of small bodies of troops' – they can play an important composite role.[11] In this context, they augment the leverage of armies by redirecting supply chains, challenging the status of allies and neutrals, and forcing greater outlays beyond the main theatre of battle, much as a blockade does but at less expense. Especially in more covert applications – involving German U-boats, for example – tactical, operational and even strategic benefits of the fleet in being can exceed the costs for the side that wields it.[12]

During the First World War, several navies possessed something akin to a fleet in being. Britain controlled the North Sea, for example, largely through the use of a fleet in being, as almost a mirror image of the Germans' own 'risk fleet' constituted just before the war, which sought to challenge British dominance simultaneously in multiple places.[13] The Italian and Austrian navies during the war promoted the use of fleets in being as well, but doing so was more likely an excuse for refusing battle, making them 'not so much defensive as inert'.[14]

The Italians pursued a similar naval strategy in the Second World War, with a similar lack of success. The German navy, by contrast, was effective in threatening and diverting British naval forces with an aggressive combined operation off the coast of Norway. Another good example of a successful fleet-in-being rationale was US Admiral Ernest King's initial Pacific strategy, summed up by his famous line: 'hold what you've got and hit them when you can'.

The fleet-in-being concept has been applied to non-maritime forces, albeit with difficulty. Union General George McClellan's inaction during the US

Civil War is not a strong endorsement of an army force in being. Air forces present a somewhat different case. The advent of airpower was seen as a critical factor vitiating the strategic potential of the fleet in being as a force immobiliser.[15] But airpower itself, particularly bombers (and, by extension, the nuclear triad), may function as a fleet in being in some circumstances.[16] Something comparable may be imagined for satellites and hypersonic weapons. Such assets may serve as a kind of insurance policy by exerting minimal deterrence against like forces. In either case, actual deployment in battle would represent a fundamental failure of the policy.

The Pentagon may have applied the concept more flexibly by orienting US forces as forward-deployed, 'supported' geographic combatant commands sustained, as regional circumstances require, by 'supporting' commands, especially in the context of increasing diplomatic roles for geographic combatant commanders. Arguably, the United States has a fleet-in-being maritime strategy today given its limited deployments of carrier strike groups and area support groups.

The value of the fleet in being has been in the eye of the beholder. Its golden age was the eighteenth century, which featured, as noted, multiple powers having alternately to deter one another and to draw one another into battle in multiple naval theatres (the Mediterranean and Caribbean seas, and the Atlantic and Indian oceans). Add to this the fluctuating politics on the European continent, and the fleet in being begins to appear like an essential strategy for managing regional security. Despite today's very different complexities and interrelationships, the fleet in being, regardless of its plausibility in any particular military scenario, always possesses an important psychological quality in aiming to influence the calculus of an adversary. Both nuclear deterrence and reassurance involve similar calculi.[17] The important point is that, like any concept, the fleet in being does not have independent or intrinsic value. It must be part of a broader strategy.

Contemporary relevance

The American geopolitical mindset of Mahan's time divided the world into three parts: Europe, the Americas and the Pacific. The prevailing view was that US interests demanded isolation (understood as neutrality) from the first, hegemony in the second and a balance of power in the third. Each component relied on the successful management of the others.

The tripartite American mind perhaps was inherited from, or at least related to, that of the British. For them, the relevant trio comprised the European continent, the overseas empire and the home islands. It was unlikely that Britain could preserve a balance of power on the first while fully defending the other two, so British strategic doctrine emphasised optimal rather than maximal arrangements of resources and political alignments. Each arrangement was the subject of regular, passionate debate over operational questions of emphasis and allocation, as well as adjustments to the underlying strategic principle: how much did the three elements enhance or diminish one another? Still, the doctrine's inherent flexibility, along with a certain British tendency for decisive action, or what some may see as reversing course, transformed geographic vulnerabilities into assets, at least for as long as it lasted – arguably, to the end of the 1950s.

Geographic vulnerabilities became assets

The contemporary analogy is the United States' need to defend its own hemisphere, protect allies and defend interests farther afield, notably in Northeast Asia and the Middle East. However, it is important to recall that a major shift in US strategic thinking took place between Mahan's time and the present day.[18] By the middle of the twentieth century, the US was no longer a continental power at home and a maritime power abroad, as it had been for Mahan's generation. It had become a superpower, sharing borders with other major powers in Asia and Europe, with an approach to the air and the sea that reinforced regional interdependence. Neither the end of the Cold War in the 1980s nor the subsequent disappearance of the Soviet Union changed that composite orientation for the United States. They may have exacerbated it.

Thirty years seems like a very long time in politics, but geopolitical mentalities take a while to evolve. Another shift in the Mahanian direction appears to have taken place. It is the result of the assertiveness of other major powers, namely China and Russia, and of the weariness of the American people with the costs of poorly conceived and badly executed military interventions during the past two decades. It is too soon to tell how lasting this shift will be, or whether it will be replaced by a counter-shift involving either doctrinaire non-intervention or something else dictated by emergent events. In the meantime, the United States has adopted an official strategic doctrine based on a traditional concept of great-power competition, which presumably allows for selective intervention. It appears to take for granted the American people's willingness to continue to pay the costs of competition, whatever it entails; but what it entails, in terms of cost and geopolitics, remains vague.

Neither competition nor greatness is a geopolitical given. They demand choice. Thus, it is not clear how much of this strategic reorientation, either for the United States or for its presumed adversaries and competitors, is rhetorical. Do they seek to weaken the United States everywhere? To overtake it economically? To acquire its allies? To make it a vassal or tributary power? To expel it from certain regions? What do they want, exactly? During the Cold War, the best strategic minds engaged in similar thought experiments over the putative capabilities and intentions of the Soviet Union and other powers.[19] Yet most people now accept that the Cold War did not end because one side defeated the other, as would occur in a traditional war. It is more convenient to say one won a competition when the other forfeited. The nature and extent of the competition – or, really, multiple competitions in different regions – are still the subjects of intense debate.[20]

To participate in this debate is also a choice. The more important question to revisit is how the Cold War ended so peacefully, and why in its aftermath there was no war of succession among the world's major powers, numerous violent conflicts notwithstanding. One possible answer to both questions is that the preponderance of US power remained a strong deterrent. Another is that regional integration mitigated conflicts between historic adversaries to the extent that many people in several regions came to understand their interests, and themselves, collaboratively – and in some places even as members of a community.

The question facing US strategists today is how best to advance and defend the country's interests in several regions while helping them to become, or remain, peaceful. There are at least 15 regions to consider spanning Africa (Central, East, South and West), America (Central, North and South), Asia (Central, Northeast, South, Southeast and Southwest), Europe (Central/South/West and Eastern) and Australasia. The Arctic and Antarctic may someday join the list, depending how intense the geopolitical contest over these places becomes. The United States is still unique in having important interests and a political and economic presence in every one.

The ranking of these interests is complicated, variable and subjective. However, any systematic effort to rank them must begin on the principle that no region is separable from its neighbours. All regions overlap to some degree. And superpowers – defined not only by their size but also by their capacity to mobilise resources from one part of the globe to another – therefore have interests that intersect regions. This principle is important because policies must account for the reality of regional interpenetration and interdependence, especially where policymakers identify an aim to deny regional mastery to any single power. If policymaking works to counter that reality, or if it seeks to impose a preferred hierarchy of interests and interest groups, it will be more likely to encounter resistance than alternatives that set community-building as their primary aim.

To imagine the world organically as a set of interlocking and interdependent regions is rather different than seeing it as a chessboard of greater and lesser powers. But either way, the operational elements of strategy must have an important regional dimension because they must align domestic preferences with interests.[21] Great-power competition does not take place exclusively on a bilateral basis. Lesser powers and their own interests matter – and are, to a significant degree, indivisible from great powers and their interests. The reasons for that are familiar: people, goods, ideas, loyalties and enmities traverse borders; geography exerts power in a manner that blurs the distinction not only between greater and lesser powers but also between their military and non-military relations; these relations are themselves indivisible from the mental maps and other forces in economics, society, culture and ideology that frame international politics. The recognition of indivisibility is the real basis for asking if the fleet-in-being concept is more viable than other concepts because it rests on the belief that no power

– large or small – has the luxury of repudiating geography or human nature, both of which tend to be connective as well as divisive.

The fleet in being versus other strategies

Once again in conscious or unconscious imitation of the British, strategic debate in the US today presents two opposing attitudes that have acquired the trappings of doctrine: hegemonic and restrained. Both are programmatic, hierarchical and implicitly imperialistic in their conception, with the US cast as the subject and the rest of the world as the object. The British once called them 'forward' and 'backward'. The distinction is quite simplistic and to some extent false, as some hegemonic policies have been restrained in their execution. Yet the debate has had relatively little to do with most realities outside the United States, or with external US interests. Debaters are not necessarily unmindful of those realities, but regional interests are again the object, rather than the subject, under discussion.[22]

The utility of the fleet-in-being concept is that it overcomes the limitations of this hierarchy by flipping the subject–object relationship on its head. A fleet in being by definition is restrained. Translated from a naval to a general policy, it is also counter-hegemonic. Its aim is to combine particular interests at certain places and times, not to design or dictate circumstances on principle. It shapes regional circumstances by adapting itself to them. Just as Torrington defended his decision to hold back his force after having noted the size and location of the opposing force, and as later war planners offered a similar justification for the repositioning of naval and related assets, contemporary American statecraft should be based empirically on the existence of a polycentric world and the role of multilateral institutions in it.

The fleet in being is not a passive or reactive strategy, however. It is active yet inductive, seeking power through the influence over others in concert. Its maxim is not 'use it or lose it' or 'you don't lose if you don't play', but instead 'collaborate and gain'. That is another way of saying that US power 'in being' is not an end in itself, but rather is wielded – or withheld, as the case may warrant – to serve US interests. It is an indirect strategy that serves to redirect US power through the enhancement of the collective power of other nations whose interests align actively or potentially with those of the United States. Or, as the late Fred Iklé once described a similar approach, it is 'that the US preserve and improve its various capabilities to help its friends defend themselves'.[23] That is different from the wishful supposition that a superpower's unilateral disengagement will compel other powers to develop and use such capabilities responsibly on their own.

In practice, today's fleet in being may be distinguished from three principal alternative concepts that have been advanced in what has become a hoary and at times narcissistic debate over whether or not US power is a force for good: unipolar hegemony, spheres of influence and offshore balancing. The first is a blanket strategy of power for its own sake: imposing or renouncing it, no matter what. The second is a more parsimonious version of the first strategy, but probably impossible to enact in the twenty-first century because of economic and related interdependence. The third is an even more parsimonious version of the first, and probably a less parsimonious version of the second, vaguely akin to the British continental commitment with the entire world standing in for Europe. Unlike the first and second, it confuses the ends and means of a policy of limited liability; conflates non-intervention with neutrality as well as disengagement; and neglects some hard lessons about interdependence and collective security inasmuch as it presumes an ability to programme the minds of regional actors and underrates the chance that military and non-military engagement (or disengagement) are understood as two sides of the same coin.

Here, too, it is hard to see how such a strategy could work today, starting with the difficulty in identifying what lies 'offshore' and in determining what actually constitutes a balance of power. Even if all that were possible for military and other planners to do with a degree of certainty, the strategy, like the other two, is based on the direct use or non-use of power, and has little to do or say about how to make optimal use of the combined or indirect use of power, allied or otherwise, in specific regions. The underlying basis for all three models is partition or rivalry, not cooperation or collaboration. If their aim is peace, it is hard to imagine it being anything other than an oppressive order that is unlikely to garner much support from the American people even if it could be made to serve US interests.

By contrast, the exercise of a fleet-in-being strategy is indirect and works through collaboration with regional powers. Multilateral institutions, and the cooperative behaviour and confidence they engender, constitute the 'fleet' in the strategy. The aim of such collaboration is to build security communities. A security community aligns power relationships among large, middle and small powers with the interests and aims of these powers, and with the overall health of the community. The history of the western hemisphere and of Western Europe demonstrate that fostering alignment is arduous, contentious and frustrating, but also that, if done well, a security community can emerge even in the most fractious of regions. There has been no major international war in either place for many decades, and none appears likely. There is no inherent reason why this cannot be true in other regions. That is not to deny the existence of rivalry in today's world, but rather to advance an approach to regional politics that does not have rivalry as its basis.

Such an approach cannot rely exclusively upon the artistry of a particular leader or government. It must gain institutional life. Much as a naval fleet in being is mobilised from place to place in order to make optimal use of its strength while diverting and dividing that of its adversaries, the energetic participation in multilateral institutions – political alliances such as NATO as well as non-governmental bodies of many shapes, colours and sizes from region to region – must continue as a renewed, collaborative form of American leadership 'in being' rather than in nominal authority. The aim of this fleet is not to 'lead from behind' or to cloak American power, but instead to give it a more lasting and versatile influence consistent with American values. Institutions are the repositories and magnets of both latent and active power. They can act to limit and proscribe the power of nation-states, including superpowers like the United States, but over time they enlist and enhance it. The more the United States works with and through such institutions, the greater and more beneficial its world position probably will be. Such a view has recently returned to official favour.[24] But unless these entities have roots in the local soil, sustaining them would likely be a major task for US diplomacy and continue to involve significant costs up front for benefits that appear at the present time to be rather distant.

*   *   *

The United States can no longer presume to govern nearly every part of the world. Nor can it afford to withdraw its attention from certain parts of the world. The United States is still too big, too powerful and too necessary, and the world has become too small. Because regional cooperation is not likely to work if it is imposed from the outside, and not likely to happen on its own from the inside, it is the responsibility of the world's major powers, including the United States, to encourage it in both places by assisting regional powers with their efforts to strengthen and extend the remit of multilateral institutions. Such assistance is self-interested and important. It can be furthered by viewing contemporary geopolitics as a naval strategist would conceptualise a fleet in being: an active but indirect force summoned by circumstances in order to stimulate, diversify, fortify and defend the efforts of others in ways that favour the national interest.

Acknowledgements

An earlier version of this essay was prepared for the nuclear-security project at the Hoover Institution on War, Revolution and Peace at Stanford University. I am grateful to James Goodby, C. Richard Nelson, Erik Sand and Heather Yeung for providing helpful comments and suggestions.

Notes

1   US Department of Defense, *Dictionary of Military Terms* (New York: Skyhorse, 2009), p. 207.

2   See Geoffrey Till, *Seapower: A Guide for the Twenty-first Century* (London: Frank Cass, 2004), pp. 160–2.

3   For a good summary, see John B. Hattendorf, 'The Idea of a "Fleet in Being" in Historical Perspective', *Naval War College Review*, vol. 67, no. 1, Winter 2014, pp. 43–61.

4   Torrington was subsequently tried by court martial and acquitted.

5   See H.H. Scullard, 'Roman Sea-power', *Classical Review*, vol. 7, no. 2, June 1957, pp. 144–7; and Graham Bower, 'National Policy and Naval Strength', *Journal of Comparative Legislation and International Law*, third series, vol. 10, no. 4, 1928, p. 342, which restates the words of Quintus Silo to Marius: 'If you are a great general, Marius, come out and fight a battle.' Marius: 'If you are one, make me do it.'

6   See J.C.M. Ogelsby, 'Spain's Havana Squadron and the Preservation of the

Balance of Power in the Caribbean, 1740–1748', *Hispanic American Historical Review*, vol. 49, no. 3, August 1969, pp. 473–88, 481.

7   Quoted in Clark G. Reynolds, 'The U.S. Fleet-in-Being Strategy of 1942', *Journal of Military History*, vol. 58, no. 1, January 1994, pp. 103–18, 104 (Reynolds's emphasis). See also Hattendorf, 'The Idea of a "Fleet in Being"' in Historical Perspective', pp. 45–6.

8   See G.S. Graham, 'The Naval Defence of British North America 1739–1763', *Transactions of the Royal Historical Society*, vol. 30, December 1948, pp. 95–110. Maintaining a flexible and mobile emphasis between the two theatres foreshadowed the kind of calculus that later became famous with the British 'continental commitment'.

9   See, for example, Paul van Hooft, 'Don't Knock Yourself Out: How America Can Turn the Tables on China by Giving Up the Fight for Command of the Seas', *War on the Rocks*, 23 February 2021, https://warontherocks. com/2021/02/dont-knock-yourself-out-how-america-can-turn-the-tables-on-china-by-giving-up-the-fight-for-command-of-the-seas/; and Shi Xiaoqin and Liu Xiaobo, 'Chinese Assessment of New U.S. Naval Strategy', *USNI News*, 19 February 2021, https://news.usni.org/2021/02/19/chinese-assessment-of-new-u-s-naval-strategy.

10   N.A.M. Rodger, *The Command of the Ocean: A Naval History of Britain 1649–1815* (New York: W. W. Norton & Co., 2005), p. 231. Rodger added: 'though the deterrence was successful, it was also costly. It needed large fleets and skilful leadership.'

11   *Ibid.*, pp. 270–1.

12   For German and British consideration of the fleet in being and new naval technologies at the turn of the twentieth century, see Keith Bird, 'The Tirpitz Legacy: The Political Ideology of German Sea Power', *Journal of Military History*, vol. 69, no. 3, July 2005, pp. 821–5; and Nicholas A. Lambert, 'Admiral John Fisher and the Concept of Flotilla Defence, 1904–1909', *Journal of Military History*, vol. 59, no. 4, October 1995, pp. 639–60.

13   See R.B. McCallum, review of A.J. Marder's *From the Dreadnought to Scapa Flow*, vol. III, in *English Historical Review*, vol. 83, no. 326, January 1968, pp. 216–17; and Bird, 'The Tirpitz Legacy'.

14   Rhodri Williams, review of Paul G. Halpern's, *The Naval War in the Mediterranean, 1914–1918*, in *English Historical Review*, vol. 103, no. 409, October 1988, p. 1,011.

15   See Andrew Gyorgy, 'The Geopolitics of War: Total War and Geostrategy', *Journal of Politics*, vol. 5, no. 4, November 1943, p. 358.

16   See McGeorge Bundy, 'Nuclear Weapons and the Gulf', *Foreign Affairs*, vol. 70, no. 4, Fall 1991, pp. 83–94.

17   It probably will do for the foreseeable future. See Walter Pincus, 'A Glimpse of the U.S.' New Nuclear Posture', *Cipher Daily Brief*, 23 March 2021, https://www.thecipherbrief.com/column_article/a-glimpse-of-the-u-s-new-nuclear-posture.

18   See Alan K. Henrikson, 'The Map as an "Idea": The Role of Cartographic Imagery During the Second World War', *American Cartographer*, vol. 2, no. 1, 1975, pp. 19–53.

19 See, for example, W. Scott Thompson, *Power Projection: A Net Assessment of U.S. and Soviet Capabilities* (New York: National Strategy Information Center, 1978).

20 Lorenz Luthi, *Cold Wars* (Cambridge: Cambridge University Press, 2020) is a recent example.

21 See Samuel P. Huntington, *The Common Defense: Strategic Programs in National Politics* (New York: Columbia University Press, 1961), esp. chapter five.

22 See Elbridge Colby and Walter Slocombe, 'The State of (Deterrence by) Denial', *War on the Rocks*, 22 March 2021, https://warontherocks.com/2021/03/the-state-of-deterrence-by-denial/; and Miranda Priebe et al., *Implementing Restraint: Changes in U.S. Regional Security Policies to Operationalize a Realist Grand Strategy of Restraint* (Santa Monica, CA: RAND Corporation, 2021), https://www.rand.org/pubs/research_reports/RRA739-1.html.

23 Fred C. Iklé, 'Discriminate Deterrence: A Response to Critics', *National Interest*, no. 13, Fall 1988, p. 134.

24 See, for example, Matthew P. Goodman, 'Variable Geometry Takes Shape in Biden's Foreign Policy', Center for Strategic and International Studies, 19 March 2021, https://www.csis.org/analysis/variable-geometry-takes-shape-bidens-foreign-policy.

Could Land Swaps Break the Kosovo–Serbia Impasse?

Fatma Aslı Kelkitli

The relationship between Serbia and Kosovo has steered a complicated and awkward course since the latter's declaration of independence in 2008. Negotiations led by the European Union to end the impasse between the two sides have yielded only meagre results. The idea of a territorial-exchange agreement between Belgrade and Pristina emerged in summer 2018 discussions between the two leaderships, but was shelved due to the objections of some European countries and domestic opposition in Serbia and Kosovo. However, since no satisfying power-sharing resolution of the two sides' political differences has been reached, the possibility of a territorial-exchange deal may return. Indeed, a territorial exchange could be the most promising disposition available, provided certain historical and political impediments can be overcome.

The search for a solution

It has been more than 13 years since Kosovo declared independence from Serbia. Out of the 193 members of the United Nations, 98 have recognised the nascent republic as a sovereign state.[1] Yet Serbia still regards Kosovo as a constituent part of its territory, and has succeeded in preventing Kosovo's recognition as a sovereign country by many states. It fell to the EU to search for a way to break the deadlock, as both Serbia and Kosovo have long aspired to Union membership. EU-mediated talks began in March 2011,

Fatma Aslı Kelkitli is an Associate Professor at Istanbul Arel University.

Survival | vol. 63 no. 3 | June–July 2021 | pp. 71–98   https://doi.org/10.1080/00396338.2021.1930408

which resulted in the signing of several agreements on technical matters. Most of these agreements have been only partially implemented, however, as many are dependent upon the settlement of the political impasse between Belgrade and Pristina. Accordingly, the EU brought together the premiers of Serbia and Kosovo to engage in political negotiations in October 2012 that culminated in the adoption of the 'First Agreement of Principles Governing the Normalization of Relations' in April 2013. The agreement called for the establishment of an 'Association/Community of Serb majority municipalities' in Kosovo, which would exercise full authority in the areas of economic development, education, health, and urban and rural planning; for the integration of all Serbian security structures and judicial authorities within the security and legal framework of Kosovo; for the holding of municipal elections in the northern municipalities in 2013; and for the agreement of both parties not to block each other's EU journey.[2] However, this agreement has remained largely unimplemented, except for the organisation of municipal elections in the northern municipalities in November 2013 and the integration of Serbian judicial personnel into Kosovo's legal system.[3] Serbia and Kosovo hammered out another set of agreements in August 2015 that addressed issues surrounding the association/community of Serb-majority municipalities in Kosovo, energy, telecommunications and the Ibar Bridge.[4] Out of these four deals, only the telecommunications agreement has been fully implemented.[5]

After the EU-mediated negotiations reached a dead end in 2016, the presidents of Serbia and Kosovo started to explore alternative solutions to the stalemate. In summer 2018, the idea of a territorial-exchange agreement was reportedly put forth by Serbian President Aleksandar Vucic and his Kosovar counterpart Hashim Thaçi.[6] According to the proposed plan, four Serbian-dominated municipalities in northern Kosovo (Leposavic, North Mitrovica, Zubin Potok and Zvecan) would merge with Serbia and in return Kosovo would be awarded two Albanian-majority municipalities in southern Serbia (Bujanovac and Presevo).

The territory of the northern municipalities measures 1,007 square kilometres. Of the 146,128 Serbians in Kosovo, 70,430 are estimated to live in these municipalities, representing approximately 90% of the population in this area.[7] Northern Kosovo shares a border with Serbia, and the Serbian flag and dinar, as well as the Cyrillic script, are widely used by the region's inhabitants. Local institutions in the fields of education, healthcare, infrastructure development and social services often function independently of, and in parallel with, Kosovar institutions

The territory occupied by the municipalities of Bujanovac and Presevo, on the other hand, measures 725 km² and is home to a population of about 68,000.[8] More than 90% of the inhabitants of Presevo, and more than half the residents of Bujanovac, are of Albanian origin.[9] The early 2000s witnessed a brief military conflict between these municipalities on one side and the Serbian state, along with the so-called Liberation Army of Presevo, Medveda and Bujanovac, on the other, which ended with the signing of the Koncul Agreement in February 2001 – an agreement mediated by the NATO secretary-general. It led to the demilitarisation of armed Albanian groups in Bujanovac, Medveda and Presevo, but relations between Albanians and Serbs in these three municipalities have remained distant and tense.[10] Just as the Serbs living in northern Kosovo refuse to recognise the authority of Pristina, the Albanians residing in southern Serbia demonstrate little sign of allegiance to Belgrade.

The territorial-exchange proposal was rebuffed by opposition parties, religious institutions and nationalist groups in both Serbia and Kosovo, and appears to have been shelved, at least for the time being. Yet the land swap may, in the long run, be the only way to achieve a permanent rapprochement between Serbia and Kosovo. The territories being proposed for the swap are comparable in size and population, and the requisite background conditions are present for a peaceful territorial exchange. If some domestic political obstacles could be overcome in both Serbia and Kosovo, there is a good chance that the Gordian knot of Belgrade–Pristina relations could finally be untangled.

Partition or power-sharing?

The establishment of a functioning democracy in a country plagued by ethnic conflict is a daunting task. In Serbia and Kosovo, many people have lost loved ones, homes and valuable belongings in violent domestic battles with erstwhile friends, neighbours and co-workers because of ethnic, religious or linguistic differences. These painful experiences have produced fear, anger and alienation among the formerly warring groups. The erosion of respect and trust, along with low levels of contact between the contending parties, has made it difficult to sustain a cohesive and harmonious society.

Military clashes between the belligerents, coupled with extensive civilian suffering during the ethnic conflicts, have given rise to a security dilemma in which the sparring groups see each other not as citizens of a joint state but as threats that need to be addressed through acts that in turn give rise to feelings of insecurity in other groups.[11] The hardening of ethnic identities has intensified the polarisation of society, as any interaction with members of an adversary group is considered treason by one's fellow community members.[12]

The difficulty of accommodating irreconcilable disagreements in the aftermath of ethnic civil wars has led to the suggestion that it is helpful or even necessary to physically separate combatant groups to reach enduring, peaceful settlements in conflict-ridden territories.[13] Partition, territorial segregation and population transfers, either agreed upon by the relevant parties or imposed on them by a stronger third party, are believed to reduce the likelihood of a recurrence of ethnic conflict.[14] Minority groups may be given the chance to break free from the shackles of a common state and go their own way. Majority groups may experience a loss of territory and population, but will have a more homogeneous and stable country.[15] Even if some minority groups continue to reside in the partitioned state, their meagre numbers will not pose a significant political or military threat to the majority.[16]

The opponents of partition schemes have long pointed out that dividing a territory can be fraught with difficulties, especially if the land in question has some tangible or intangible value for the parties. The territory under discussion may hold significant economic potential, such as abundant energy resources or mineral deposits; be geographically close to the homeland; or contain ancient religious sites or ancestral graves which are of historical, sentimental or symbolic importance.[17] Another criticism is that dividing a territory among the contending sides may not end the violence and may even trigger further conflicts as left-behind minorities mobilise for autonomy or independence. The historical cases of India, Ireland and Pakistan are often cited. Furthermore, the population transfers that usually accompany partition arrangements tend to violate basic human rights as people are ripped from their native lands, immovable belongings and friends.[18]

Power-sharing models in the Balkans

The popular alternatives entail strong power-sharing mechanisms, which ensure that no single group makes decisions without the involvement of the other groups, deemed the best way to achieve democratisation, decentralisation and identity reconstruction in war-torn societies. In line with this reasoning, several power-sharing models have been introduced in the Balkans since the mid-1990s, in Bosnia-Herzegovina, North Macedonia and Kosovo.

The power-sharing system embraced by Bosnia-Herzegovina in the wake of the Dayton Agreement that ended the bloody three-year war there largely corresponds to the consociational-governance system advanced by Arend Lijphart. This consensual form of democracy rests on the joint exercise of governmental power by all significant segments of society in a grand coalition; a mutual veto that serves to protect vital minority interests; proportionality in political representation, civil-service appointments and the allocation of public funds; and a high degree of autonomy for each segment to manage its internal affairs.[19] The constitution of Bosnia-Herzegovina designates Bosniaks, Croats and Serbs as constituent peoples of the republic, and most governmental organs reflect this ethno-national definition via the presence of ethnic quotas for these three groups.[20] Moreover, representatives of each group are granted the right to veto any legislation they deem destructive to their group's vital interests. Bosnia-Herzegovina is also a highly decentralised state. It is composed of two entities, the Federation of Bosnia-Herzegovina and Republika Srpska, plus the autonomous Brcko district. The federation is further divided into ten cantons. All these entities enjoy a high degree of autonomy.

The consociational-democracy model established in Bosnia-Herzegovina fell short of creating a stable and efficient political system in that country. As underlined by Lijphart, this model necessitates the commitment and cooperation of segmented leaders to preserve the unity of the country.[21]

The segmented elites in the Bosnian case, however, find it difficult to compromise on even minor issues. The long-time leader of Republika Srpska, Milorad Dodik, has repeatedly voiced his lack of faith in the sustainability of the Bosnian state.[22] Another source of gridlock is the lawmaking process. Passing legislation at the state level is a long and arduous process due to the extensive veto rights of the constituent groups.

The power-sharing system in Macedonia took shape following the signing of the Ohrid Framework Agreement in August 2001, which brought an end to the six-month armed conflict between the National Liberation Army (an Albanian paramilitary organisation) and the Macedonian security forces. The agreement envisaged governmental decentralisation, non-discrimination and equitable representation in the public sector; a double-majority system in parliament; and acceptance of Albanian as an official state language.[23]

The Law on Local Self-government of 2002 enlarged the competencies of municipalities and granted them responsibility for urban planning, pre-school and primary education, basic healthcare, and sports and cultural issues.[24] The Law on Territorial Organization of 2004, on the other hand, redrew municipal boundaries to increase the number of municipalities with an Albanian majority.[25] This led to discomfort among Macedonians, who claimed they were being denied access to public services in Albanian-majority municipalities.[26]

The implementation of the principles of non-discrimination and equitable representation, which aimed to correct imbalances in public bodies through the recruitment of members of under-represented communities, has been partially successful. Albanians and other minorities are recruited in greater numbers to the public sector compared to the pre-2001 period. However, the use of this principle by the political parties as a bargaining chip in political negotiations, and the introduction of the spoils system into recruitment processes to the benefit of the Albanian minority, increased societal tensions and raised doubts about the future viability of the Ohrid Framework Agreement.[27]

Kosovo introduced its power-sharing system in June 2008 with the coming into force of its constitution, which guaranteed representation of non-majority communities in Kosovo's parliament, and required government and majority consent from communities that held reserved seats regarding legislation on vital interests, such as laws concerning communities, municipalities, education, local elections, the protection of cultural heritage, religious freedom, language use and symbols.[28] Yet Article 149 of the constitution stated that laws of vital interest might initially be adopted by a simple majority, which decreased the impact of minority representatives in the formulation of the legal framework.[29] A Committee on Rights and Interests of Communities, a permanent body mostly made up of minority representatives to which all proposed laws could be submitted for further scrutiny, was also established within the Kosovo parliament, but was not equipped with a veto power.[30]

Serbs reject Kosovar institutions

The most serious problem encountered by Kosovo since its independence has been the integration of the Serbian minority into the country's political system. While Serbs who live in the central and southern parts of Kosovo in scattered enclaves have acknowledged Kosovar institutions to some extent, Serbs living in northern Kosovo totally reject them. Serbs who reside south of the Ibar River have acquired Kosovo identity cards, accepted jobs from the Kosovo government and started to use Kosovo number plates.[31] They have also participated in local and general elections. The Independent Liberal Party, founded in Gracanica in 2006 and comprising mostly Serb members, won the municipalities of Gracanica, Klokot and Strpce in the November 2009 municipal elections. The party also sent eight representatives to the Kosovo Assembly after the December 2010 parliamentary election.[32] Although it was difficult to claim that party supporters felt a close affinity to the Kosovo state, their geographical distance from Serbia led them to adopt a more conciliatory approach.

Meanwhile, the four municipalities in the northern part of Kosovo that are overwhelmingly inhabited by Serbs and contiguous with Serbia have never come under the jurisdiction of the Kosovo state. In these municipalities, institutions in the fields of education, healthcare, infrastructure and security are controlled by Serbia. Pristina's attempt to integrate these four municipalities into its own state structures through the creation of the association/community of Serb-majority municipalities, which was granted wide autonomy in internal affairs, backfired amid rejection from the Kosovo Constitutional Court and internal opposition.

Serbia's intervention in Kosovo's politics through the propping up of the political party Srpska Lista (Serb List) further complicated the integration of the Serbian minority into Kosovo's political system. The party has played a significant role in local and general elections in Kosovo since 2013. It won all ten seats reserved in the Kosovo Assembly for the Serbian community in October 2019, and party members serve as mayors in all ten Serb-majority municipalities. It has been alleged that Srpska Lista's electoral success relied to a great extent on generous funds from Serbia and the intimidation of rival Kosovar Serbian parties.[33] The Serbian government itself, which had once urged Serbs in northern Kosovo to reject Kosovar institutions in a February 2012 referendum, encouraged voting in the local and general elections in Kosovo starting with the municipal election in November 2013.[34] This encouragement was not necessarily intended to bolster Serbs' confidence in Kosovo's government, however. Its main aim was to keep Serbia's EU-membership aspiration on track through cooperation in the elections. The fact that there were approximately 5,600 Kosovo Serb voters in the October 2019 elections who lacked Kosovar identity cards, almost all of whom lived in the four northern municipalities in Kosovo, demonstrated the unwillingness of Serbs living in northern Kosovo to recognise the institutions of Kosovo.[35]

The low level of contact between Albanians and Serbs in northern Kosovo undermines the workability of the power-sharing system. Kosovar Albanians, who constitute the overwhelming majority of the population in Kosovo, have yet to fully accustom themselves to the idea of a multi-ethnic Kosovo state. Serbs living in northern Kosovo do not recognise the statehood of Kosovo and retain deep suspicions regarding the recognition of their rights in an Albanian-dominated state. Taking into account the dim prospects of integrating the Serbian minority in the north into Kosovo's state structures, a land swap between Serbia and Kosovo may well be the only way to achieve permanent peace.

Peaceful territorial exchange: the solution for Kosovo?

A peaceful territorial change is defined as an alteration in the territorial status quo via bargaining and negotiation between the concerned parties, which rules out war or other unilateral, coercive means of ending a conflict.[36] Such a change may take place in the form of a purchase, an exchange or a cession of the disputed territory. The land swaps between the Czech Republic and Slovakia in 1997, and between Bangladesh and India in 2015, are good examples of peaceful and successful territorial exchanges. After a land-swap agreement was clinched in 1996, the border between the Czech Republic and Slovakia was redrawn in 1997 to bring the Czech-controlled but overwhelmingly Slovak-populated U Sabotu under the jurisdiction of Slovakia. In return, Sidonie, which belonged to Slovakia but whose population was mainly made up of Czechs, was ceded to the Czech Republic. Bangladesh and India exchanged 162 enclaves in 2015: 51 Bangladeshi enclaves became Indian territory and 111 Indian enclaves became part of Bangladesh.[37]

Many studies have examined the factors that may influence the realisation of a peaceful territorial exchange. Paul Huth, Todd Allee and Krista Wiegand have focused on regime type. While Huth and Allee claim that democratic regimes may find it difficult to make the concessions required for peaceful territorial transfers due to pressures from civil society, Wiegand finds that single-party regimes are more likely to pursue peaceful dispute resolutions compared to other authoritarian regimes.[38] Mark Zacher concentrates on the influence of international norms, especially the norm of territorial integrity, on perceptions of territorial matters by states.[39] Sara Mitchell and Allee and Huth have looked into the reasons why states resort to third-party intervention for the resolution of territorial disputes.[40] Several scholars have scrutinised the impact of former military conflicts or failed settlement attempts on the peaceful resolution of territorial issues.[41]

Of all the available models, Arie Marcelo Kacowicz's is the most comprehensive. It encompasses all the factors listed above, along with considerations of power asymmetry, third-party threats and domestic politics. Kacowicz posits six background conditions or variables for the realisation of a peaceful territorial exchange. Such an exchange is more likely to occur where the distribution of power between the parties is somewhat asymmetrical, preferably to the advantage of the power that is in control of the territory; where the parties' political regimes are of a similar type; where there is a consensus between the parties about the implementation of norms and the rules of international law; where third parties offer good offices, mediation or arbitration; where the parties have been involved in a war within the ten-year period preceding the negotiations on territorial change; and where there is a third-party threat against at least one of the parties.[42]

The process of peaceful territorial exchange, especially in democratic countries, is open to the monitoring, scrutiny and criticism of the political opposition, non-governmental organisations, religious institutions and the media. These organisations may limit the bargaining space of the negotiating parties because they have the power to shape public opinion. Therefore, Kacowicz adds the impact of domestic politics as a variable that can potentially derail the process of peaceful territorial exchange if it is not properly handled by the negotiating parties.[43]

Power disparity

Kacowicz's model requires a power disparity that favours the status quo power on the grounds that equal power paves the way for attempts to use military means to resolve the dispute. Indicators of power capabilities include territorial size, population, the number of armed-forces personnel, defence expenditures, gross national product, government revenue, trade value and energy consumption.[44]

It is clear from these indicators that there is a power asymmetry between Serbia and Kosovo. With an area of 77,474 km², Serbia is more than seven times larger than Kosovo, which measures 10,887 km².[45] While Kosovo is home to a population of approximately 1.8 million people, Serbia has nearly seven million inhabitants.[46] The Serbian Armed Forces comprise 28,000 troops, whereas the newly formed Kosovo army has only 5,000 members.[47] Kosovo also hosts approximately 4,000 NATO troops, but they are mostly involved in border security, de-mining and the protection of heritage sites.[48] Serbia earmarked €792m for its defence expenditures in 2019.[49] Kosovo allocated €58.7m.[50]

Serbia recorded a gross national product of €40.22 billion in 2018, while Kosovo's gross national product that year was €7.03bn.[51] The Serbian government had revenues of €15.96bn in 2017, compared to Kosovo's €1.85bn.[52] Serbia's trade value hit €40.7bn in 2018, while Kosovo's was €3.7bn.[53] Serbia consumes 29.81bn kilowatt-hours of electric energy per year, compared to Kosovo's yearly consumption of 3.96bn kWh.[54] All these indicators demonstrate that Kosovo is a smaller power than Serbia.

Regime type

Kacowicz's model underlines the importance of the negotiating states having similar political regimes. Where regimes display differing norms, ideologies or views, these might present obstacles during the bargaining phase and hinder the prospects for peaceful territorial exchange.[55] Both Serbia and Kosovo have been described as 'partly free', 'defective' or 'flawed' democracies by democracy indexes because they do not always comply with the basic principles of liberal democracy, such as the holding of free, fair and competitive elections, the separation of powers, the rule of law, and the protection of civil liberties and political freedoms.[56] Although the latest municipal, presidential and parliamentary elections took place in a free and competitive atmosphere in Serbia, unbalanced coverage in the state-owned media favouring the ruling Serbian Progressive Party (SNS) and Vucic, the incumbent candidate; the misuse of public resources by the SNS; and strong allegations regarding the ruling party's exertion of pressure on voters employed in the public sector cast a shadow on the fairness of the electoral process.[57] The executive in Serbia controls the legislative process to a significant extent, and the judiciary is open to the influence and interference of the executive as well. Press freedom has significantly declined in Serbia, especially since Vucic's inauguration as president in 2017.

The parliamentary and municipal elections in Kosovo were considered generally fair and competitive by international observers. However, Srpska Lista, the leading Serbian party in Kosovo which, as noted, enjoys close links with Serbia, was occasionally accused of harassing rival parties to sustain its dominance in Kosovo's politics.[58] Also of concern is the spending of public funds on election campaigns and biased media coverage.[59] Kosovo's executive, much like Serbia's, intervenes continuously in legislative and judicial affairs. Threats and intimidation against journalists who criticise politicians undermine the country's press freedoms, and free expression more generally. The similarities between these two struggling democracies may facilitate a political dialogue between them for a peaceful territorial exchange.

Norms, principles and rules

Despite the existence of a conflict between Serbia and Kosovo over the norm of sovereignty, both states demonstrate a desire to join the EU, an organisation that rejects rigid interpretations of concepts such as political independence, territoriality and non-interference in states' internal affairs. Belgrade and Pristina have been striving for some time to adhere to the standards established by the EU as prerequisites to acceptance into the club. Referred to as the 'Copenhagen criteria', these standards oblige candidate states to have institutions that guarantee democratic governance, the rule of law, human rights, and respect for and protection of minorities; to maintain a functioning market economy and demonstrate a capacity to cope with competition and market forces within the EU; and to demonstrate the administrative and institutional capacity to take on the obligations of membership.[60] Both Serbia and Kosovo have been taking legislative steps to attune their laws to the EU's accession criteria, which may increase the prospects for successful territorial exchange between them.

Third-party contributions

Kacowicz's model highlights the potential of third-party diplomatic intervention to help resolve territorial disputes. The EU and the United States seem to be key third parties with regard to the possible territorial exchange between Serbia and Kosovo. As noted, Belgrade and Pristina both regard EU membership as a strategic goal, and the United States proved itself a critical actor during the Kosovo War of 1998–99. It has remained engaged with Kosovo ever since.

The proposal to exchange territory between Serbia and Kosovo met with mixed reactions in the EU. High Representative for Foreign Affairs and Security Policy Josep Borrell stated: 'It is not up to us to tell Kosovans and

Serbs what they should agree on. Our role will be to facilitate dialogue. But … we cannot be more Catholic than the Pope.'[61] European Commissioner for Neighbourhood and Enlargement Oliver Várhelyi indicated that a 'land swap … [is] a secondary issue. What is necessary is that first of all we have both actors/entities at that table, engaging in a meaningful way, and coming up with a solution.'[62] Germany, a powerful political and economic player in the Balkans, has explicitly opposed the idea of a territorial change in the region. German Chancellor Angela Merkel said that the borders of the Western Balkan region were inviolable, whereas German Foreign Minister Heiko Maas stressed that discussions on a land swap could open up old wounds among the Balkan people.[63]

Washington under the Trump administration appeared open to the idea of a territorial exchange between Serbia and Kosovo. In August 2018, John Bolton, then national security advisor, stated that if the two parties could work out a solution that might include territorial adjustments, the United States would not stand in the way.[64] In August 2019, US secretary of state Mike Pompeo appointed Matthew Palmer, the deputy assistant secretary of the Bureau of European and Eurasian Affairs and a veteran diplomat with significant experience in the Balkans, as his special representative for the Western Balkan region.[65] In October 2019, Richard Grenell, the United States' ambassador to Germany, became the special presidential envoy for Serbia and Kosovo's peace negotiations. There were also reports that Grenell was mediating secret talks between Vucic and Thaçi for the realisation of a territorial-exchange agreement, though Grenell dismissed these claims.[66] In January 2020, the United States mediated an agreement between Kosovo, Serbia and the German airline Lufthansa on the resumption of commercial flights between Serbia and Kosovo after a 21-year hiatus.[67] Finally, in September 2020, Vucic and Kosovar prime minister Avdullah Hoti signed economic-normalisation agreements at the White House that encompassed the construction of highways and rail networks, and the opening and management of the joint Merdare crossing.[68] These developments indicate that the backing of the EU and the US might be crucial for the smooth functioning of any territorial-exchange process between Serbia and Kosovo. Although US President Joe Biden sent a letter to Vucic in February 2021 urging Serbia to recognise Kosovo, the administration's attitude towards a possible land swap is yet to be determined. Even so, there has been nothing to suggest that the United States would impede a land-swap deal between the parties.

The EU, however, has been more ambivalent. The Union's misgivings may be linked to concerns that a land-swap deal could strengthen separatist groups in Bosnia-Herzegovina and North Macedonia, and thus have a destabilising effect across the Western Balkans. Yet the land-swap deal between Serbia and Kosovo, if it ever materialises, will not be the result of a unilateral decision. Rather, it will be a mutually agreed settlement, and therefore will not necessarily set a precedent for secessionist factions in Bosnia-Herzegovina or North Macedonia. Neither the Dayton Agreement nor the constitution of Bosnia-Herzegovina offers entities the option of unilateral secession. Furthermore, the Dayton Agreement was endorsed by the UN Security Council many times, and any unilateral attempt to secede will not only contravene UN regulations but also draw the fury of leading international actors, which may prevent other countries from recognising the secessionist entity.[69] Serbia and Croatia signed the Dayton Agreement, taking responsibility for the territorial integrity of Bosnia-Herzegovina. And despite Dodik's divisive rhetoric, Republika Srpska does not enjoy the necessary economic self-sufficiency to function as an independent state. It relies on funds from the central government to pay its debts, which by 2020 represented more than 50% of its GDP.[70] Serbia may not be enthusiastic about a possible union with Republika Srpska as its Sandzak region, which is mainly populated by Bosniaks, may demand to secede if any such union takes place. Sandzak had voted in favour of autonomy in an October 1991 referendum that was declared unconstitutional by the Serbian authorities.[71] Today, it is one of the poorest regions in Serbia; its Bosniak residents often complain about poor infrastructure, inadequate investment opportunities and difficulties in gaining access to public-sector jobs. The region's problems only worsened with the COVID-19 pandemic, which revealed the incapacity of its local healthcare system and strained ties with Belgrade. It is highly probable that Serbia will refrain from encouraging secessionist tendencies in Republika Srpska, which would further alienate and radicalise its own Bosniak population. North Macedonia, on the other hand, has come a long way towards accommodating the grievances of its ethnic Albanian citizens by expanding their democratic representation and cultural rights. The 2019 Law on the Use of Languages, for example, made Albanian a co-official language at the state level. The inclusive and integrative approach of the North Macedonian government towards its Albanian minority seems likely to attenuate separatist currents in the country.

Wars and threats

Kacowicz's model holds that a history of war between the parties to a territorial-exchange negotiation may help them reach a settlement. The Kosovo War of 1998–99 may have ended more than 20 years ago, but it was an important learning experience, especially for Serbia, which has demonstrated much more caution, restraint and moderation in its international dealings compared to the pre-war period. Although Vucic has consistently refused to atone for the violence inflicted by Serbia during the Kosovo War, and has even claimed that the Racak massacre of January 1999, in which Serbian forces killed 45 Albanian civilians, is a fabrication, he has also acknowledged that Serbia lost Kosovo and should move to normalise relations by reaching an agreement.[72]

The presence of a third-party threat against one of the negotiating sides may also contribute to the resolution of a territorial dispute. Although neither Serbia nor Kosovo appears to be experiencing such a threat, Serbia's progressive tilting towards the EU has triggered some problems with Russia, whose intelligence services have taken action in that country.[73] Russia's meddling may increase if Serbia's EU-membership journey, which is very much dependent on the normalisation of its relations with Kosovo, is put on hold. This situation may serve as another motivating factor for a land swap between Belgrade and Pristina.

Domestic politics

In many ways, conditions appear to be favourable for a possible territorial exchange between Belgrade and Pristina. Yet domestic politics remain a factor to be reckoned with in both states. In Serbia, the prospective land-swap arrangement was vehemently rejected by nationalist and conservative opposition parties, and the Serbian Orthodox Church. The Serbian Radical

Party, the Democratic Party of Serbia, the Dveri Movement and the People's Party all declared that they would oppose any solution that would relinquish Serbia's authority over Kosovo.[74] The Serbian Orthodox Church, which sees Kosovo as the heartland of Serbian Orthodox spirituality and identity, also came out strongly against the division of Kosovo on the grounds that the Serbian community living south of the Ibar River and its sacred sites would be deprived of adequate protection in such a scenario.[75]

The well-being of the Serbian population residing south of the Ibar River and the protection of Serbian religious sites will loom large in any land-swap deal between Serbia and Kosovo. Most of the Serbs in the central and southern parts of Kosovo live in the municipalities of Gracanica, Klokot, Novo Brdo, Partes, Ranilug and Strpce. The livelihood of these communities mostly depends on agriculture, dairy production, cattle-breeding and low-level trade. Illegal logging and frequent thefts of agricultural machinery and live-stock vehicles, coupled with an insufficient response to such crimes by the Kosovo police, have undermined living conditions in these communities and eroded their trust in Kosovar institutions.[76] Improving the infrastructure of these municipalities by building sewage systems and wells, paving roads, and solving problems of public lighting and electricity supply, along with more serious action by the Kosovo police on crimes against minorities, would help to remedy the woes of Serbs living south of the Ibar.

The Orthodox Church rejected the swap

Kosovo hosts about 1,300 Orthodox churches, monasteries and other religious sites, four of which (Bogorodica Ljeviska Church, Gracanica Monastery, Peja Patriarchate and Visoki Decani Monastery) appear on UNESCO's World Heritage List.[77] Kosovo is equipped with the requisite legislation (its Cultural Heritage Law and Law on Special Protective Zones) to ensure the protection and security of these religious institutions. Yet the occasional desecration or robbery of churches and cemeteries, as well as construction near protected areas, caused tension to build between the Serbian Orthodox Church and Albanian-majority municipalities. Municipalities are responsible for the maintenance of public cemeteries and therefore should be attentive to the complaints of the Serbian minority concerning the upkeep of such places. Likewise, the Kosovo government should not allow municipal officials to ignore the implementation of court decisions regarding sacred sites. The religious diversity of Kosovo's population should also be taken into consideration when setting up police units to protect religious sites. The implementation of much-debated amendments to the Law on Freedom of Religion, which permit religious groups to acquire legal status, conduct business, acquire real and personal property, and open bank accounts, should have positive implications for the relationship between the Serbian Orthodox Church and Kosovar institutions.

The SNS received nearly 61% of votes in the June 2020 election and captured 157 seats in Serbia's 250-member parliament, which demonstrated that Vucic and his party continued to retain credibility in the eyes of the Serbian public. The party formed a coalition government with the contribution of 31 deputies. The SNS has the majority to call for a national referendum concerning a possible territorial exchange with Kosovo. Guarantees that the Serbian community and Serbian sacred sites south of the Ibar River will be protected may persuade the Serbian public to tilt towards the deal, as nearly half of Serbs think that it is not possible for Serbia to regain full control or sovereignty over Kosovo.[78]

Rumours of a possible territorial exchange with Serbia have aroused the ire not only of the parliamentary opposition but of some members of the ruling coalition as well. Then-prime minister Ramush Haradinaj called the partition proposal irrational, and his party, the Alliance for the Future of Kosovo, declared that it might lead to more war.[79] The Democratic Party of Kosovo, the Social Democratic Initiative, the Democratic League of Kosovo, the Social Democratic Party of Kosovo and the Alliance for a New Kosovo all voiced their objections to the proposed scheme and criticised Thaçi sharply.[80]

One of the plan's most vocal critics was Albin Kurti, the leader of the Vetëvendosje (Self-determination) party, who accused Thaçi of bargaining Kosovo's territory with Vucic and insisted that there was no room for discussion of Kosovo's partition.[81] Kurti became prime minister of Kosovo in February 2020, but his government collapsed on 25 March that same year after a vote of no confidence initiated by its coalition partner, the

Democratic League of Kosovo. In the February 2021 parliamentary election, the Vetëvendosje party won a landslide victory, acquiring 50.28% of the vote. This electoral success returned Kurti to the prime ministerial post in March 2021.

Progress on any territorial-exchange scheme with Serbia will be complicated by the need to pass constitutional amendments to allow a referendum on the deal, which will require a two-thirds majority vote in Kosovo's Assembly.[82] None of the political parties is willing to back such a move at present. However, Kosovar politicians are aware of Kosovo's dire economic conditions, which are only worsened by the feud with Serbia. Kosovo is the third-poorest country in Europe in terms of GDP per capita, and its economy is still highly dependent on remittances from the diaspora.[83] Youth employment hovers at around 50%, and 100,000 people leave the country for good every year.[84] The coronavirus pandemic also took its toll, resulting in GDP contraction and job losses. Capital investments that were slow even before the pandemic nearly came to a halt.[85] The country's egregious financial situation is keenly felt by the public, who give unemployment (84%), corruption (53%) and fighting the coronavirus (48%) as the biggest problems Kosovo faces.[86] It does not help that the government has been paying rent for unused state offices in Leposavic, North Mitrovica and Zubin Potok, and paying salaries to former Civil Protection Corps members in northern Kosovo who, despite being employed at various ministries and state agencies, do not show up for work.[87]

Convincing the public

Serbian and Kosovar politicians, as well as the publics of both countries, should keep in mind that the normalisation of relations between them is a prerequisite for achieving political stability, economic prosperity and EU membership. Serbia, by taking back at least a part of Kosovo, may finally accept the independence of the country. Kosovo may finally be able to focus on internal state-building without striving in vain to integrate an unruly Serb population into its state structures.

Any territorial-exchange agreement between Serbia and Kosovo would almost certainly be subjected to referendums in both countries to ensure popular consent. The full and direct participation of the citizens of Serbia and Kosovo in this crucial decision is needed as it will affect their daily lives. Furthermore, territorial adjustment goes beyond the mandate granted to politicians in general elections, so referendums are needed to legitimise any action.

If the land-swap deal is accepted in a referendum, the acquired rights of people living in territories which are subject to the exchange should be protected. They may also be given the choice to retain their existing nationality. Even if the land-swap deal goes through, there will still be Albanians, Bosniaks and Roma living in northern Kosovo, and Serbs and Roma residing in Bujanovac and Presevo. These stay-behind minorities should retain the right to be educated in their own language, to profess and practise their own religion, and to enjoy their own culture. Forcible population transfers are out of the question as they would violate fundamental human rights such as the right to family life, the right to freedom of movement and the right to own property.

Most of the prospective new minorities in Kosovo and Serbia live in rural areas and engage in farming and the raising of livestock. Developing rural infrastructure and creating a secure and suitable environment for the sale of agricultural products to other regions may speed up the adaptation of these minorities to their new countries. Another important issue that should be handled carefully is the language barrier. Kosovo's Roma speak Serbian, and the language of Bosniaks is similar to that of Serbs. However, Albanians in northern Kosovo, especially the young generation, do not speak Serbian, and Serbs and Roma in Bujanovac and Presevo have little knowledge of Albanian. The Serbian and Kosovar governments may prepare learning programmes to help their new Albanian and Serbian minorities to learn the language of the majority, which will accelerate their integration into their respective societies. Albanian-language classes may also encompass the Kosovar Serbs living south of the Ibar River.

It is to be expected that some members of the affected minorities may want to leave their places of residence due to the difficulties of becoming accustomed to new political, legal and economic systems. People who make this decision should be compensated for their material losses. Another risk is the possibility of future amendments to Kosovo's constitution, which may result in the curtailment of some of the privileges enjoyed by the remaining Serbian minority. In order to prevent this from happening, the prospective territorial-exchange agreement should contain strong clauses to guarantee the political and legal rights of minorities in both countries.

*   *   *

The mediocre performance of the power-sharing systems that have been introduced in the Western Balkans since the mid-1990s has encouraged a search for alternative solutions to conflicts there, particularly partition schemes. The proposed territorial-exchange plan between Serbia and Kosovo is one such alternative.

The material power imbalance between Serbia and Kosovo, Serbia's new foreign-policy outlook – which eschews military adventures and attaches special importance to potential EU membership despite the displeasure of its long-term ally Russia – and the similar political regimes of the two countries are factors that could facilitate the realisation of a land-swap deal.

The support of the EU and the US, the most important third parties with a stake in the peaceful resolution of the Serbia–Kosovo dispute, will also be crucial for the achievement of any agreement. While the US seems ready to discuss any kind of peace deal so long as the parties are in agreement, Germany, an influential EU member, has been more circumspect, probably because of concerns that a deal may incite conflict in Bosnia-Herzegovina and North Macedonia. Yet the current stalemate is not to the benefit of the EU either, because it strengthens hardliners in both Serbia and Kosovo. For this reason, many high-ranking EU representatives have expressed the view that the Union may demonstrate flexibility concerning the adjustment of borders so long as the parties reach an agreement that brings stability.

The success of a possible territorial exchange between Serbia and Kosovo is, however, very much dependent on overcoming domestic political obstacles in both states. Inserting extensive guarantee clauses into the prospective agreement for the protection of the political and legal rights of minority communities in Serbia and Kosovo, and subjecting the deal to a referendum in both countries, may attenuate opposition. Ultimately, the decision should be left to the inhabitants of Serbia and Kosovo, as it is their future well-being that is at stake. The current situation appears unsustainable, however, as not only is it hindering an enduring rapprochement between Belgrade and Pristina, but it also presents a major stumbling block in each country's European journey.

Notes

1 See Paul Antonopoulos, 'U.S. Could Push the Remaining EU States That Do Not Recognize Kosovo to Do So', BRICS Information Portal, 29 October 2020, http://infobrics.org/post/32130/.
2 Government of the Republic of Serbia, Office for Kosovo and Metohija, 'First Agreement of Principles Governing the Normalization of Relations', 28 November 2019, http://kim.gov.rs/eng/p03.php.
3 See European Commission, 'Kosovo 2020 Report', p. 63, https://ec.europa.eu/neighbourhood-enlargement/sites/near/files/kosovo_report_2020.pdf.
4 The Ibar Bridge is also known as the New Bridge or the Mitrovica Bridge.
5 See European Commission, 'Kosovo 2020 Report', p. 63.
6 See Michael Rossi, 'Partition in Kosovo Will Lead to Disaster', *Foreign Policy*, 19 September 2018, https://foreignpolicy.com/2018/09/19/partition-in-kosovo-will-lead-to-disaster-serbia-vucic-thaci-mitrovica-ibar/.
7 See Minority Rights Group, 'Kosovo-Serbs', 29 November 2019, https://minorityrights.org/minorities/serbs-3/; and Aleksander Zdravkovski and Sabrina P. Ramet, 'The Proposed Territorial Exchange Between Serbia and Kosovo', *Insight Turkey*, vol. 21, no. 2, 2019, p. 19, doi: 10.25253/99.2019212.01.
8 Zdravkovski and Ramet, 'The Proposed Territorial Exchange Between Serbia and Kosovo', p. 19.
9 Arsim Ejubi and Zoran Stiperski, 'The Geopolitical Background of the Preševo Valley Crisis', *Politische Geographie*, vol. 160, 2018, p. 234, https://pdfs.semanticscholar.org/e7f6/80ee3be99fa781d9c8199a1d84c39a5f0082.pdf?_ga=2.163379642.707107523.1575147199-369430686.1562488808.
10 See Linda Pressly and Albana Kasapi, 'Serbia–Kosovo: Where Neighbours Do Not Share a Coffee', BBC News, 10 January 2019, https://www.bbc.com/news/world-europe-46808673.
11 See Barry R. Posen, 'The Security Dilemma and Ethnic Conflict', *Survival*, vol. 35, no. 1, 1993, p. 28, doi: 10.1080/00396339308442672.
12 See Alexander B. Downes, 'The Problem with Negotiated Settlements to Ethnic Civil Wars', *Security Studies*, vol. 13, no. 4, 2004, p. 241, doi: 10.1080/09636410490945893.
13 See, for example, Chaim Kaufmann,

'Possible and Impossible Solutions to Ethnic Civil Wars', *International Security*, vol. 20, no. 4, 1996, pp. 136–75, https://www.jstor.org/stable/2539045?seq=1; Robert A. Pape, 'Partition: An Exit Strategy for Bosnia', *Survival*, vol. 39, no. 4, 1997, pp. 25–8, doi: 10.1080/00396339708442941; and John J. Mearsheimer, 'The Case for Partitioning Kosovo', in T.G. Carpenter (ed.), *NATO's Empty Victory: A Postmortem on the Balkan War* (Washington DC: CATO Institute, 2000), pp. 133–8.

14 See Chaim D. Kaufmann, 'When All Else Fails: Ethnic Population Transfers and Partitions in the Twentieth Century', *International Security*, vol. 23, no. 2, 1998, p. 125, https://www.jstor.org/stable/2539381?seq=1.

15 See Jan Tullberg and Birgitta S. Tullberg, 'Separation or Unity? A Model for Solving Ethnic Conflicts', *Politics and the Life Sciences*, vol. 16, no. 2, 1997, p. 239, https://www.jstor.org/stable/4236353?seq=1.

16 See Jaroslav Tir, 'Letting Secessionists Have Their Way: Can Partitions Help End and Prevent Ethnic Conflicts?', *International Interactions*, vol. 28, no. 3, 2002, pp. 270–1, doi: 10.1080/03050620213654.

17 See Gary Goertz and Paul Diehl, *Territorial Changes and International Conflict* (London: Routledge, 1992), pp. 14–19.

18 See Carter Johnson, 'Partitioning to Peace: Sovereignty, Demography, and Ethnic Civil Wars', *International Security*, vol. 32, no. 4, 2008, p. 150, https://www.jstor.org/stable/30129794?seq=1.

19 Arend Lijphart, *Democracy in Plural Societies: A Comparative Exploration* (New Haven, CT: Yale University Press, 1977), p. 25.

20 Constitutional Court of Bosnia and Herzegovina, 'Preamble', Constitution of Bosnia and Herzegovina, 15 December 2019, http://www.ccbh.ba/osnovni-akti/ustav/?title=preambula.

21 Lijphart, *Democracy in Plural Societies*, p. 53.

22 See 'Protests Show Bosnia Needs to Dissolve, Dodik Says', Balkan Insight, 14 February 2014, https://balkaninsight.com/2014/02/14/dodik-blaims-international-community-for-bosnian-protests/; and Sabina Niksic, 'Bosnian Serb Leader Calls for Dissolution of Bosnia', AP, 20 February 2020, https://apnews.com/article/14663362ce4801d69dd2cf73c9429918.

23 Organisation for Security and Cooperation in Europe, 'Ohrid Framework Agreement', 22 December 2019, https://www.osce.org/skopje/100622?download=true.

24 See Olimpija Hristova, '(Dis) Integrative Power of Decentralization: Multi-ethnic Municipalities in Macedonia', Zip Institute, 2013, p. 7, http://civicamobilitas.mk/wp-content/uploads/2018/03/PAPER-2-FOR-WEB2.pdf.

25 See Ognen Vangelov, 'The Primordialisation of Ethnic Nationalism in Macedonia', *Europe–Asia Studies*, vol. 71, no. 2, 2019, p. 211, doi: 10.1080/09668136.2018.1562043.

26 See Eben Friedman, 'The Ethnopolitics of Territorial Division in the Republic of Macedonia', *Ethnopolitics*, vol. 8, no. 2, 2009, p. 216, doi: 10.1080/17449050802243418.

27 See Marija Risteska, 'Insiders and Outsiders in the Implementation of the Principle of Just and Equitable Representation of Minority Groups in Public Administration in Macedonia', *International Journal of Public Administration*, vol. 36, no. 1, 2013, p. 32, doi: 10.1080/01900692.2012.691239.

28 Office of the Prime Minister of Kosovo, 'Constitution of the Republic of Kosovo', 28 December 2019, available at http://www.kryeministri-ks.net.

29 See Florian Bieber, 'Power Sharing and Democracy in Southeast Europe', *Taiwan Journal of Democracy*, 2013, p. 141, https://pdfs.semanticscholar.org/b9b9/b045bcef3d6dd80b5cf2c730a0d5321808a4.pdf.

30 Office of the Prime Minister of Kosovo, 'Constitution of the Republic of Kosovo'.

31 See Chris van der Borgh and Laura Lasance, 'Parallel Governance and Boundary Strategies in Gracanica, Kosovo', *Nationalism and Ethnic Politics*, vol. 19, no. 2, 2013, pp. 201–2, doi: 10.1080/13537113.2013.788916.

32 'Kosovo Serb Political Landscape: Independent Liberal Party', KoSSev, 3 October 2019, https://kossev.info/kosovo-serb-political-landscape-independent-liberal-party/.

33 See European Commission, 'Kosovo 2020 Report', p. 4.

34 See Nora Stel and Chris van der Borgh, 'Political Parties and Minority Governance in Hybrid Political Orders: Reflections from Lebanon's Palestinian Settlements and Kosovo's Serbian Enclaves', *Journal of Intervention and Statebuilding*, vol. 11, no. 4, 2017, p. 499, doi: 10.1080/17502977.2017.1376948.

35 European Union Election Observation Mission, 'Kosovo 2019 Early Legislative Elections Final Report', 2019, p. 15, https://www.ecoi.net/en/file/local/2024495/Kosovo_early-legislative-elections_6-October-2019_final-report.pdf.

36 See Arie M. Kacowicz, 'The Problem of Peaceful Territorial Change', *International Studies Quarterly*, vol. 38, 1994, p. 219, https://www.jstor.org/stable/2600976?seq=1.

37 See Hosna J. Shewly, 'India and Bangladesh Swap Territory, Citizens in Landmark Enclave Exchange', Migration Policy Institute, 9 March 2016, https://www.migrationpolicy.org/article/india-and-bangladesh-swap-territory-citizens-landmark-enclave-exchange#:~:text=India%20and%20Bangladesh%20formally%20exchanged,located%20inside%20another%20sovereign%20territory.

38 Paul K. Huth and Todd L. Allee, *The Democratic Peace and Territorial Conflict in the Twentieth Century* (Cambridge: Cambridge University Press, 2003); and Krista E. Wiegand, 'Peaceful Dispute Resolution by Authoritarian Regimes', *Foreign Policy Analysis*, vol. 15, no. 3, 2019, pp. 303–21, doi: 10.1093/fpa/orz006.

39 Mark W. Zacher, 'The Territorial Integrity Norm: International Boundaries and the Use of Force', *International Organization*, vol. 55, no. 2, 2001, pp. 215–50, doi: 10.1162/00208180151140568.

40 Sara McLaughlin Mitchell, 'A Kantian System? Democracy and Third-party Conflict Resolution', *American Journal of Political Science*, vol. 46, no. 4, 2002,

pp. 749–59, doi: 10.2307/3088431; and Todd. L. Allee and Paul K. Huth, 'The Pursuit of Legal Settlements to Territorial Disputes', *Conflict Management and Peace Science*, vol. 23, no. 4, 2006, pp. 285–307, doi: 10.1080/07388940600972644.

41 See, for example, Paul R. Hensel et al., 'Bones of Contention: Comparing Territorial, Maritime, and River Issues', *Journal of Conflict Resolution*, vol. 52, no. 1, 2008, pp. 117–43, doi: 10.1177/0022002707310425.

42 Arie M. Kacowicz, *Peaceful Territorial Change* (Columbia, SC: University of South Carolina Press, 1994), pp. 9–10.

43 *Ibid.*, p. 232.

44 *Ibid.*, p. 42.

45 Central Intelligence Agency, 'Serbia', *World Factbook*, 18 January 2020, https://www.cia.gov/library/publications/the-world-factbook/geos/ri.html; and Central Intelligence Agency, 'Kosovo', *World Factbook*, 18 January 2020, https://www.cia.gov/library/publications/the-world-factbook/geos/kv.html.

46 CountryMeters, 'Kosovo Population', 18 January 2020, https://countrymeters.info/en/Kosovo; and Statistical Office of the Republic of Serbia, 'Population', 18 January 2020, https://www.stat.gov.rs/en-US/.

47 Barbara Surk, 'Kosovo Parliament Votes to Create an Army, Defying Serbia and NATO', *New York Times*, 14 December 2018, https://www.nytimes.com/2018/12/14/world/europe/kosovo-army-serbia-nato.html.

48 See North Atlantic Treaty Organization, 'NATO's Role in Kosovo', 16 March 2020, https://www.nato.int/cps/en/natolive/topics_48818.htm.

49 Maja Zivanovic, 'Serbia to Hike Budget for Army and Police', Balkan Insight, 30 November 2018, https://balkaninsight.com/2018/11/30/serbian-government-plan-increase-for-army-and-police-11-28-2018/.

50 Die Morina, 'Kosovo Hikes Defence Budget to Fund New Army', Balkan Insight, 8 February 2019, https://balkaninsight.com/2019/02/08/kosovo-splashes-money-for-newly-established-army-02-08-2019/.

51 Macrotrends, 'Serbia GNP 1997–2020', 18 January 2020, https://www.macrotrends.net/countries/SRB/serbia/gnp-gross-national-product; and Macrotrends, 'Kosovo GNP 2006–2020', 18 January 2020, https://www.macrotrends.net/countries/XKX/kosovo/gnp-gross-national-product.

52 Central Intelligence Agency, 'Serbia'; and Central Intelligence Agency, 'Kosovo'.

53 Statistical Office of the Republic of Serbia, 'External Trade of Goods', 18 January 2020, https://data.stat.gov.rs/Home/Result/1701?languageCode=en-US; and Kosovo Agency of Statistics, 'International Trade Statistics, 2018', 18 January 2020, https://ask.rks-gov.net/en/kosovo-agency-of-statistics/add-news/international-trade-statistics-2018.

54 WorldData, 'Energy Consumption in Serbia', 18 January 2020, https://www.worlddata.info/europe/serbia/energy-consumption.php; and WorldData, 'Energy Consumption in the Kosovo', 18 January 2020, https://www.worlddata.info/europe/kosovo/energy-consumption.php.

55 Kacowicz, *Peaceful Territorial Change*, p. 45.

56 See Freedom House, 'Freedom in the World 2019: Serbia', 22 January 2020, https://freedomhouse.org/report/freedom-world/2019/Serbia; Freedom House, 'Freedom in the World 2019: Kosovo', 22 January 2020, https://freedomhouse.org/report/freedom-world/2019/Kosovo; BertelsmannStiftung Transformation Index, 'BTI 2018 Scores', 22 January 2020, https://www.bti-project.org/en/data/rankings/status-index/; and Snezana Bjelotomic, 'The Economist Intelligence Unit: Serbia Is a Flawed Democracy', Serbianmonitor.com, 11 January 2019, https://www.serbianmonitor.com/en/the-economist-intelligence-unit-serbia-is-a-flawed-democracy/.

57 See Organisation for Security and Cooperation in Europe, *Republic of Serbia Presidential Election 2 April 2017: OSCE/ODIHR Election Assessment Mission Final Report* (Warsaw: Office for Democratic Institutions and Human Rights, 2017), p. 1, https://www.osce.org/odihr/elections/serbia/322166?download=true; and Organisation for Security and Cooperation in Europe, *Republic of Serbia Early Parliamentary Elections 24 April 2016: OSCE/ODIHR Limited Election Observation Mission Final Report* (Warsaw: Office for Democratic Institutions and Human Rights, 2016), p. 1, https://www.osce.org/odihr/elections/serbia/256926?download=true.

58 See Freedom House, 'Freedom in the World 2019: Kosovo'.

59 See BertelsmannStiftung Transformation Index, 'BTI 2018 Kosovo Country Report', 23 January 2020, https://www.bti-project.org/en/reports/country-reports/detail/itc/RKS/.

60 European Commission, 'Accession Criteria', 25 January 2020, https://ec.europa.eu/neighbourhood-enlargement/policy/glossary/terms/accession-criteria_en.

61 'Borrell: If Kosovo and Serbia Agree on Territorial Exchange, We Can't Be More Catholic than the Pope', Euronews Albania, 6 May 2020, https://euronews.al/en/kosovo/2020/05/06/borrell-if-kosovo-and-serbia-agree-on-territorial-exchange-we-can-t-be-more-catholic-than-the-pope.

62 'Commissioner Várhelyi: Kosovo–Serbia Land Swap Is Secondary, Solution Is Important', Exit News, 8 May 2020, https://exit.al/en/2020/05/08/commissioner-varhelyi-kosovo-serbia-land-swap-is-secondary-solution-is-important/.

63 See Laurence Norman and Drew Hinshaw, 'U.S., Germany at Odds Over Serbia–Kosovo Land Swap', *Wall Street Journal*, 31 August 2018, https://www.wsj.com/articles/u-s-germany-at-odds-over-serbia-kosovo-land-swap-1535729377.

64 'Bolton Says U.S. Won't Oppose Kosovo–Serbia Land Swap Deal', Radio Free Europe/Radio Liberty, 24 August 2018, https://www.rferl.org/a/bolton-says-u-s-won-t-oppose-kosovo-serbia-land-swap-deal/29451395.html.

65 US Embassy in Montenegro, 'Matthew Palmer's Appointment as Special Representative for the Western Balkans', 31 January 2020, https://me.usembassy.gov/matthew-palmers-appointment-as-special-representative-for-the-western-balkans/.

66 See 'Kurti Accuses Grenell of Discussing the Exchange of Territories; Grenell Denies', European Western Balkans, 21 April 2020, https://europeanwesternbalkans.com/2020/04/21/kurti-accuses-grenell-of-discussing-the-exchange-of-territory-grenell-denies/.

67 See 'Kosovo PM Hails as "Positive Signs" Recent Deals with Serbia', AP, 27 January 2020, https://apnews.com/article/0d6f87e98f9d82e5e275fb1137a0932d.

68 See Sandra Maksimovic, 'What Did Serbia and Kosovo Sign in Washington?', European Western Balkans, 17 September 2020, https://europeanwesternbalkans.com/2020/09/17/what-did-serbia-and-kosovo-sign-in-washington/.

69 See James Ker-Lindsay, 'The Hollow Threat of Secession in Bosnia and Herzegovina: Legal and Political Impediments to a Unilateral Declaration of Independence by Republika Srpska', LSEE-Research on South Eastern Europe, 2016, pp. 16–18, http://www.lse.ac.uk/LSEE-Research-on-South-Eastern-Europe/Assets/Documents/Publications/Paper-Series-on-SEE/KerLindsay-Hollow-Threat-of-Secession-in-BiH.pdf.

70 Valerie Hopkins, 'Old Tensions Still Alive in Bosnia 25 Years After Dayton', Financial Times, 4 January 2021, https://www.ft.com/content/2704c51b-0e46-4891-81ad-00c23d70ed5c.

71 See Peter Geoghegan, 'At Balkan Crossroads, Anger at "Black Sheep" Image', Politico, 9 August 2017, https://www.politico.eu/article/serbia-sandzak-islam-caught-between-competing-worlds/.

72 Ivana Sekularac and Aleksandar Vasovic, 'Accept Reality, Serbia Does Not Control Kosovo: Vucic', Reuters, 27 May 2019, https://www.reuters.com/article/us-serbia-kosovo/accept-reality-serbia-does-not-control-kosovo-vucic-idUSKCN1SX1U2.

73 See Shaun Walker, 'Serbian President Accuses Russia of Spy Plot Involving Army', Guardian, 21 November 2019, https://www.theguardian.com/world/2019/nov/21/serbia-investigates-video-claiming-to-show-russian-spy-paying-off-official.

74 See Fitim Salihu, 'Could Kosovo and Serbia Really Exchange Territory?', Kosovotwopointzero.com, 14 August 2018, https://kosovotwopointzero.com/en/could-kosovo-and-serbia-really-exchange-territory/; and Jamie Dettmer, 'Serbian President's Trip to Kosovo to Discuss Land-swap Blocked', Voice of America, 10 September 2018, https://www.voanews.com/europe/serbian-presidents-trip-kosovo-discuss-land-swap-blocked.

75 Serbian Orthodox Church, 'Communiqué of the Holy Assembly of Bishops of the Serbian Orthodox Church on Kosovo and Metohija', 2 February 2020, http://www.spc.rs/eng/communique_holy_assembly_bishops_serbian_orthodox_church_kosovo_and_metohija.

76 See Marcoandrea Spinelli, 'Threatening Archipelagos: Serbian Enclaves and Minorities in Kosovo', Journal of Geography, Politics and Society, vol. 8, no. 4, 2018, pp. 20–1, doi: 10.4467/24512249JG.18.024.9011; and 'Life in Gorazdevac: We Have Survived the Worst, but We Are Slowly

Disappearing', KoSSev, 27 December 2019, https://kossev.info/life-in-goraz-devac-we-ve-survived-the-worst-but-we-are-slowly-disappearing/.

77 See Tamara Rastovac Siamasvili, 'Serbian Cultural and Religious Heritage in Kosovo and Metohija', NewEurope, 16 September 2019, https://www.neweurope.eu/article/serbian-cultural-and-religious-heritage-in-kosovo-and-metohija/.

78 'Survey: 77% of Serb Citizens Would Not Support Kosovo's Independence in Exchange for Faster EU Accession for Serbia', KoSSev, 29 July 2020, https://kossev.info/survey-77-of-serb-citizens-would-not-support-kosovos-independence-in-exchange-for-faster-eu-accession-for-serbia/.

79 See 'Proposing Change of Kosovo–Serbia Border, Irrational', *Gazeta Express*, 27 August 2019, https://g22.gazetaexpress.com/proposing-change-of-kosovo-serbia-border-irrational/; and Salihu, 'Could Kosovo and Serbia Really Exchange Territory?'

80 See Salihu, 'Could Kosovo and Serbia Really Exchange Territory?'

81 See 'Thousands Protest in Kosovo over Possible Serbia Land Swap', Radio Free Europe/Radio Liberty, 29 September 2018, https://www.rferl.org/a/protest-in-kosovo-over-possible-land-swap-with-serbia/29516478.html.

82 Office of the Prime Minister of Kosovo, 'Constitution of the Republic of Kosovo'.

83 World Bank, 'Kosovo', 24 March 2020, https://www.worldbank.org/en/country/kosovo/overview#3.

84 Alida Vracic, 'The Way Back: Brain Drain and Prosperity in the Western Balkans', European Council on Foreign Relations, 9 May 2018, https://www.ecfr.eu/publications/summary/the_way_back_brain_drain_and_prosperity_in_the_western_balkans.

85 See 'Outlook 2021 Kosovo', Bne IntelliNews, 7 January 2021, https://www.intellinews.com/outlook-2021-kosovo-199066/.

86 National Democratic Institute, 'Kosovo Public Opinion Survey', May 2020, p. 8, https://www.ndi.org/sites/default/files/NDI%20Kosovo%20Public%20Opinion%20Poll%20-%20May%202020.pdf.

87 See Doruntina Baliu, 'Millions Lost on Integration Efforts', Prishtina Insight, 27 October 2020, https://prishtinainsight.com/millions-lost-on-integration-efforts-mag/.

Israel's Right-wing Populists: The European Connection

Dani Filc and Sharon Pardo

In February 2019, during a visit by Hungarian Prime Minister Viktor Orbán to Israel, Israeli Prime Minister Benjamin Netanyahu sent a clear message from Jerusalem to Brussels by declaring that a strong bond exists between Israel and Orbán's Hungary, one based on the 'many things' that these two countries 'have shared in the past' as well as in the present. According to Netanyahu, Israel and Hungary 'are both small nations, democracies, that share common values and common interests'.[1] The partnership between Netanyahu's Israel and Orbán's Hungary is indicative of the enormous change that Israel has undergone during Netanyahu's era. Israel has become, much like Orbán's Hungary, a right-wing, populist, illiberal powerhouse. And it is not above joining forces with a European far right with anti-Semitism in its lineage.

Populism in Israel

Populism is a contested concept.[2] It has been understood as an ideology, a discourse, a disease of liberal democracy, a mobilisation strategy or a political style. Most researchers of populism tend to view it as a 'thin' ideology, or a discourse.[3] Under this interpretation, populism is an ideology that loosely connects a set of recurrent themes, among them a conviction that the common people are a source of virtue, nostalgia for a mythical heartland,

Dani Filc and **Sharon Pardo** are professors in the Department of Politics and Government at Ben-Gurion University of the Negev.

Survival | vol. 63 no. 3 | June–July 2021 | pp. 99–122   https://doi.org/10.1080/00396338.2021.1930409

anti-elitism, anti-intellectualism and a lack of confidence in liberal democracy.[4] For Cas Mudde, populism promotes two main beliefs: that society is divided between the pure people and the corrupted elites, and that democracy is solely the expression of popular sovereignty. This characterisation has been widely accepted. However, it could fit some illiberal or limited democratic movements other than populist ones.[5] Moreover, the characterisation of populism as an ideology or a discourse does not discriminate between clearly distinct movements, such as European right-wing populism and Evo Morales's indigenous movement in Bolivia.

Others consider populism the antithesis of liberal democracy.[6] By their lights, populists oppose liberal democracy, since its emphasis on civil processes as well as individual and minority rights limits popular sovereignty. For these critics, liberalism is 'good democracy' and populism 'bad democracy', and they tend to disregard historical cases in which populist movements enhanced and broadened democracy. A third group sees populism as a political strategy whereby a charismatic leader uses a direct, quasi-personal manner to approach a heterogeneous mass of followers, bypassing intermediary links. Yet populism may also be highly institutionalised, and develop intermediate associations (like, say, Peronism) as well as mobilising discrete sectors of society.[7] In addition, populism can be construed as a political style, defined as 'the repertoires of performance that are used to create political relations'. The populist political style is distinguished by its appeal to the people, a sense of crisis or threat, the use of 'bad manners' and a coarsening of political discourse.[8]

For our purposes, populism most crucially consists of political formations that emerge in situations of conflict over the inclusion or exclusion of certain social groups, mobilising people by stressing elitist antagonism. Such movements see society as polarised between a presumptively homogeneous people and its enemies, which consist of elites and their foreign allies.

The people can mean the whole political community, the plebs as opposed to the ruling elites, or an ethno-cultural closed community (the *volk*).[9] Inclusive populist movements stress the notion of the people as plebeians, thereby allowing, at least partially, the political integration of excluded social groups and, in the process, enlarging the boundaries of democracy.[10] In contrast, exclusionary populism emphasises the organic understanding of the 'people' as an ethnically or culturally homogeneous unit. This is a nativist perspective, which promotes the belief that states should be inhabited exclusively by members of the nation widely held to be the native group and that non-native persons and ideas represent a threat.[11]

Populism is prevalent in Israeli politics because conflicts concerning the inclusion or exclusion of subordinate social groups have marked Israeli society since its inception. Such conflicts stem from the interplay of several factors: the tension between the conceptualisation of the Jewish people as a religious unity and its heterogeneous character; the enduring conflict with the Palestinian people; and the ongoing Israeli colonialism in the occupied territories. Israel is marked by persistent clashes over the place in Israeli society of different social groups, among them Israeli Arabs, Jews who emigrated from Muslim countries (*Mizrahim*) and immigrants from the former Soviet Union or Ethiopia. The lack of a territorial definition of 'we the people', and the conflation between demos and ethnos, explain why most populist movements, including contemporary Israel's, are essentially exclusionary. Scholars have defined Israel as a limited democracy, an ethnic democracy or an ethnocracy.[12] But there is a consensus that Israel is not a full liberal democracy. Almost two million people are living under Israeli occupation without civic and political rights; there are legal differences between the Jewish majority and the Arab-Palestinian minority; and there is no separation between state and religion. Hence, populist movements have emerged whose conception of democracy is illiberal.[13]

Populism is prevalent in Israeli politics

In a divided society, the signifier *people* has become a major reference point for the constitution of political identities, and populism a central feature of the political system. In the late 1950s, the 1960s and the 1970s, the currently dominant party, Likud, developed as an inclusive populist movement under Menachem Begin's leadership. As such, it reached power in 1977. The party developed a narrative of Israeli history that symbolically included *Mizrahim* in the common 'we', implemented economic and social policies aimed at their material inclusion, and politically included *Mizrahim* by opening the party to a young *Mizrahi* political leadership that emerged at the local level and achieved national standing.[14]

Today, there are three parties in Israel that can be considered populist: Shas, an ultra-orthodox religious *Mizrahi* party; Yisrael Beiteinu (Israel Our Home), a party led by former minister of foreign affairs and minister of defence Avigdor Lieberman; and Likud. In the March 2021 elections, the three parties combined received almost 37% of the vote, reflecting the centrality of populism in Israeli politics. With 1,066,892 votes, Likud, led by Netanyahu, was Israel's most popular party. Under Netanyahu's leadership, Likud has become an overtly exclusionary party, with an anti-liberal conception of democracy. Netanyahu has turned to nativism and xenophobia, mostly in the form of Islamophobia. He has fomented opposition to purportedly elitist institutions such as academia, media and the judicial system, and encouraged an anti-liberal understanding of democracy.

Ernesto Laclau argued that for populist purposes, the people is constructed through a chain of equivalences between the claims of different social groups.[15] For Netanyahu, however, the identity of the people is crystal clear: 'us' means the Jewish people, which Netanyahu tacitly defines, in accord with the Orthodox religious view, as those born to a Jewish mother. The 'anti-people' is marked by anti-Semitism: 'I have a message to all the antisemites out there – whether they live in modern Persia, in the palaces of Tehran or the bunkers of Beirut; whether they march through the streets of Charlottesville or murder worshippers in a synagogue in Pittsburgh; whether they voice their hatred in political parties in Britain, or Europe, or the United States.'[16] Netanyahu turns Laclau on his head, building a chain of equivalences in which the Islamic State (ISIS) is like Iran, Iran is like Hizbullah, Hizbullah is like Hamas, Hamas is like Mahmoud Abbas and the Palestinian Authority (PA), the Palestinians in the occupied territories are like Israeli-Arab citizens, and Israeli-Arab citizens are like the Israeli left. All the links in the chain are enemies of the 'true people'.

An example of this chain of equivalences is his statement during the 2015 election campaign after the prosecutor of the International Criminal Court opened a preliminary examination into the situation in Palestine. 'Israel totally rejects the scandalous decision of the International Court prosecutor', said Netanyahu.

> Following her absurd decision Hamas already declared that they will sue the state of Israel. I won't be surprised if we will hear similar things from Hezbollah, ISIS and Al Qaeda. A few days after Islamist terror committed a massacre in France, the prosecutor decided to investigate Israel that [sic] defends its citizens from the extremist Islamic terrorist organization Hamas that aims to massacre Jews. It is the same Hamas that has a pact with the [PA].[17]

Netanyahu's chain of equivalences was not limited to Muslims but included the Israeli left and centre-left (all of them referred to as 'the Left'), since the 'leftist elites' were not part of the 'true' people. Commenting on United Nations Security Council Resolution 2334, which reaffirms that the settlements in the West Bank are illegitimate, Netanyahu stated: 'Left parties, politicians and TV journalists were extremely pleased with the Security Council's resolution; almost as [much as] the [PA] and Hamas.'[18] Leftists, for Netanyahu, are not really Jews. As he explained to Rabbi Yitzhak Kaduri in October 1997, 'the Left has forgotten what it is to be a Jew'.[19] Commenting on Israeli Members of Knesset (MKs) visiting Palestine Liberation Organization (PLO) leader Marwan Barghouti in jail, Netanyahu declared: 'The news about leftist MKs' visits to terrorists convicted for murdering Jews show how perverted and dangerous the Left's way is.'[20] In the April 2019 elections, Likud's electoral campaign extended the chain of equivalences even further. Likud claimed that Benny Gantz, leader of the centrist Blue and White party, would 'form a government with the Arab parties'. This, Likud argued, was 'proof' that Gantz was not a legitimate alternative and that such a government would be supported by Tehran.[21]

The demonisation of Arabs and Muslims is central to Netanyahu's chain of equivalences. During an 'emergency meeting' called to help prevent the election of a centrist government supported by the United Arab List, Netanyahu declared that if such a government were established, 'Teheran, Ramallah and Gaza will celebrate'. Moreover, for Netanyahu, the enemy is not really human, at least not to the extent that the people and its allies are:

> After a terrorist attack, we mourn. They make the terrorists their heroes. They name streets and squares after them … He who indiscriminately kills innocent citizens does not struggle for human rights or for liberty, he aims at extermination and tyranny … as in Iran, Gaza or under ISIS … The time has come for the civilized world to build a united front against this barbaric fanaticism. We in Israel understand this well, since we fight terror for already 100 years.[22]

In this apocalyptic view, confronting the definitive evil is the Jewish people – a people defined biologically and facing eternal threats of extermination. For Netanyahu, Israel is destined to 'live by the sword' forever. As he expressed in May 2019: 'During the last 100 years our enemies tried to exterminate us once and again, but they failed. We will continue to fight against those who want to kill us, and we make our roots deeper in the motherland.'[23]

Likud's nativism has distinctive characteristics. It is not territorial – Arabs born in Israel are not native in the eyes of exclusionary populists – but defined by the boundaries of Judaism. The non-native 'other' is represented by Israeli Arabs, migrant workers from developing countries and asylum seekers (mostly African). Likud went from allowing the inclusion of *Mizrahim* to excluding Israel's Arab citizens, whose citizenship the party considers conditional. In 2014, Netanyahu said that he 'would instruct the Minister of the Interior to deny citizenship to those who call for the elimination of Israel'.[24]

On the day of the 2015 elections, Netanyahu called Jewish citizens to come and vote because 'the Israeli Arabs are galloping to the ballot boxes driven by buses paid by leftist Non-Governmental Organizations'.[25] In November 2016, Israel suffered several serious wildfires. Likud's leadership – with no proof at all – claimed they were the result of 'fire terrorism' perpetrated by Arab citizens.[26] Official investigators later refuted the claim. During the September 2019 elections campaign, Netanyahu's chatbot warned: 'Israeli Arabs want to exterminate all of us, men women and children.'[27]

Politicians such as Minister of Transportation Miri Regev promoted legislation aimed at banning specific Israeli-Arab MKs, and Likud MK David Bitan declared that he would be happier if Israeli Arabs did not vote at all. Recalling Turkish President Recep Tayyip Erdogan's approach to Kurdish members of parliament, Regev called Arab MKs 'Trojan Horses'.[28] In both the April and the September 2019 elections, Likud promoted an initiative to forbid Arab MKs from running for parliament. They also put forward legislation advancing the installation of video cameras in polling stations in Arab villages and cities – purportedly to avoid fraud, but in fact to intimidate Arab voters. The Likud government passed a bill allowing for an elected MK to be expelled from parliament if such action were approved by three-quarters of MKs, clearly targeting Arab MKs.

Regev called Arab MKs 'Trojan Horses'

Likud also expressed its nativism in attacks against asylum seekers. Regev, when not yet in her ministerial role, called Sudanese refugees 'a cancer in the nation's body'.[29] Danny Danon, former minister of science, technology and space, and former Israeli ambassador to the UN, wrote: 'The influx of undocumented men … did real damage to the social fabric of our society … The Likud government … will work tirelessly until there are no more infiltrators crossing our borders.'[30]

The cultural elites are depicted as leftist and attacked as enemies of the people and accomplices of non-Jews. When the Israeli High Court of Justice ruled against a law to imprison asylum seekers, Regev declared: 'The court is disconnected from the people. The Court's decision is essentially calling everyone in Africa to come to Israel, because infiltrators can move around freely. The Court didn't think of the good of the Israeli public in its decision and will make the situation intolerable.'[31] Yariv Levin, speaker of the Knesset and former minister of tourism, directly accused the High Court of Justice of being a nest of left-wingers.[32] Like Levin, Netanyahu dubs journalists who criticise him and his government 'ultra-leftists', and has attempted to close the public broadcasting corporation for being 'infiltrated by leftists'.[33]

Over the past decade, Likud has developed an anti-liberal conception of democracy according to which democracy is mostly about the majority rule of the Jewish people. Likud opposes core elements of liberal democracy such as judicial review, the independence of the judiciary and individual rights, deeming them inimical to the people's will. Human-rights groups and anti-occupation non-governmental organisations have been tagged anti-Israeli, anathema to the common people's interests and hospitable only to 'infiltrators'. In the words of Regev, then chairwoman of the Internal Affairs and Environment Committee: 'Thousands of infil-trators … are helped by human rights organizations, leftist human rights' organizations … There are no organizations caring for the human rights of the [Israeli] citizens, of those that pay taxes and serve in the army … Human rights are only for infiltrators.'[34]

The Israeli right and the eurosceptics

In line with the morphing of its domestic identity, Israel has become a soft eurosceptic country, developing strong political alliances and institutional connections with populist and eurosceptical political actors that do not support the norms informing European Union policies.[35] From the time of Israel's establishment in 1948, the country's leaders were concerned with gaining international recognition and legitimacy, and breaking out of the political and diplomatic isolation that the Arab countries were imposing on the nascent state. Over the years, in order to break this isolation, to save Jews from persecution and to secure the future of the Jewish state, Zionist underground groups in Mandatory Palestine and the Israeli leadership were willing to cooperate with certain dubious actors in Europe and elsewhere.[36] Although Israel denounced apartheid for years after its establishment, and during the 1960s formed alliances with the newly independent African coun-tries, following the Arab–Israeli War of October 1973, many African states severed diplomatic ties with Israel. In turn, Israel established unabashedly close relations with South Africa that continued well into the 1980s.[37]

When Netanyahu first came to power in 1996, Jews were not persecuted in Europe and Israel was no longer an isolated country. Yet, like some of his predecessors, Netanyahu and the Likud party were still anxious to cooperate with radical-right populist parties and governments. And these new partners were quick to return their diplomatic appreciation.

A case in point is Belgium's Vlaams Belang (Flemish Interest) party. The party, whose founders collaborated with the Nazis and whose past leadership cast doubts on the reality of the Holocaust, is today an enthusiastic supporter of Israel. Filip Dewinter, its former leader, notes that its cosiness with Israel has prompted some to say that 'we are the accomplices of international Jewry and that we betrayed nationalism in return for Jewish money, that we kowtow for international Zionism'.[38] This suggests that an equilibrium of joint legitimation is emerging: since the early 2000s, notes Mudde, 'the party has only rarely been accused of anti-Semitism' and has been perceived as a defender of the Jewish community.[39] In fact, according to Dewinter, 'there is a common interest between Jewish and Flemish people in the struggle against Islam in Europe'. Hence, Dewinter called on Jews to join in the battle against Muslims: Jews 'are our brothers-in-arms in the battle against extremist Islam … [They] are part of European culture. Islam is not.'[40]

Perceiving itself as Israel's 'ally against radical Islam', in December 2010 the party joined a delegation of other European populist parties on a trip to Israel. They visited the Knesset and met with a deputy minister, as well as with the leadership of the Jewish settlers in the occupied territories. During the trip Dewinter and his colleagues issued the 'Jerusalem Declaration', a manifesto in which they announced their commitment to the 'existence of the State of Israel' and to Israel's right 'to defend itself against any aggression, especially against Islamic terror'.[41]

Since the Alternative für Deutschland (Alternative for Germany, or AfD) party was founded in April 2013, it has stormed national politics and is today the largest opposition party in the German Bundestag.[42] Elements of the AfD are openly racist, unabashedly anti-Semitic and supportive of neo-Nazi movements, and its co-founder and former co-leader Alexander Gauland has questioned Germany's special relationship with Israel.[43] Yet some in Israel have voiced sympathy for the party and are advocating closer relationships with its leadership. Thus, Rafi Eitan, a former minister for senior citizens and minister for Jerusalem affairs under Netanyahu, and an influential voice on Israeli security until his death in early 2019, vociferously advocated closer Israeli relations with the AfD. In 2018, on the occasion of

International Holocaust Remembrance Day, Eitan filmed a video message of support for the AfD, which the AfD posted on its social-media accounts. In his message, Eitan offered greetings to the party's leadership and stated that 'we all in Israel appreciate your attitude towards Judaism'. Eitan further advised the AfD that 'if you work wisely, strongly, and most important, realistically … instead of "Alternative for Germany," you might become an alternative for all Europe'. On his personal Facebook page, Eitan further explained his support for the party: 'The Muslim world and its culture are very different from those of the West', he said. 'Anywhere there are Muslims today, in any European country, one can expect violence and terror because

of these differences.' Eitan also expressed confidence that the AfD would 'help Israel with anything we'll ask of them'.[44]

Yair called for the death of the EU

In August 2019, *Israel Hayom*, an Israeli daily closely associated with Netanyahu, campaigned for an official dialogue between Israel and the AfD, calling on Israel to 'take care of its own national interests and look at where it can find those who will help promote them', and observing that the 'AfD has already tried to promote a few pro-Israel initiatives'.[45] More recently, in May 2020, Yair Netanyahu, the prime minister's son, literally became a poster boy for the AfD. After Yair called for the death of the EU and the return of a 'Christian' Europe in a tweet, Joachim Kuhs, an AfD member of the European Parliament, turned the tweet into a graphic featuring a picture of the young Netanyahu.[46]

Matteo Salvini, the leader of Italy's far-right Lega party, has called Israel 'a fortress for the protection of Europe' and a 'bulwark of Western rights and values', and has been critical of the EU for its 'unbalanced' position on the Israeli–Palestinian conflict and its condemnation of Israel 'every 15 minutes'.[47] He is one of Netanyahu's closest allies in the EU, touting himself as 'a friend and brother of Israel', while Netanyahu calls Salvini 'a great friend of Israel'.[48] Gilad Erdan, the Israeli ambassador to the US and the UN, has said of Israel and Lega that 'we are partners in the fight against radical Islamic terror, which threatens Europe and Israel'.[49] Salvini conflates anti-Semitism with hostility to Israel and ascribes anti-Semitism in Europe to

Islamist extremists. He has promised to 'take it upon himself' to fight 'anti-Israeli bias' at the EU.[50]

Netanyahu's Israel has also developed a special relationship with Geert Wilders and his anti-Islam, anti-immigrant Partij voor de Vrijheid (Party for Freedom) in the Netherlands. Unlike other far-right parties in Europe, this one is not perceived in Israel as an anti-Semitic party with a fascist past. Wilders himself, who in his youth lived in Israel for 18 months and volunteered at an Israeli settlement, has visited Israel dozens of times and openly admires the country as 'a shining light in the Middle East's darkness'.[51] Even so, the relationship is ambiguous. Publicly, although Israel does not boycott Wilders and his party, it refrains from hosting him at the highest levels. Unofficially, Wilders is a welcome guest in Israel. Privately, top Israeli officials, including Lieberman and the foreign ministry's director general, have met with Wilders regularly.[52] For Likud's leadership, Wilders is a strong ally because he believes that the conflict between Islam and the West, and between Israel and the Arabs, is deeply ideological. For Wilders, Israel is a model state: 'I wish we in the Netherlands would have half the courage that you have to fight the Arabs … We must learn from you. To be tougher.'[53]

Likud's links with Austria's Freiheitliche Partei Österreichs (Freedom Party of Austria, or FPÖ) – founded by a former Nazi SS officer – are complicated but on balance positive. In 1999, Israel recalled its ambassador to Vienna after the party first joined Austria's coalition government. Over the years, however, Israel has warmed to the FPÖ. What seemed to temper Israel's attitude were former party chairman and Austrian vice-chancellor Heinz-Christian Strache's views on Islam and the Israeli–Palestinian conflict.[54] In a 2017 letter to Netanyahu, Strache asserted that 'Israel possess the right to build wherever is required in the Land of Israel', including in the occupied territories and East Jerusalem. Strache further committed himself to do all in his power to move the Austrian Embassy to Jerusalem.[55] Immediately after being appointed Austria's vice-chancellor in December 2017, Strache said that Vienna was 'striving for an honest, sustainable and friendly contact with Israel', and vowed that his party would be 'an essential partner in Europe's fight against anti-Semitism'. The 2017–19 Kurz–Strache government was probably the most Israel-friendly in

Austria's history. On the day of its inauguration, the government committed itself to advancing legislation granting citizenship to the descendants
of Austrian Holocaust victims, which was enacted and entered into force
in September 2020. Vice-Chancellor Strache and his party's foreign minister, Karin Kneissl, have repeatedly stated – on the record – that they are
in full support of the new legislation.[56] A year later, in September 2018,
Netanyahu expressed his appreciation.[57]

Strache has visited Israel several times, often as a guest of settlers or of
Likud. Despite an official diplomatic boycott, Likud's top leadership, including Netanyahu, have all met with Strache. Indeed, former Likud MK Yehudah
Glick, who for many years had advocated closer relations with the FPÖ, confirmed to us that the informal embrace of Strache came from the very top:
'Every time that I traveled, I informed Netanyahu. He encouraged me and
gave me his blessing.'[58] Similar voices can be heard in the Israeli Ministry of
Foreign Affairs. Talya Lador-Fresher, former Israeli ambassador to Austria
and current head of the Bureau for European Affairs, is also a strong advocate of Israel–FPÖ relations. In February 2017, she became the first Israeli
ambassador to Vienna to establish direct contacts with Strache.[59] Since then,
Lador-Fresher has staunchly supported the relationship.[60] Furthermore,
under the Kurz–Strache government the Austrian Cultural Forum strengthened and deepened its cultural activities in Israel. Following the COVID-19
outbreak, Netanyahu and Chancellor Sebastian Kurz closely cooperated in
the fight against the pandemic. In May 2020, Kurz hosted the leaders of the
countries at the forefront of the pandemic response for an exchange of ideas
and courses of action. Netanyahu was among the invited leaders, alongside
the prime ministers of Australia, the Czech Republic, Denmark, Greece,
Norway and Singapore. The leaders agreed that the Israeli cyber directorate
would lead consultations within this group regarding databases.[61] In March
2021, the two countries, together with Denmark, agreed to join forces in
investing in research for and rolling out COVID vaccines.[62]

The Netanyahu government's relationship with the Visegrad Group of
countries (V4) – the Czech Republic, Hungary, Poland and Slovakia – is
overtly friendly, and increasingly so.[63] In July 2017, when Netanyahu was
visiting Hungary for a V4 summit, he could be heard during a closed-door

meeting with V4 leaders over a 'hot mic' sharply attacking the EU and asking the V4 countries to help erode the consensus among EU members regarding Iran and the Israeli–Palestinian conflict.[64] His larger goal is to establish a new diplomatic alliance in which Israel would provide the V4 with aid in different fields, such as security, cyber, high tech, medicine and agriculture, in return for the group's support of Israel in the EU and the UN.[65] He appears to be succeeding. In February 2019, Jerusalem was to host the first-ever V4 summit outside Europe. While the event was ultimately cancelled due to a diplomatic row between Israel and Poland over comments by the acting Israeli foreign minister about Polish anti-Semitism, Netanyahu did host the Czech, Hungarian and Slovak prime ministers at his residence. In the months bracketing the aborted summit, in violation of official EU policy, Slovakia announced the establishment of a cultural and trade office in Jerusalem, Hungary opened a trade office there and the Czech Republic opened a diplomatic office in the city.[66]

Strong relationships with the Jewish state insulate the V4 – especially Orbán's Hungary – against criticism that they are pushing anti-Semitic and xenophobic discourses and policies.[67] Moreover, as supporters of ethno-nationalism at home, V4 leaders genuinely admire Netanyahu for his tough position in advancing Israel's diplomatic and security interests, and for the internal policies he has enacted to ensure the ethnic character of Israel. During his visit to Jerusalem in March 2021, Orban said to his Israeli audience: 'In Hungary, not just your country, but your prime minister, has a very high reputation as the friend of Hungary, which is not just expressed by culture and political gestures … I just congratulate you [Netanyahu] and your government for [a] successful decade. What I can do is nothing else … just try to copy it for Hungary.' Andrej Babis, the Czech prime minister, was equally admiring. After inaugurating the Jerusalem office of the embassy of the Czech Republic in Israel, Babis called Netanyahu a 'great leader', adding that 'the reason why I came here to Israel is to learn about your experience. Under the guidance of Prime Minister Benjamin Netanyahu, [a] great leader, the State of Israel has become the example to follow.'[68] These European leaders do not share the EU's official criticism of the Israeli government's stance on the Israeli–Palestinian conflict, and sympathise with Israeli viewpoints on issues such as migration, security and regional threat perceptions that tend to clash with the EU's.[69] Like Wilders, Orbán has voiced the belief that 'the biggest common adversary to our common civilization is the force of militant Islam'.[70]

Israel has reciprocated with material support to the V4 countries. During 2017–19, Israeli imports from the V4 countries surged.[71] While available data for 2020 indicates a sharp global decline in trade growth of about 8%, largely due to the pandemic, trade between Israel and Hungary, for example, grew about 1% that year.[72] Israel supplied both Hungary and the Czech Republic with Moderna COVID-19 vaccines, and assisted them and at least one other V4 country in acquiring Pfizer-BioNTech vaccines.[73] The diplomatic affection between Netanyahu and the V4 has also made for closer cultural ties. In November 2018, Czech President Milos Zeman inaugurated the new 'Czech House' cultural centre in Jerusalem, and in 2019 Hungary launched 'The Hungarian Culture Year in Israel' to win over the Israeli public with a cavalcade of cultural events and Hungarian cuisine.[74]

Under Netanyahu's premiership, Israel has operated and behaved as a populist, soft eurosceptic country for whom relations with the V4 members, as well as other Eastern European countries, are a strategic tool for modifying EU foreign policy. In August 2019, Netanyahu visited Lithuania to attend the summit of the Baltic states. Like his visit to Hungary two years earlier, this was the first visit to Lithuania by an Israeli prime minister, and as such a historic opportunity to underscore the deepening relations between the two countries. In the event, he revealed a pan-European strategy. 'I want to achieve a balance in the [EU's] not always friendly relations with Israel in order to maintain fairer and genuine relations', he said upon arriving in Vilnius. 'I am doing it through contacts with blocs of [EU] countries, Eastern European countries, and now with Baltic countries.'[75]

*   *   *

Since 1967, the Arab–Israeli conflict has defined the contours of Israeli–European relations.[76] Israel has viewed European positions manifesting sympathy with the Palestinians as inimical to its security and as uncritically reflecting the positions of the Arab world. During the 1990s, Europe launched a series of multilateral initiatives, most notably the Euro-Mediterranean Partnership and the Union for the Mediterranean, through which it sought to manage relations between Israel and the Arab world. The EU's linkage of these multilateral efforts to the Arab–Israeli conflict has only further undermined Israel's confidence in the EU.[77] Furthermore, Israel's isolation within these arrangements may have encouraged it to seek political shelter in European radical-right populist parties and governments.

To a significant degree, the relationships between Netanyahu's Israel and European radical-right populist parties and governments are based on transactional calculations and a fairly straightforward quid pro quo: the European players forgive Israel for its expansion in the occupied territories and are even willing to recognise Jerusalem as Israel's capital, in return for which Netanyahu's Israel forgives them for their historical and ideological links with neo-Nazism, and even their present-day anti-Semitism at home. As a senior diplomat at the Israeli Ministry of Foreign Affairs explained to us:

> The EU has different shades of democracy. With Hungary and the other V4 countries, we share interests, we understand democracy in a similar way and we have the same analysis regarding the Middle East and the Muslim world. We get all the support we need from them and they are always open to our arguments. As for anti-Semitism, none of them is anti-Semitic. We simply have different narratives regarding the Holocaust. Above all, we share common values with them.[78]

The rationalisation is quite obvious and confirms an equilibrium of joint legitimisation.

Yet, on a deeper level, the convergence between the European right and Israel aims to weaken core liberal EU norms that are contested within the EU itself.[79] The convergence thus subverts Brussels's efforts to construct normative internal and foreign policies, as well as its ability to exert meaningful pressure on Israel.[80] Like European right-wing populists, Netanyahu perceives the European left and the Arab and Muslim immigrant communities as the main problem for the continent, and the key European threat today to Israel and to European Jewry. For Israel, European populists are ideological allies, harnessing ethnic nationalism in an overarching struggle against global Islam.[81] They oppose both immigration in general and Arab and Muslim immigration in particular. As Netanyahu and Orbán declared in 2018 in Jerusalem: 'We both understand that the threat of radical Islam is a real one. It could endanger Europe … By being here, at the frontline of the battle against radical Islam, in many ways Israel is defending Europe.'[82] Cementing the relationship, both Netanyahu's Likud and his European partners of the populist radical right despise multiculturalism, detest political correctness, have little respect for international organisations and international law, and abhor probing and uncooperative media. Netanyahu's Israel is not merely instrumentalising the European right to alleviate external pressures on Israel or to blackmail and divide EU member states and institutions; his government and its European partners share deep ideological affinities and common values, and hostility to the EU project itself.

Notes

1   Israel Ministry of Foreign Affairs, 'PM Benjamin Netanyahu Meets with Hungarian PM Viktor Orban', Press Release, 19 February 2019, https://mfa. gov.il/MFA/PressRoom/2019/Pages/ PM-Benjamin-Netanyahu-meets-with-Hungarian-PM-Viktor-Orban-19-Feb-2019.aspx.

2   See Margaret Canovan, *Populism* (New York: Harcourt Brace Jovanovich, 1981); Gino Germani, *Authoritarianism, Fascism and National Populism* (New Brunswick, NJ: Transaction Books, 1978); Ghita Ionescu and Ernest Gellner (eds), *Populism: Its Meanings and National Characteristics* (London: Macmillan, 1969); Erik Jones, 'Populism in Europe: What Scholarship Tells Us', *Survival*, vol. 61, no. 4, August–September 2019, pp. 7–30; Ernesto Laclau, *The Populist Reason* (London: Verso, 2005); Ernesto Laclau, *Politics and Ideology in Marxist Theory* (London: Verso, 1977); Michael Lee, 'Populism or Embedded Plutocracy? The Emerging World Order', *Survival*, vol. 61, no. 2, April–May 2019, pp. 53–82; Cas Mudde, *Populist Radical Right Parties in Europe* (Cambridge: Cambridge University Press, 2007); and Matthijs Rooduijn and Tjitske Akkerman, 'Flank Attacks: Populism and Left–Right Radicalism in Western Europe', *Party Politics*, vol. 23, no. 3, July 2015, pp. 193–204.

3   See Carlos de la Torre, 'Populismo, Cultura Politica y Vida Cotidiana en Ecuador', in Felipe de Lara Burbano

(ed.), *El Fantasma del Populismo: Aproximacion a un Tema Siempre Actual* (Venezuela: Nueva Sociedad, 1998), pp. 136–60; Kirk A. Hawkins, *Venezuela's Chavismo and Populism in Comparative Perspective* (Cambridge: Cambridge University Press, 2010); Mudde, *Populist Radical Right Parties in Europe*; and Mario E. Poblete, 'How to Assess Populist Discourse Through Three Current Approaches', *Journal of Political Ideologies*, vol. 20, no. 2, May 2015, pp. 201–18.

4   See Donald MacRae, 'Populism as an Ideology', in Ionescu and Gellner (eds), *Populism: Its Meanings and National Characteristics*, pp. 153–65; and Paul Taggart, *Populism* (Buckingham: Open University Press, 2000).

5   See Paulina Ochoa Espejo, *The Time of Popular Sovereignty: Process and the Democratic State* (University Park, PA: Pennsylvania State University Press, 2011).

6   See, for example, Lee, 'Populism or Embedded Plutocracy?'; Takis S. Pappas, *Populism and Crisis Politics in Greece* (Basingstoke: Palgrave, 2014); and Jan-Werner Müller, *What Is Populism?* (Philadelphia, PA: University of Pennsylvania Press, 2016).

7   See Kurt Weyland, 'Neopopulism and Neoliberalism in Latin America: Unexpected Affinities', *Studies in Comparative International Development*, vol. 31, no. 3, February 1996, pp. 3–31; and Robert S. Jansen, 'Populist Mobilization: A New Theoretical Approach to Populism', *Sociological Theory*, vol. 29, no. 2, June 2011, pp. 75–96.

8   See Benjamin Moffitt and Simon Tormey, 'Rethinking Populism: Politics, Mediatisation and Political Style', *Political Studies*, vol. 62, no. 2, May 2013, p. 387.

9   See Margaret Canovan, *The People* (Cambridge: Polity Press, 2005).

10 See Nicos Mouzelis, 'On the Concept of Populism: Populist and Clientelist Modes of Incorporation in Semiperipheral Polities', *Politics & Society*, vol. 14, no. 3, September 1985, pp. 329–48; de la Torre, 'Populismo, Cultura Politica'; and Carlos de la Torre, 'Populist Redemption and the Unfinished Democratization of Latin America', *Constellations*, vol. 5, no. 1, June 2008, pp. 85–95.

11 See Mudde, *Populist Radical Right Parties in Europe*.

12 See Sammy Smooha, 'Ethnic Democracy: Israel as an Archetype', *Israel Studies*, vol. 2, no. 2, Fall 1997, pp. 198–241; and Oren Yiftachel, *Ethnocracy: Land and Identity Politics in Israel/Palestine* (Philadelphia, PA: University of Pennsylvania Press, 2006).

13 See Mabel Berezin, *Illiberal Politics in Neoliberal Times: Culture, Security and Populism in the New Europe* (Cambridge: Cambridge University Press, 2016); and Pappas, *Populism and Crisis Politics in Greece*.

14 See Dani Filc, *The Political Right in Israel: Different Faces of Jewish Populism* (London: Routledge, 2010).

15 Laclau, *The Populist Reason*.

16 Benjamin Netanyahu, 'Video Address to the 2019 AIPAC Policy Conference in Washington', Press Release, Israel Ministry of Foreign Affairs, 26 March 2019, https://mfa.gov.il/MFA/PressRoom/2019/Pages/PM-Netanyahu-s-video-address-to-the-2019-AIPAC-Policy-Conference-26-March-2019.aspx.

17 Elior Levi and Itamar Eichner, 'Hamas: "We Will Submit Evidence to The Hague"; Netanyahu Approached Kerry', Ynet, 17 January 2015, https://www.ynet.co.il/articles/0,7340,L-4615994,00.html.

18 Benjamin Netanyahu, Facebook post, 24 December 2016, available at http://www.facebook.com/Netanyahu.

19 'Netanyahu to Rabbi Kaduri: "The Left Has Forgotten What It Is to Be a Jew"', YouTube, October 1997, https://www.youtube.com/watch?v=N_5rVMDUI18.

20 Yaron Avraham, 'The MK's Visits of Terrorists: "Moral Horror"', News 12, 6 August 2019, https://www.mako.co.il/news-military/2019_Q3/Article-ba623dcd0586c61027.htm.

21 'Likud Against Gantz: "Will Form a Government with the Arabs' Support"', Srugim News, 20 February 2019, available at https://www.srugim.co.il.

22 Prime Minister's Office, 'Prime Minister Netanyahu's Remarks at the Memorial Ceremony for Victims of Terror on Mount Herzl', 8 May 2019, https://www.gov.il/he/departments/news/event_mounthatred080519.

23 Prime Minister's Office, 'Prime Minister Netanyahu's Remarks at the Memorial Ceremony for the Fallen Soldiers', 8 May 2019, https://www.youtube.com/watch?v=Mhe8fyt20Jg.

24 'Prime Minister: "We Will Consider Striping Citizenships to Those Calling for Our Destruction"', News 12, 9 November 2014, https://www.mako.co.il/news-military/politics-q4_2014/Article-dadac21c5929941004.htm.

25 Shabtai Bandet, Omri Nahmias and Yair Altman, 'Netanyahu Distributed a Video: "The Arabs are Galloping to the Ballot Boxes"', Walla News, 17 March 2015, https://elections.walla.co.il/item/2838603.

26 'MK Nava Boker Who Lost Her Husband at the Carmel: "The Fire Is Bringing Me Back Six Years"', Maariv, 24 November 2016, https://www.maariv.co.il/news/politics/Article-564589.

27 Rafaella Goichman, 'Netanyahu's Chatbot: "The Arabs Want to Destroy Us All"', Marker, 11 September 2019, https://www.themarker.com/technation/1.7831338.

28 'Arab MKs Are "Trojan Horse" Seeking to Destroy Israel, Claims Israeli Minister', MEMO Middle East Monitor, 4 February 2019, https://www.middleeastmonitor.com/20190204-arab-mks-are-trojan-horse-seeking-to-destroy-israel-claims-israeli-minister/.

29 Asher Schechter, 'How Likud MK Miri Regev Talked Her Way to the Top', Haaretz, 21 December 2012, https://www.haaretz.com/.premium-how-a-likud-mk-talked-her-way-to-the-top-1.5277198.

30 Danny Danon, 'We're on the Tight Track', Jerusalem Post, 19 December 2013, https://www.jpost.com/Opinion/Op-Ed-Contributors/Were-on-the-right-track-335462.

31 Lahav Harkov, 'Court Ruling on Migrants Irks Critics of Judicial Activism', Jerusalem Post, 22 September 2014, https://www.jpost.com/israel-news/court-ruling-on-migrants-irks-critics-of-judicial-activism-376067.

32 See Gilad Zwick, 'Yariv Levin: The High Court of Justice Is the Extreme Left, Prefers the Infiltrators to

Southern Tel Aviv Residents', *Mida*, 6 November 2017, available at https://mida.org.il.

33 Dror Halavy, 'Kachlon: I'll Veto Closure of Public Broadcasting Body', *Hamodia*, 31 October 2016, https://hamodia.com/2016/10/31/kachlon-ill-veto-closure-of-public-broadcast-body/.

34 Miri Regev, 'The 187th Meeting of the 19th Knesset: Miri Regev (Chairwoman of the Internal Affairs and Environment Committee)', *Knesset Protocols*, 8 December 2014, p. 130, http://online.knesset.gov.il/PDF/41188/PDF_41188.PDF.

35 See Sara B. Hobolt and Catherine E. de Vries, 'Public Support for European Integration', *Annual Review of Political Science*, vol. 19, no. 1, May 2016, pp. 413–32; Liesbet Hooghe and Gary Marks, 'Sources of Euroscepticism', *Acta Politica*, vol. 42, nos 2–3, July 2007, pp. 119–27; Ian Manners, 'Normative Power Europe: A Contradiction in Terms?', *Journal of Common Market Studies*, vol. 40, no. 2, December 2002, pp. 235–58; Matthias Matthijs, 'The Three Faces of German Leadership', *Survival*, vol. 58, no. 2, March 2016, p. 143; and Sharon Pardo and Neve Gordon, 'Euroscepticism as an Instrument of Foreign Policy', *Middle East Critique*, vol. 27, no. 4, October 2018, pp. 399–412. Paul Taggart and Aleks Szczerbiak explain that 'soft' euroscepticism 'involves contingent or qualified opposition to European integration'. By contrast, 'hard' euroscepticism 'implies outright rejection of the entire project of European political and economic integration, and opposition to one's

country joining or remaining a member of the EU'. Paul Taggart and Aleks Szczerbiak, 'Contemporary Euroscepticism in the Systems of the European Union Candidate States of Central and Eastern Europe', *European Journal of Political Research*, vol. 43, no. 1, January 2004, pp. 3–4.

36 See Lorena De Vita, *Israelpolitik: German–Israeli Relations, 1949–1969* (Manchester: Manchester University Press, 2020); and Dan Tamir, *Hebrew Fascism in Palestine, 1922–1942* (London: Palgrave Macmillan, 2018).

37 See Sasha Polakow-Suransky, *The Unspoken Alliance: Israel's Secret Relationship with Apartheid South Africa* (New York: Pantheon, 2010).

38 Stewart Ain, 'The Season of Dewinter?', *Jewish Week*, 9 December 2005, https://www.amren.com/news/2005/12/the_season_of_dewinter/.

39 Cas Mudde, *The Ideology of the Extreme Right* (Manchester: Manchester University Press, 2002), p. 100.

40 Assaf Uni, 'Belgian Extreme Right-winger Calls on Jews to Join in Battle Against Muslims', *Haaretz*, 8 October 2006, https://www.haaretz.com/1.4872759.

41 Patrick Moreau, 'The Victorious Parties: Unity in Diversity?', in Uwe Backes and Patrick Moreau (eds), *The Extreme Right in Europe: Current Trends and Perspectives* (Göttingen: Vandenhoeck and Ruprecht, 2012), p. 122.

42 See Kai Arzheimer, 'The AfD: Finally a Successful Right-wing Populist Eurosceptic Party for Germany?', *West European Politics*, vol. 38, no. 3, January 2015, pp. 535–56.

43 See Ofer Aderet, 'Day After Election Success: Far-right AfD Leader Questions Germany's Special Relationship with Israel', *Haaretz*, 25 September 2017, https://www.haaretz.com/world-news/europe/far-right-afd-leader-questions-germany-s-special-relationship-with-israel-1.5453408.

44 Itamar Eichner, 'Rafi Eitan Not Aware of AfD's Anti-Semitic Comments', Ynet, 2 April 2018, https://www.ynetnews.com/articles/0,7340,L-5086344,00.html.

45 Eldad Beck, 'Israel's Boycott of Alternative for Germany: The Right Thing to Do?', *Israel Hayom*, 12 August 2019, https://www.israelhayom.com/opinions/is-israel-right-to-boycott-alternative-for-germany/.

46 See 'Netanyahu's Son Becomes Star of German Nationalist Party After Calling EU "Evil"', *Haaretz*, 8 May 2020, https://www.haaretz.com/israel-news/.premium-yair-netanyahu-becomes-the-star-of-a-german-nationalist-party-after-calling-eu-evil-1.8825923.

47 Davide Lerner, 'Italian Far-right Leader Salvini Calls Western Wall Place that "Belongs to Everyone"', *Haaretz*, 11 December 2018, https://www.haaretz.com/israel-news/.premium-italy-s-salvini-faces-backlash-at-home-for-slamming-hezbollah-in-israel-visit-1.6741045. See also Erik Jones, 'Italy, Its Populists and the EU', *Survival*, vol. 60, no. 4, August–September 2018, pp. 113–22.

48 Ariel David, 'Communist, Separatist, Nationalist: What You Need to Know about Italian Strongman Matteo Salvini', *Haaretz*, 9 December 2018, https://www.haaretz.com/world-news/europe/.premium-what-you-need-to-know-about-italian-strongman-matteo-salvini-1.6726833; and Noa Landau and Davide Lerner, 'In Jerusalem Meeting, Netanyahu Hails Italy's Salvini as a "Great Friend of Israel"', *Haaretz*, 12 December 2018, https://www.haaretz.com/israel-news/.premium-in-jerusalem-meeting-netanyahu-hails-italy-s-salvini-as-a-great-friend-of-israel-1.6741620.

49 Yori Yalon, 'Italy's Interior Minister: Israel Is a Bulwark Defending Europe, Middle East', *Israel Hayom*, 12 December 2018, https://www.israelhayom.com/2018/12/12/italys-interior-minister-israel-is-a-bulwark-defending-europe-middle-east/.

50 Landau and Lerner, 'In Jerusalem Meeting, Netanyahu Hails Italy's Salvini as a "Great Friend of Israel"'.

51 Arieh Eldad, 'An Interview with Geert Wilders Leader of the Dutch Party for Freedom', Prof. Arieh Eldad's Website, 4 October 2014, available at https://www.ariehledad.co.il.

52 Author interview with senior Israeli official, Tel Aviv, 30 March 2017.

53 Eldad, 'An Interview with Geert Wilders'.

54 See Toby Greene and Jonathan Rynhold, 'Europe and Israel: Between Conflict and Cooperation', *Survival*, vol. 60, no. 4, August–September 2018, pp. 104–5; and Toby Greene, 'Judeo-Christian Civilizationism: Challenging Common European Foreign Policy in the Israeli–Palestinian Arena', *Mediterranean Politics*, March 2020.

55 'Austria's Far-right Freedom Party Commits to Moving Embassy to Jerusalem', i24News, 22 June 2017, https://www.i24news.

tv/en/news/international/
europe/148524-170621-austria-
s-far-right-freedom-party-com-
mits-to-moving-embassy-to-jerusalem.

56 See Raphael Ahren, 'Vienna Says
Still Wants to Give Citizenship to
Descendants of Holocaust Victims',
Times of Israel, 14 December 2018,
https://www.timesofisrael.com/
vienna-says-still-wants-to-give-
citizenship-to-descendants-of-
holocaust-victims/.

57 Raphael Ahren and Staff,
'Netanyahu Hails Ties with
Austria After Meeting with Kurz',
Times of Israel, 27 September 2018,
https://www.timesofisrael.com/
netanyahu-hails-ties-with-austria-
after-meeting-with-kurz/.

58 Author telephone interview with
Yehudah Glick, 18 August 2019.

59 See Ariel Kahana, 'First Israeli Move
Towards Recognizing the Austrian
Freedom Party', *Maariv*, 27 February
2017, https://www.makorrishon.co.il/
nrg/online/1/ART2/866/528.html.

60 Author interview with senior Israeli
diplomat, Tel Aviv, 3 May 2021.

61 See Prime Minister's Office,
'PM Netanyahu Participates in
Conference of Leaders of Countries
at the Forefront of Dealing with
the Coronavirus, Hosted by
Austrian Chancellor Sebastian
Kurz', 7 May 2020, https://www.
gov.il/en/departments/news/
event_conference070520.

62 See Laurie Kellman, 'Israel, Denmark
and Austria Join Forces Against COVID-
19', AP News, 4 March 2021, https://
apnews.com/article/israel-denmark-
austria-join-forces-covid-19-7491318d2e
d32c5c5dc00c521c293e5e.

63 See Veronica Anghel, 'Together
or Apart? The European Union's
East–West Divide', *Survival*, vol. 62,
no. 3, June–July 2020, pp. 179–202;
Greene and Rynhold, 'Europe and
Israel', p. 98; Noa Landau, 'Splitting
the EU: Israel's Tightening Alliance
with Central Europe's Nationalist
Leaders', *Haaretz*, 8 July 2018, https://
www.haaretz.com/israel-news/.
premium-splitting-the-eu-israel-s-
tightening-alliance-with-central-
europe-1.6247069; and Kamil
Zwolski, 'Poland's Foreign-policy
Turn', *Survival*, vol. 59, no. 4, August–
September 2017, pp. 167–82.

64 See Landau, 'Splitting the EU'.

65 See Joanna Dyduch, 'The Visegrád
Group's Policy Towards Israel:
Common Values and Interests as
a Catalyst for Cooperation', SWP,
Comment no. 2018/C 54, December
2018, https://www.swp-berlin.
org/fileadmin/contents/products/
comments/2018C54_Dyduch.pdf;
and Bálint Molnár, 'Israel and the
Visegrád (V4) Group: Challenges
and Opportunities', *Israel Journal
of Foreign Affairs*, vol. 13, no. 1, July
2019, pp. 3–21.

66 See Herb Keinon, 'Hungary, Slovakia
to Establish Diplomatic Delegations
in Jerusalem', *Jerusalem Post*, 20
February 2019, https://www.jpost.
com/israel-news/hungary-to-establish-
trade-office-in-jerusalem-581087;
and Judy Maltz, 'Czech Republic
Officially Opens Diplomatic Office
in Jerusalem', *Haaretz*, 11 March
2021, https://www.haaretz.com/
israel-news/.premium-czech-republic-
officially-opens-diplomatic-office-in-
jerusalem-1.9611621.

67 On Orbán's anti-Semitism and his attacks on the Jewish philanthropist George Soros, see, for example, Ira Forman, 'Viktor Orbán Is Exploiting Anti-Semitism', *Atlantic*, 14 December 2018, https://www.theatlantic.com/ideas/archive/2018/12/viktor-orban-and-anti-semitic-figyelo-cover/578158/.

68 'Press Conference: Israel's Prime Minister Benjamin Netanyahu and His Czech and Hungarian Counterparts', YouTube, 11 March 2021, https://www.youtube.com/watch?v=ar-YYu_wZDs.

69 See Dyduch, 'The Visegrád Group's Policy Towards Israel', p. 1.

70 Israel Ministry of Foreign Affairs, 'PM Benjamin Netanyahu Meets with Hungarian PM Viktor Orban'.

71 Central Bureau of Statistics, 'Exports and Imports, by Commodities and Countries – Annual Data, 2017–2019', https://old.cbs.gov.il/fortr17/impexp/menu_e.html.

72 See UN Conference on Trade and Development, *Key Statistics and Trends in International Trade 2020* (Geneva: United Nations, 2021), p. v; and 'Press Conference: Israel's Prime Minister Benjamin Netanyahu and His Czech and Hungarian Counterparts'.

73 Patrick Kingsley, 'Israel Gives Vaccine to Far-off Allies, as Palestinians Wait', *New York Times*, 23 April 2021, https://www.nytimes.com/2021/02/23/world/middleeast/israel-palestinians-vaccine-diplomacy.html; and author interview with senior Israeli diplomat, Tel Aviv, 3 May 2021.

74 See Noa Landau, 'Czech President Arrives in Israel to Inaugurate Cultural Center in Jerusalem', *Haaretz*, 24 November 2018, https://www.haaretz.com/israel-news/.premium-czech-president-to-inaugurate-cultural-center-in-jerusalem-during-upcoming-visit-1.6680456; and Itamar Sharon, 'Danube Days: Hungary Launches Culture Year in Israel with Song and Dance', *Times of Israel*, 20 February 2019, https://www.timesofisrael.com/danube-days-hungary-launches-culture-year-in-israel-with-song-and-dance/.

75 Vaidotas Beniusis, 'Netanyahu Lands in Lithuania, Grandma's Birthplace, in Search of European Allies', *Times of Israel*, 23 August 2018, https://www.timesofisrael.com/netanyahu-arrives-in-lithuania-in-search-of-european-allies/.

76 See Raffaella A. Del Sarto, 'Stuck in the Logic of Oslo: Europe and the Israeli–Palestinian Conflict', *Middle East Journal*, vol. 73, no. 3, Autumn 2019, pp. 376–96.

77 See Dimitris Bouris, *The European Union and Occupied Palestinian Territories: State-building Without a State* (Abingdon: Routledge, 2014); Raffaella A. Del Sarto, *Contested State Identities and Regional Security in the Euro-Mediterranean Area* (London: Palgrave Macmillan, 2006); Raffaella A. Del Sarto, *Israel Under Siege: The Politics of Insecurity and the Rise of the Israeli Neo-revisionist Right* (Washington DC: Georgetown University Press, 2017); Patrick Müller, *EU Foreign Policymaking and the Middle East Conflict: The Europeanization of National Foreign Policy* (Abingdon: Routledge, 2012); Sharon Pardo and Joel Peters, *Uneasy Neighbors: Israel and the European Union* (Lanham, MD: Lexington Books, 2010); Anders Persson, *The EU and the*

Israeli–Palestinian Conflict 1971–2013: In Pursuit of a Just Peace (Lanham, MD: Lexington Books, 2014); and Anders Persson, *EU Diplomacy and the Israeli–Arab Conflict, 1967–2019* (Edinburgh: Edinburgh University Press, 2020).

78 Author interview with senior Israeli diplomat, Jerusalem, 22 November 2018.

79 See Manners, 'Normative Power Europe'; Pardo and Gordon, 'Euroscepticism as an Instrument of Foreign Policy'; and Sharon Pardo, *Normative Power Europe Meets Israel: Perceptions and Realities* (Lanham, MD: Lexington Books, 2015).

80 See Raffaella A. Del Sarto, 'Normative Empire Europe: The European Union, Its Borderlands, and the "Arab Spring"', *Journal of Common Market Studies*, vol. 54, no. 2, March 2016, pp. 215–32; and Anders Persson, 'Shaping Discourse and Setting Examples: Normative Power Europe Can Work in the Israeli–Palestinian Conflict', *Journal of Common Market Studies*, vol. 55, no. 6, August 2017, pp. 1,415–31.

81 Author email correspondence with Cas Mudde, 19 March 2017.

82 Israel Ministry of Foreign Affairs, 'PM Netanyahu Meets with Hungarian PM Viktor Orbán', Press Release, 19 July 2018, https://mfa.gov.il/MFA/PressRoom/2018/Pages/PM-Netanyahu-meets-with-Hungarian-PM-Orb%C3%A1n-19-July-2018.aspx.

Russia's Deceptive Nuclear Policy

Dave Johnson

On 2 June 2020, Russian President Vladimir Putin signed and made public the Basic Principles of the State Policy of the Russian Federation on Nuclear Deterrence (State Policy on Nuclear Deterrence, or State Policy).[1] About a week later, the Ministry of Foreign Affairs promulgated an English version.[2] The new document attracted significant attention from Western analysts. This was, in part, because of Putin's deliberate, and largely successful, efforts to return nuclear weapons to the forefront of the global security environment, and to make nuclear deterrence a central element of Russia's relations with the United States and its NATO allies.

Like any nuclear-weapons state, Russia no doubt has secret guidance for the operational employment of nuclear weapons. It defies belief that such a document would be publicly released. Nevertheless, for the last ten years, Russian officials have raised the expectation that the previously secret State Policy would constitute definitive guidance on Russia's nuclear-deterrence policy. Contrary to that expectation, however, it does not reveal much if anything new or meaningful in terms of how Russia uses nuclear weapons for deterrence, or how it would use them for escalation control and operational effect in crises and military conflicts.

Dave Johnson is a staff officer in the NATO International Staff Defence Policy and Planning Division. He previously served as an officer in the US Air Force in posts at Supreme Headquarters Allied Powers Europe (SHAPE), US Strategic Command, the US Defense Attaché Office Moscow and the Pentagon. The views expressed are those of the author and do not necessarily reflect those of the North Atlantic Treaty Organization.

Survival | vol. 63 no. 3 | June–July 2021 | pp. 123–142   https://doi.org/10.1080/00396338.2021.1930410

The document's central assertion is that Russia's concept for the employment of nuclear weapons does not include pre-emptive nuclear strikes (превентивные удары) and relies on retaliatory strike (ответно-встречный удар, literally retaliatory-meeting strike, and comparable to launch-on-warning). Contradicting this assertion are existing Russian strategic-guidance documents and their previous iterations; related statements by Russian officials and authoritative military experts; the nuclear dimension of Russian exercises and operations; and, most importantly, Russia's nuclear capabilities, force structure and posture. The State Policy on Nuclear Deterrence presents a selective and distorted picture of Russia's nuclear strategy for external messaging purposes and, to a lesser extent, for domestic political ones.

The State Policy's selective message

The State Policy purports to set out official Russian views on the tenets of nuclear deterrence, the military dangers and threats that nuclear deterrence is intended to neutralise, and conditions for the Russian Federation's use of nuclear weapons.[3] But it omits or downplays important known elements of Russia's deterrence policy and approaches, and related nuclear-deterrence and nuclear-war-fighting capabilities. Additionally, the State Policy provides no new programmatic guidance on Russia's nuclear forces. It conveys a simple message with three elements: 1) Russian nuclear capabilities are entirely defensive; 2) they are intended to have a deterrent effect against a host of threatening developments emanating from the United States and its allies; and 3) Russia implements nuclear deterrence in line with international norms and agreements, and in compliance with its arms-control obligations.

This characterisation carefully draws elements from stated policy that support an essentially benign message. But the idea that a growing array of potential threats implicitly emanating from the United States and NATO necessitates Russia's nuclear posture ignores Moscow's very deliberate campaign since 2008 to give nuclear weapons a prominent role in its efforts to destabilise European geopolitics and Western alliance relations. NATO's efforts to strengthen its deterrence and defence posture in response to Russian territorial aggression are portrayed as unprovoked encroachment by adversary military forces. Similarly, Russia's development and fielding of the SSC-8 *Screwdriver* (Russian designation: 9M729) land-based, dual-capable cruise missile, which violated the now-defunct Intermediate-Range Nuclear Forces Treaty, are conveniently ignored. Having made the case for a Russia set upon from all sides by myriad external threats, the State Policy asserts that Russia nevertheless implements its nuclear-deterrence policy in a purely defensive manner in line with universally recognised principles and norms, and Russia's international commitments and treaty obligations.

Policy and doctrine

Major-General (Retd) Vladimir Dvorkin, who spent a career developing concepts for the employment of Russia's strategic nuclear forces, has himself observed that documents such as the Russian Military Doctrine provide only a partial and fragmentary depiction of Russia's nuclear policy.[4] Indeed, the State Policy on Nuclear Deterrence, which is derived from the Russian Military Doctrine and other guidance documents, is far from comprehensive and definitive. As Dvorkin pointed out, forces and capabilities represent the real nuclear policy. Documents such as the Military Doctrine and the State Policy validate observable trends rather than revealing and driving major shifts. Considered in the broader context, they are useful reference points when handled with care. But it is important to remember that they always have a messaging component. Such documents reveal some elements of Russian policy and doctrine for deterrence purposes, while concealing others for military advantage.

Three inconsistencies between the State Policy, on the one hand, and existing guidance and known Russian approaches to deterrence, on the other, stand out. They involve the treatment of nuclear deterrence versus Russia's concept of strategic deterrence; the role of nuclear weapons in regional conflicts, including their limited use; and Russia's military strategy of active defence.

Strategic deterrence

Strategic deterrence is an overarching concept for Russian security. It integrates non-military and military elements of national power, including conventional capabilities, non-strategic nuclear capabilities, and strategic

Figure 1: **Mechanisms of strategic deterrence**

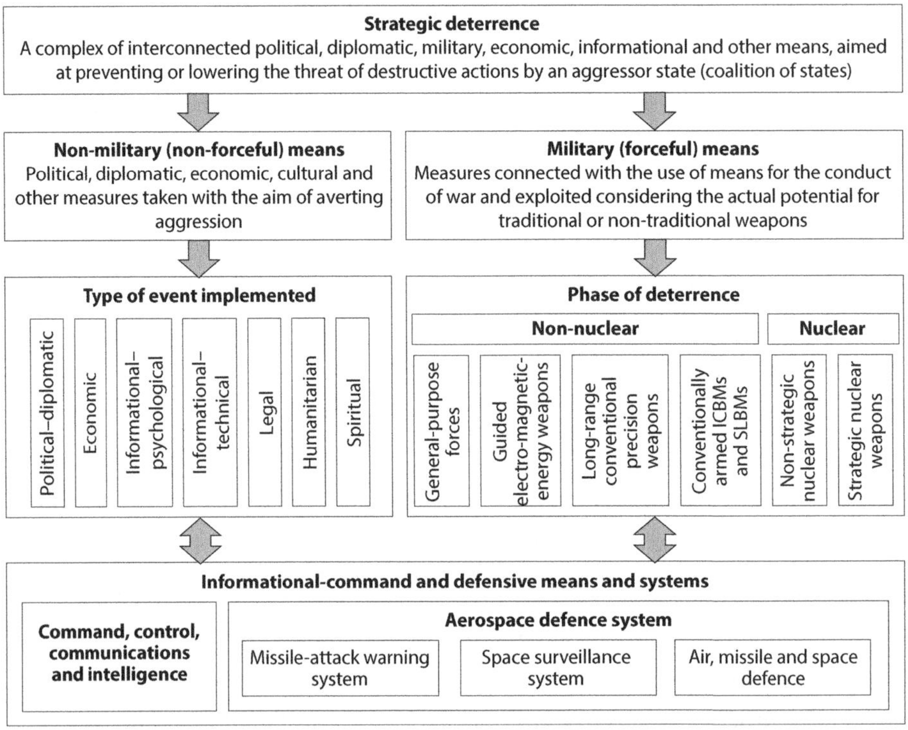

Source: This illustration was translated by the author from A.V. Skrypnik, 'O Vozmozhnom Podkhode k Opredeleniyu i Mesta Oruzhiya Napravlennoi Elektromagnitnoi Energii v Mekhanizme Silovogo Strategicheskogo Sderzhivanya' [On a possible approach to the definition and place of directed-energy weapons in the mechanism of forceful strategic deterrence], *Vooruzheniya I Ekonomika*, vol. 3, no. 19, 2012, p. 46.

nuclear capabilities for deterrence in peacetime and escalation control during a crisis or conflict, and for successful war termination.[5] The components of strategic deterrence are divided into non-military and military means (see Figure 1). The military component of strategic deterrence comprises general-purpose forces (that is, conventional forces), non-nuclear or pre-nuclear forces (conventional precision weapons) and nuclear forces (strategic and non-strategic nuclear capabilities). In practice, the military component of strategic deterrence combines a wide array of dual-capable and nuclear missile systems able to deliver conventional precision and non-strategic nuclear strikes, as well as strategic nuclear strikes.

Strategic deterrence 'is carried out in peacetime and in periods of direct threat of aggression up to the stage of use of military forces' and 'can occur in the course of an already beginning military conflict with the aim of deter-

Table 1: **The distinctions between global and regional nuclear deterrence**

Aspects of the nuclear threat	Nuclear deterrence	
	Global	Regional
Aim	Retaliation	Defeat of the aggressor's military potential
Form	Retaliatory employment of nuclear weapons	First use of nuclear weapons
Scale	Unlimited use of nuclear weapons	Limited use of nuclear weapons
Targets	Predominately value objects of the aggressor	Predominately military objects of the aggressor
Possible time of implementation	At the final stages of aggression	At any stage of the escalation of aggression

Source: This table was translated by the author from 'Voennaya Mysl no. 4/1999', *Diskussionnaya Tribuna*, April 1999, pp. 71–80, http://militaryarticle.ru/voennaya-mysl/1999-vm/9712-diskussionnaja-tribuna-4.

ring its escalation'. Moreover, 'strategic deterrence should be conducted constantly right up to the stage of mass employment of nuclear weapons'. The omission of strategic deterrence from the State Policy obscures the integration of conventional precision-strike and nuclear weapons for combined deterrent and operational purposes, which is clear in other Russian guidance statements, force structure and observable operational approaches.[6]

Regional deterrence

Russia's adoption of nuclear weapons for regional deterrence and their limited use in escalating regional conflicts are further major omissions from the State Policy on Nuclear Deterrence. The Russian concept of strategic deterrence envisions two tightly interconnected levels – global deterrence and regional deterrence – which are viewed as complementary (see Table 1). Russian military theoreticians and planners also regard precision conventional and nuclear weapons as complementary in supporting strategic deterrence at these interconnected levels. According to Russian military experts:

> The threat of mass employment of, for the most part, strategic nuclear weapons for infliction of deterrent damage to the military–economic potential of the aggressor under any conditions is the basis for global deterrence. Regional deterrence is based on the threat of mass employment

of non-strategic nuclear forces and strategic non-nuclear forces in any wars
launched against Russia and her allies, the result of which could be the
smashing of the enemy strike formations participating in the aggression
and the infliction of deterring damage on the economy of the aggressor.[7]

Two important assertions in the State Policy begin to break down when
compared to Russia's theatre nuclear capabilities and the associated concepts. The first is the claim that Russia's nuclear-deterrence policy is entirely
defensive, the second that Russia's nuclear policy does not include options
for first use or pre-emption.[8]

For example, Russia's 2017 naval policy clearly sets out a role for non-
strategic nuclear weapons in a regional conflict that does not align with
these central elements of the State Policy on Nuclear Deterrence. The 2017
document states that 'in conditions of escalation of a military conflict,
demonstration of readiness and determination to use force by employment
of a non-strategic nuclear weapon is an efficient deterrence factor'.[9] It goes
on to frame as a measure of naval effectiveness 'the capability of the Navy
to inflict not less than critical damage on the enemy fleet by use of non-
strategic nuclear weapons'.[10]

Russia's active-defence concept
A third key incongruity is that between the profile of Russian nuclear
deterrence presented in the State Policy and Russia's military strategy of
active defence. Active defence is based on the capability of high-readiness
forces to seize and hold the strategic initiative through pre-emption.[11] This
relatively new label for Russian operational-strategic approaches is in
keeping with long-standing Russian (and Soviet) concepts, practices and
strategic culture. There is an obvious tension between the main elements
of active defence and the almost passive image of nuclear-deterrence
policy portrayed in the State Policy document. It is also worth noting the
elastic meaning of 'defensive' in the context of active defence, as well as
in Russia's characterisation of military operations carried out in support
of its revisionist agenda, which has included aggression against Georgia
and Ukraine.

Military capabilities and force posture

The State Policy focuses on Russia's strategic nuclear forces and their primary mission of strategic nuclear deterrence. It omits any mention of Russia's large stockpile of non-strategic nuclear weapons, their role in regional deterrence and war fighting, and their conceptual and operational linkages to strategic nuclear deterrence.[12] Thus, the State Policy obscures the role of dual-capable and nuclear-weapon systems observed in Russian exercises, Russia's introduction of a nuclear dimension into its aggression against Georgia in 2008 and Ukraine in 2014, and its ominous nuclear

Figure 2: **Approximate coverage of five operational/operational-strategic precision-strike weapons from illustrative positions within Russian and Russian-controlled territory**

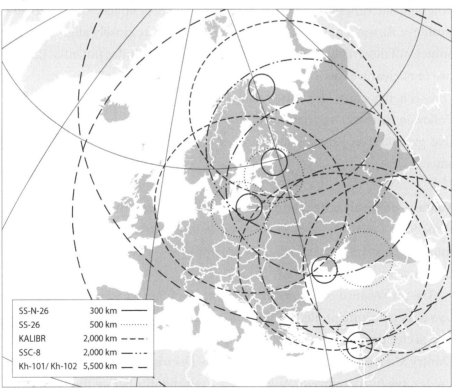

SS-N-26	300 km ———
SS-26	500 km ··········
KALIBR	2,000 km —– —– ·
SSC-8	2,000 km —– ·· —
Kh-101/ Kh-102	5,500 km —– —–

Source: This illustration of Russia's redundant, overlapping coverage of most of Europe with its various dual-capable precision-strike platforms is adapted from Dave Johnson, 'Russia's Conventional Precision Strike Capabilities, Regional Crises, and Nuclear Thresholds', Livermore Papers on Global Security No. 3, Center for Global Security Research, Lawrence Livermore National Laboratory, February 2018, p. 40, https://cgsr.llnl.gov/content/assets/docs/Precision-Strike-Capabilities-report-v3-7.pdf. Approximate scale 1:8, 425,000. Prepared by the author using a public-domain map: 'File:Germany on the globe (Germany centered).svg', CC BY-SA 3.0, https://commons.wikimedia.org/wiki/File:Germany_on_the_globe_(Germany_centered).svg.

rhetoric in general.[13] This truncated depiction of Russia's deterrence posture does not pass a reality check against its forces and capabilities.

Incongruously, one element of language contained in the State Policy cuts against efforts by Russian leaders and commentators to depict a restrained nuclear strategy. The document mentions as a principle of nuclear deterrence 'unpredictability for a potential adversary in terms of scale, time and place for possible employment of forces and means of nuclear deterrence'. This political guidance is well reflected in the large and growing set of dual-capable and nuclear missile systems that can deliver nuclear warheads of various explosive yields by air, land and sea at battlefield, theatre and intercontinental ranges (see Figure 2). The guidance and resulting capabilities also contradict any notion that Russian leaders would only consider potential nuclear employment in response to nuclear attack. The observable profile of Russia's nuclear forces and posture is more closely aligned with a strategy of deterrence and counter-escalation that includes potential limited use of nuclear weapons in escalating conventional regional conflicts.

Given the gaps, disconnects and internal contradictions in the State Policy on Nuclear Deterrence, it clearly is not the comprehensive and definitive guidance on Russia's nuclear-deterrence policy that Russian officials say it is.

Military–political context and information environment

If the State Policy does not make sense in its putative role, its primary aim must be to shape the information sphere in the West on Russia, nuclear deterrence and arms control.[14]

The provenance of the document casts doubt on its status as a substantive policy document. Released in June 2020, it is supposed to be a version of a secret document signed in 2010 at the same time that then-president Dmitry Medvedev signed the 2010 Military Doctrine.[15] Russian officials took the trouble to announce in August 2010, four months before that document was signed, that a nuclear-policy document was being developed as a secret annex to the forthcoming Military Doctrine. During the interval between August and December that year, periodic commentary by Russian officials appeared in Russian media disclosing aspects of the related debate over how aggressive or restrained the policy should be in response to purported developments in US nuclear-deterrence policy. In this time frame, negotiations on NATO–Russia missile-defence cooperation, which ultimately failed, were increasingly strained.

Eventually both documents were signed and, again, Russian officials made sure to point out the existence of the secret 'Fundamentals of the Russian Federation State Policy of Nuclear Deterrence to 2020', and Russian media subsequently referred openly to it. This extended flogging of the supposed secret document paid substantial dividends in Russia's efforts to increase the profile and salience of nuclear weapons in the international security environment. The mysterious document became a regular reference point in Russian and Western media, and for several Western analysts who speculated that it might hold the key to the various aspects of Russia's nuclear strategy and doctrine then being debated.[16]

Given that the State Policy turned out not to be the Rosetta Stone of Russian nuclear doctrine that Russian officials and the press had portrayed it as and others had anticipated, it is worth speculating whether anything close to the current document actually existed in 2010, or if the whole 2010 episode and its aftermath simply amounted to a disinformation effort. In any case, having drawn attention to a 2010 version of the State Policy and burnished its cachet by acknowledging its supposedly secret status, Russian experts are now retrofitting the story of the 2010 document in order to serve new aims. After the 2020 publication of the State Policy, the Russian news agency TASS reported that, according to General-Colonel (Retd) Viktor Esin, former Chief of the Main Staff of the Strategic Rocket Forces, 'such a document had appeared as an annex to the (2010) military doctrine' and that 'it was not secret, but was not published'.[17] But news reports of Medvedev's signing of the 2010 revision of the Military Doctrine and the Basic Principles of the State Policy of the Russian Federation on Nuclear Deterrence, based on a statement by Medvedev's press secretary, describe the 2010 State Policy on Nuclear Deterrence as classified (засекречен).[18]

General Esin, commenting on the 2020 State Policy, has depicted its publication as a transparency move intended to counter 'fake' Western claims about the Russian nuclear doctrine:

> The expert community has long insisted on publishing too, so that we are not accused of doctrines invented by the Americans, such as 'escalate to de-escalate', that is, the use of nuclear weapons to achieve victory in a military conflict with conventional weapons. An open visor was necessary so that they wouldn't make fakes out of our realities.[19]

Additionally, Esin and other Russian experts speaking in state-controlled media have characterised the State Policy as a message to the US and its allies in advance of potential renewed arms-control negotiations, including then-anticipated negotiations on the potential (now actual) extension of the Strategic Arms Reduction Treaty (New START), and a response to what they assert is the US adoption of a strategy of limited nuclear war.[20]

The Russian General Staff reinforced and elaborated the original messages set out by Russian experts immediately after the publication of the State Policy in an article co-authored by Major-General Andrei Sterlin, Chief of the General Staff's Main Operational Directorate, published in *Red Star*, the official newspaper of the Russian Ministry of Defence. Two months after the publication of the State Policy, Sterlin claimed that it had 'resonated widely' in foreign and domestic media, and had surprised most nuclear-weapons experts in its divergence in several key points from their opinions. According to Sterlin, the release of such a significant document was intended to counter false assertions by the United States and its NATO allies of the aggressiveness of Russia's nuclear policy. He emphasised, in particular, that the US falsely attributed an 'escalate to de-escalate' strategy to Russia in order to 'scare its NATO allies, especially on the eastern flank'.[21] Sterlin asserts that Russia's nuclear policy is totally defensive and responds to a range of aggressive or destabilising moves by the US, implicitly unprovoked, with respect to missile defence, space, arms treaties and nuclear-deterrence posture.

Russia and China appear to have coordinated on public messaging and exploitation of the State Policy prior to its release. The day after the document's publication, it featured as the third item in the regular press conference of the spokesperson for the Chinese Ministry of Foreign Affairs in response to a question from Russia's RIA Novosti news agency. The ministry spokesperson had a ready response, saying that 'rising unilateralism and hegemonism in international strategic security is having a severe impact on global strategic equilibrium and stability. China respects and understands Russia's efforts to safeguard national security interests. We stand ready to work with all sides to uphold international strategic stability and promote global peace and security.'[22] This joint choreography on the roll-out of the State Policy fits a pattern of Russian–Chinese cooperation and coordination on issues related to strategic stability, including nuclear weapons, against their perceived common adversary. It also reinforces the idea that messaging, as part of information confrontation, is a primary aim of the document.

The statements by Russian officials and informed Russian experts, and the apparent Russian–Chinese coordination on messaging, help clarify the information-confrontation aims of the document. These include scene-setting for strategic-arms-control negotiations (in particular, to delegitimise US and allied nuclear-deterrence approaches), clouding perceptions of Russia's nuclear strategy and keeping nuclear weapons at the forefront of the security environment. It would not have been possible to credibly advance these aims while depicting Russia's nuclear strategy accurately.

When might Russia employ nuclear weapons?

In February 2018, the United States' Nuclear Posture Review cited Moscow's preparedness for limited nuclear first use and related coercive nuclear threats.[23] To counter that claim, Russian leaders and expert commentators conducted a disinformation campaign against measured US nuclear-posture adaptations prescribed by the Nuclear Posture Review. The leading parries, frequently picked up in Western media and expert analyses, were that the US was 'lowering the nuclear threshold' and that it was preparing for limited nuclear war in response to a non-existent threat.[24] Russia's misrepresentations peaked in October 2018, when Putin said that Russian strategy did not contemplate pre-emptive nuclear strikes and relied on retaliatory strikes. Russians martyred in a nuclear attack, he claimed, would go to heaven and the aggressors, not having time to repent after Russia's retaliatory strike, would simply perish.[25] Such themes have been carried over into the State

Policy document and the Russian messaging around it in an effort to airbrush out Russia's persistent nuclear sabre-rattling and the capabilities behind it.

A discerning reading of the text of the State Policy indicates a wide range of circumstances in which Russia might employ nuclear weapons, some that could arise before any use of nuclear weapons by an adversary. One would be a conventional attack that put the Russian regime at risk.[26] Two more that qualify are warning of a ballistic-missile attack (apparently without distinction as to whether the missiles are delivering conventional or nuclear weapons – a possible response to hypersonic weapons) and disruption of command and control of nuclear forces (which brings cyber and space activities into play as possible triggers for Russian nuclear use). Less controversially, an adversary's use of nuclear or other weapons of mass destruction could prompt Russian use of nuclear weapons. There are also several conditions that could prompt first use of non-strategic nuclear weapons in regional conflict scenarios identified in several Russian guidance documents and military writings, and evident in Russian capabilities, force structure and posture, and exercises.

While documents such as the State Policy do provide insight into some Russian red lines, in crisis or conflict Russia would be relatively unconstrained by practical limitations as to when, where and how it would first employ nuclear weapons. Russia's wide array of dual-capable and nuclear-delivery systems affords it abundant options for the flexible employment of nuclear weapons in conflict.[27] Its military capabilities and vital interests, apprehended extemporaneously in operational conditions of maximum stress and fragmentary information, will be more relevant to the question of when Russia might first use nuclear weapons in an escalating regional conflict than a policy announced in peacetime for messaging purposes.[28]

*   *   *

The Russian authorities, starting with Putin, have carried on continuous large-scale, high-profile messaging that mixes fact, fiction, half-truths and distortions to achieve their ends. Russia's intensification of these efforts with respect to nuclear policy and strategy since 2018 suggests that the adjustments proposed in the United States' 2018 Nuclear Posture Review got Moscow's attention. Russia's apparent preference is to use disinformation to obfuscate the fact that the American adjustments may be responses to its own aggressive nuclear posture. Even so, the State Policy will be a key frame of reference for some Western analysts.

The document should be understood for what it is, not what Russian officials claim it is. Pushing back on its distortions will be an ongoing and sometimes complex and vexing task. General Dvorkin's advice is a great clarifier: financed and fielded nuclear capabilities are the best indicators of Russian nuclear policy and strategy. Russia's array of theatre-range dual-capable delivery systems fielded in the last decade undercuts recent Russian assertions of a posture centred on strategic nuclear forces in a strictly retaliatory or launch-on-warning posture.[29] Instead, those systems support flexible options, including limited use of nuclear weapons in escalating regional conflicts.

The United States and its allies should also recognise the deceptive intent and potentially corrosive effects of Russia's disinformation efforts, including its characterisation of the State Policy, as part of Russia's 'hybrid' approach to conflict, which is 'a well-thought out, well-funded, and coordinated strategy'.[30] The French Ministry of Defence has noted that 'disinformation … is intended to exacerbate tensions within the targeted society, as well as to influence and to foster political paralysis'.[31] Russia has sought to increase public ambivalence towards nuclear deterrence in adversary states, undermine political support for related defence expenditures in such states and fuel domestic political pressure in them that it could exploit in future arms-control negotiations.[32] Especially in this light, Russian statements and guidance documents on nuclear policy and strategy should continuously be held up to the mirror of actual capabilities, force structure and posture, related exercises and operations, and, more broadly, Russia's evident revanchism. One rejoinder to Russian disinformation could be for the United States, individual allies or NATO to correct the record by making specific information publicly available. NATO used this approach in 2014 to counter false Russian assertions that its forces were not engaged in military operations inside Ukraine.[33]

Several observable developments would have to occur for claims such as Putin's 'only launch-on-warning' representations to be credible. These include substantial changes to Russia's current and planned non-strategic nuclear capabilities; their disentanglement from Russia's conventional precision-strike capabilities; a reversal in the trend of Russia's nuclearisation of conventional military exercises; a cessation of its nuclear sabre-rattling; and a substantial overhaul of associated military guidance.[34] None of these developments appears to be in the offing.

Acknowledgements

This article is based on a paper presented by the author in August 2020 at a seminar conducted by the Center for Global Security Studies at Lawrence Livermore National Laboratory. The author would like to thank Brad Roberts for reviewing the article and providing valuable insights.

Notes

1   Order of the President of the Russian Federation, 'On the Fundamentals of the Russian Federation State Policy in the Field of Nuclear Deterrence', Decree No. 355, 2 June 2020, http://kremlin.ru/acts/news/63447.

2   President of the Russian Federation, Executive Order, 'Basic Principles of State Policy of the Russian Federation on Nuclear Deterrence' (hereafter State Policy on Nuclear Deterrence, or State Policy), Ministry of Foreign Affairs of the Russian Federation, 8 June 2020, https://www.mid.ru/en/web/guest/foreign_policy/international_safety/disarmament/-/asset_publisher/rpofiUBmANaH/content/id/4152094.

3   State Policy on Nuclear Deterrence, paragraph 1.

4   Vladimir Zinovievich Dvorkin, 'Prazhskii Rubezh Proiden – Kakovy Dal'neishie Tseli?' [The Prague milestone has been passed – what are your further goals?], *Nezavisimoe Voennoe Obozrenie*, 4 February 2011, http://nvo.ng.ru/concepts/2011-02-04/1_snv.html?print=Y. General Dvorkin wrote this in 2011 with reference to the first three public iterations of Russia's Military Doctrine, whose texts were similarly parsed by Russian and foreign analysts to discern Russia's nuclear doctrine. Vipin Narang makes the same point as Dvorkin, saying that 'because posture focuses on observable capabilities, organizational procedures and interests, and patterns of behavior that are measurable both to adversaries and analysts, posture is a more consistent indicator than declaratory doctrine (though the two may often be consistent)'. Vipin Narang, *Nuclear Strategy in the Modern*

Era: Regional Powers and International Conflict (Princeton, NJ: Princeton University Press, 2014), pp. 230–1. Narang elaborates this idea and its implications in detail. See *ibid.*, pp. 14–24, 226–33.

5 See, for example, Kremlin, 'Voennaya Doktrina Rossiiskoi Federatsii' [Military Doctrine of the Russian Federation], 25 December 2014, http://kremlin.ru/media/events/files/41d527556bec8deb3530.pdf.

6 See A.L. Khryapin, D.A. Kalinkin and V.V. Matvichuk, 'Strategicheskoe Sderzhivanie v Usloviakh Sozdaniya SShA Global'noi Sistemy PRO I Sredstv Global'nogo Udara' [Strategic deterrence in conditions of creation by the USA of a global missile-defence system and means of global strike], Voennaya Mysl, no. 1, *Diskussionnaya Tribuna*, January 2015, p. 20.

7 *Ibid.*, pp. 19–20.

8 Gustav Gressel draws conclusions similar to those outlined in this section regarding the role of nuclear weapons in Russia's nuclear strategy for escalation control, including potential pre-emptive limited nuclear strikes. In particular, he observes that Article 4 of the State Policy indicates a role for nuclear deterrence in preventing further escalation once conflict has started, and for terminating it on conditions acceptable for the Russian Federation. This is another example of the internal contradictions in the State Policy. See Gustav Gressel, 'Russia's Nuclear Deterrence Principles: What They Imply, and What They Do Not', Commentary, European Council on Foreign Relations, 12 June 2020, https://ecfr.eu/article/commentary_russias_nuclear_deterrence_principles_what_they_imply_and_what_n/. In contrast, several other authors find that the State Policy clarifies more than it obfuscates. See, for example, Ankit Panda, 'What's in Russia's New Nuclear Deterrence "Basic Principles"?', *Diplomat*, 9 June 2020, https://thediplomat.com/2020/06/whats-in-russias-new-nuclear-deterrence-basic-principles/; Nikolai Sokov, 'Russia Clarifies Its Nuclear Deterrence Policy', Vienna Center for Disarmament and Non-Proliferation, 3 June 2020, https://vcdnp.org/russia-clarifies-its-nuclear-deterrence-policy/; and Dmitri Trenin, 'Decoding Russia's Official Nuclear Deterrence Paper', Carnegie Moscow Center, 5 June 2020, https://carnegie.ru/commentary/81983.

9 Kremlin, 'Ukaz Prezidenta Rossiiskoi Federatsii ot 20.07.2017 g. No. 327' [Decree of the president of the Russian Federation of July 20, 2017, No. 327], 20 July 2017, p. 15, http://kremlin.ru/acts/bank/42117.

10 *Ibid.*, p. 20.

11 See Dave Johnson, 'General Gerasimov on the Vectors of the Development of Military Strategy', NATO Defense College, Russian Studies Series 4/19, 30 March 2019, http://www.ndc.nato.int/research/research.php?icode=585.

12 See, for example, Dave Johnson, 'Russia's Conventional Precision Strike Capabilities, Regional Crises, and Nuclear Thresholds', Livermore Papers on Global Security No. 3, Center for Global Security Research, Lawrence Livermore National Laboratory, February 2018, pp. 63–99, https://cgsr.llnl.gov/content/assets/docs/Precision-

Strike-Capabilities-report-v3-7.pdf;
and Katarzyna Zysk, 'Escalation and
Nuclear Weapons in Russia's Military
Strategy', *RUSI Journal*, vol. 163, no.
2, May 2018, pp. 4–15.

13 On Georgia, see remarks by Frank
Miller, Air Force Association, National
Defense Industrial Association and
Reserve Officers Association Capitol
Hill Forum, 22 May 2015. He notes:
'And in fact, the Russians did go to
a nuclear alert in 2008 over Georgia
when a U.S. cruiser went into the
Black Sea and the Russians made
a hyper-leap of imagination and
decided it might be carrying nuclear-
tipped cruise missiles, which had
been retired in 1992. But okay, they
went to nuclear alert anyway.' A good
precis of regional and global activity
by Russian dual-capable aircraft in the
context of the Ukraine crisis and the
general downturn in relations with
Russia can be found in Alexandre
Sheldon-Duplaix, 'Qui Menace Qui?
Les Raisons d'une "Nouvelle Guerre
Froide"', *Stratégie, Defense & Sécurité
Internationale*, no. 112, March 2015,
pp. 54–61. See also Adrian Croft,
'Insight: Russia's Nuclear Strategy
Raises Concerns in NATO', Reuters, 4
February 2015, https://www.reuters.
com/article/instant-article/idINL-
6N0VE2RV20150204; Dave Johnson,
'Nuclear Weapons in Russia's
Approach to Conflict', Recherches &
Documents, No. 06/2016, Fondation
pour la Recherche Stratégique,
November 2016, p. 53, https://www.
frstrategie.org/sites/default/files/
documents/publications/recherches-
et-documents/2016/201606.pdf; and
Thomas C. Moore, 'The Role of

Nuclear Weapons During the Crisis in
Ukraine', Lugar Center, 29 July 2014,
https://www.thelugarcenter.org/pp/
publication-8.pdf.

14 The Russian Ministry of Defence
defines information confrontation
(информационное противоборство)
as 'an integral part of relations and
a form of battle of the parties (state,
social and political movements and
organisations, armed forces, etc.),
each of which seeks to inflict defeat
(damage) by means of information
effects on its information sphere (the
totality of information, information
infrastructure, entities involved in
the collection, formation, distribution
and use of information, as well as
the regulatory system for the resulting social relations), (while) fending
off or reducing such an impact on its
part'. Russian Ministry of Defence,
'Information Confrontation', *Military
Dictionary*, https://encyclopedia.mil.
ru/encyclopedia/dictionary/details.
htm?id=5221@morfDictionary.

15 See 'Medvedev Utverdil Voennuyu
Doktrinu i "Osnovy Gospolitiki v
Oblasti Yadernogo Sderzhivaniya"'
[Medvedev approved the Military
Doctrine and 'Fundamentals of
State Policy in the Field of Nuclear
Deterrence'], *Rossiiskaya Gazeta*, 5
February 2010, https://rg.ru/2010/02/05/
voennaya-doktrina-anons.html.

16 References to the 2010 'secret'
document, centring on what
undisclosed information it may
contain about Russia's 'nuclear
threshold', include Elbridge Colby,
'Russia's Evolving Nuclear Doctrine
and Its Implications', Note no.
01/2016, 12 January 2016, Fondation

pour la Recherche Stratégique, p. 8, https://www.frstrategie.org/sites/default/files/documents/publications/notes/2016/201601.pdf; Olga Oliker, 'Russia's Nuclear Doctrine: What We Know, What We Don't, and What That Means', Center for Strategic and International Studies, 5 May 2016, p. 4, https://csis-website-prod.s3.amazonaws.com/s3fs-public/publication/160504_Oliker_RussiasNuclearDoctrine_Web.pdf; Olga Oliker and Andrey Baklitskiy, 'The Nuclear Posture Review and Russian "De-escalation": A Dangerous Solution to a Non-existent Problem', *War on the Rocks*, 20 February 2018, https://warontherocks.com/2018/02/nuclear-posture-review-russian-de-escalation-dangerous-solution-nonexistent-problem/; and Kristin Ven Bruusgaard, 'The Myth of Russia's Lowered Nuclear Threshold', *War on the Rocks*, 22 September 2017, https://warontherocks.com/2017/09/the-myth-of-russias-lowered-nuclear-threshold/. On the idea that the 2010 State Policy on Nuclear Deterrence is a red herring, and on the Russian leadership's exploitation of it and its supposedly secret status for messaging and information-confrontation purposes in the context of Russia's renewal of geopolitical competition in Europe, see Johnson, 'Nuclear Weapons in Russia's Approach to Conflict', pp. 54–8.

17 See 'Eksperty: Osnovy Politiki Yadernogo Sderzhivaniya Prizvany Razoblachit Feiki o Planakh Rossii' [Experts: the foundations of nuclear-deterrence policy are intended to expose fakes about Russia's plans],

ITAR-TASS, 3 June 2020, https://tass.ru/politika/8632743.

18 See Aliya Samigullina and Olga Bolotova, 'Pervym ne Udaryat': Voennaya Doktrina Utverzhdena' [Don't hit first: Military Doctrine approved], Gazeta.ru, 5 February 2010, https://www.gazeta.ru/politics/2010/02/05_a_3320394.shtml; and 'Medvedev Approved the Military Doctrine and "Fundamentals of State Policy in the Field of Nuclear Deterrence"'.

19 'Experts: The Foundations of Nuclear Deterrence Policy are Intended to Expose Fakes About Russia's Plans'.

20 See *ibid.*

21 A.E. Sterlin and A.L. Khryapin, 'Ob Osnovakh Gosudarstvennoi Politiki Rossiiskoi Federatsii v Oblasti Yadernogo Sderzhivaniya' [On the foundations of the State Policy of the Russian Federation in the Field of Nuclear Deterrence], *Krasnaya Zvezda*, 7 August 2020, http://redstar.ru/ob-osnovah-gosudarstvennoj-politiki-rossijskoj-federatsii-v-oblasti-yadernogo-sderzhivaniya/.

22 Ministry of Foreign Affairs of the People's Republic of China, 'Foreign Ministry Spokesperson Zhao Lijian's Regular Press Conference on 3 June 2020', https://www.fmprc.gov.cn/mfa_eng/xwfw_665399/s2510_665401/t1785528.shtml.

23 Office of the Secretary of Defense, 'Nuclear Posture Review', US Department of Defense, February 2018, pp. 30–1, 51–5, https://media.defense.gov/2018/Feb/02/2001872886/-1/-1/1/2018-NUCLEAR-POSTURE-REVIEW-FINAL-REPORT.PDF.

24 See, for example, the assertion by a

representative of the Russian Security Council that the 2018 US Nuclear Posture Review amounted to an 'unjustified lowering of the nuclear threshold' in Anastasia Evdokimova, 'Tsena Oshibki – Voina: SovBez o Snizhenii Poroga Primeneniya Yadernogo Oruzhiya SShA' [The price of error is war: Security Council on lowering the threshold for the use of US nuclear weapons], TV Zvezda News, 1 March 2018, https://tvzvezda.ru/news/vstrane_i_mire/content/201803010910-26lv.htm. Foreign Minister Sergey Lavrov characterised the Nuclear Posture Review's proposal to field a low-yield warhead in the same way. See Sergey Guryanov, 'Lavrov Ob'yasnil Opasnost' Proizvodstva Malomoschnikh Yadernykh Boegolovok v SShA' [Lavrov explained the danger of produc-ing low-yield nuclear warheads in the United States], Vzglyad, 30 January 2019, https://vz.ru/news/2019/1/30/961836.html.

25 President of Russia, 'Zasedanie Diskussionnogo Kluba Valdai' [Meeting of the Valdai Discussion Club], 18 October 2018, http://kremlin.ru/events/president/news/58848. Launch-on-warning might be Russia's steady-state posture in peacetime but it is nothing new. That option has been enabled for decades by Soviet and then Russian investment in 360-degree ballistic-missile-attack warning-radar coverage and satellite-based missile-launch detection systems.

26 On why the phrase 'existence of the state' relates to Russia's govern-ing structures and not the nation

as a whole, see Johnson, 'Nuclear Weapons in Russia's Approach to Conflict', pp. 60–1. In the context of nuclear war, 'existence of the state' serves as a deterrent signal against regime change. It sets a much lower bar for potential first use of nuclear weapons by Russia than if the phrase were taken to refer to the existence of Russia as a nation.

27 On the flexible options and related employment concepts that Russia has developed for use of conventional precision strike and limited use of nuclear weapons for deterrence and escalation control in regional conflicts, see Johnson, 'Russia's Conventional Precision Strike Capabilities, Regional Crises, and Nuclear Thresholds', pp. 66–92.

28 The differences between thresholds indicated in peacetime declaratory policy and those that can emerge during actual crisis or conflict and related implications, primarily risk, are elaborated in Forest E. Morgan et al., *Dangerous Thresholds: Managing Escalation in the 21st Century* (Santa Monica, CA: RAND Corporation, 2008), pp. 11–14. On a related note, Vipin Narang draws a distinction between declaratory doctrine as set out in public documents and opera-tional doctrine as made evident by a country's nuclear posture, observ-ing that 'the operational doctrine generates deterrent power against an opponent'. Narang, *Nuclear Strategy in the Modern Era*, pp. 4, 226–33.

29 See, for example, Hans Kristensen and Matt Korda, 'Russian Nuclear Forces, 2020', *Bulletin of the Atomic Scientists*, vol. 77, no. 2, March 2020, Table 1, pp.

103–4, and its preceding iterations. The modernisation and diversification of Russia's theatre-range systems have proceeded in parallel with the comprehensive modernisation of Russia's strategic nuclear forces.

30 Lord Jopling, 'Countering Russia's Hybrid Threats: An Update', Special Report, Committee on the Civil Dimension of Security, NATO Parliamentary Assembly, 1 October 2018, pp. 1, 7, https://www.nato-pa.int/download-file?filename=/sites/default/files/2018-12/166%20CDS%2018%20E%20fin%20-%20HYBRID%20THREATS%20-%20JOPLING_0.pdf.

31 French Ministry of Defence, 'Defence and National Security Strategic Review 2017', p. 47, https://espas.secure.europarl.europa.eu/orbis/sites/default/files/generated/document/en/DEFENCE%20AND%20NATIONAL%20SECURITY%20STRATEGIC%20REVIEW%202017.pdf.

32 For an assessment of Russian (and Soviet) information-confrontation tactics against NATO nuclear-sharing arrangements specifically, see Lesley Kucharski, 'Russian Multi-domain Strategy Against NATO: Information Confrontation and US Forward Deployed Nuclear Weapons in Europe', Center for Global Security Research, Lawrence Livermore National Laboratory, 2018, https://cgsr.llnl.gov/content/assets/docs/4Feb_IPb_against_NATO_nuclear_posture.pdf.

33 NATO, 'NATO Releases Satellite Imagery Showing Russian Combat Troops Inside Ukraine', 28 August 2014, https://www.nato.int/cps/en/natohq/news_112193.htm. In 2020, nine US combatant commanders jointly pointed out the need for more 'ammunition in the ongoing war of narratives' and advocated for the US intelligence community to give them more evidence, including satellite photos, to share with allies and partners, 'to counter such propaganda, which means broadcasting to the world that Russia and China are undermining global order and democratic institutions'. Betsy Woodruff Swan and Bryan Bender, 'Spy Chiefs Look to Declassify Intel After Rare Plea from 4-Star Commanders', Politico, 27 April 2021, https://www.politico.com/news/2021/04/26/spy-chiefs-information-war-russia-china-484723.

34 See James Acton's work on the dimensions of what he has called nuclear entanglement in articles collated in 'Nuclear Entanglement', Carnegie Endowment for International Peace, https://carnegieendowment.org/programs/npp/nuclear-entanglement.

Using Force to Protect Civilians in UN Peacekeeping

Alex J. Bellamy and Charles T. Hunt

The protection of civilians (PoC) has emerged over the past two decades to become one of the core functions of United Nations peace operations. Yet practice remains uneven, and concerns linger that the use of force to protect civilians might make it more difficult for peacekeepers to achieve their goals in other areas. It is therefore important to understand and learn from past experience and to draw some preliminary conclusions about how, when, and to what effect force can be employed in pursuit of civilian protection. We argue that, overall, there is clear evidence that robust peacekeeping operations can improve the protection of civilians, and that the mandating of peacekeepers to use 'all necessary means' to achieve this goal is an important step in that regard. Using force to protect civilians is difficult in practice, however, and can produce unintended negative consequences. Thus, more thought must be given to precisely how force is used – in particular to ensure that peace operations are capable of exploiting tactical gains and translating those gains into political progress – and to how missions are trained and configured to forcefully pursue civilian protection.

A moral imperative

The protection of civilians emerged as a moral imperative after some high-profile failures by UN forces to do so. In 1994, peacekeepers stood aside as

---

Alex J. Bellamy is Professor of Peace and Conflict in the School of Political Science and International Studies at the University of Queensland. **Charles T. Hunt** is Associate Professor of International Relations in the School of Global, Urban and Social Studies at RMIT University and a Senior Fellow at the United Nations University Centre for Policy Research.

Survival | vol. 63 no. 3 | June–July 2021 | pp. 143–170   https://doi.org/10.1080/00396338.2021.1930411

more than 800,000 people were slaughtered during the Rwandan genocide. The following year, the Bosnian Serb Army overran the UN's designated 'safe area' in Srebrenica and killed more than 8,000 men and boys. Peacekeepers in Rwanda and Bosnia were not tasked with preventing genocide or with protecting civilians within their areas of operation, yet it was widely acknowledged that UN peacekeeping – indeed, the whole UN system – had failed badly. The UN's blunt report on Srebrenica, drafted by David Harland and submitted to the General Assembly by UN secretary-general Kofi Annan, reached some important conclusions about the enterprise of peacekeeping. Annan emphasised 'the failure to fully comprehend the extent of the Serb war aims' and 'an inability to recognize the scope of the evil confronting us'.[1] In his view, 'the men who have been charged with this crime against humanity reminded the world and, in particular, the United Nations, that evil exists in the world. They taught us also that the United Nations global commitment to ending conflict does not preclude moral judgements, but makes them necessary.'[2] There had been a failure to comprehend that the Serbian policy of 'ethnic cleansing' contemplated 'employing savage terror, primarily mass killings, rapes and brutalization of civilians, to expel populations'.[3] As a result, the international community had conducted negotiations that 'amounted to appeasement', resisted the use of force, and applied 'a philosophy of impartiality and non-violence wholly unsuited to the conflict in Bosnia'.[4]

The UN's failure in Srebrenica, Annan insisted, had its roots in the organisation's own institutional culture, and in a lack of will among major member states. The secretary-general criticised 'the pervasive ambivalence within the United Nations regarding the role of force in the pursuit of peace; an institutional ideology of impartiality even when confronted with attempted genocide'.[5] In his words, 'the cardinal lesson of Srebrenica is that a deliberate and systematic attempt to terrorize, expel or murder an entire people must be met decisively with all necessary means, and with the political will to carry the policy through to its logical conclusion'.[6] Annan's message was clear. The UN and its member states could not hope to protect 'we the peoples' from the horrors of genocide and other atrocity crimes unless they fundamentally changed the way they went about mandating, equipping and practising peace operations.[7]

The Security Council's landmark Resolution 1265 (1999) recognised the threat to international peace and security posed by human suffering and committed the council to taking appropriate steps to protect civilians directly targeted in war.[8] The following year, the council responded to the deteriorating situation in Sierra Leone by extending the mandate of UNAMSIL, the peacekeeping mission deployed there, and increasing its authorised size to 11,000 soldiers. UN Security Council Resolution (UNSCR) 1289 mandated UNAMSIL to 'take the necessary action' to 'afford protection to civilians under imminent threat of physical violence', noting that the mission should take into account 'the responsibilities of the Government of Sierra Leone'.[9] This was the first time that peacekeepers had been explicitly mandated to protect civilians. Since then, the council has increasingly used Chapter VII (enforcement) of the UN Charter to authorise peacekeepers to employ 'all necessary means' – encompassing actions up to and including the use of force – to protect civilians under threat of physical violence. In 2019, seven of the UN's 14 peacekeeping missions had protection-of-civilian mandates, with more than 95% of the UN's peacekeepers deployed on such missions.

Over time, the protection of civilians has become the centre of gravity for UN peace operations, the principal issue on which missions are judged, irrespective of their mandate.[10] As noted in the 2015 report of the High-Level Independent Panel on Peace Operations, PoC is a core obligation of the UN.[11] The Security Council increasingly identifies PoC as a 'strategic objective' for peacekeeping missions, and previously commonplace caveats on the exercising of this mandate have been loosened. Where the council once imposed geographic restrictions on the implementation of PoC, such as limiting protection to 'civilians within areas of operations', it now just as often calls for missions to expand their areas of operations to cover the protection of civilians in more areas. For example, in UNSCR 2364 (2017), the UN's mission in Mali (MINUSMA) was authorised to extend its PoC activities into central regions.[12] Meanwhile, explicit commitments to limit PoC activities to meeting threats from non-state actors to avoid prejudicing the host government's responsibilities to protect civilians (as evident in UNAMSIL) have been occasionally supplanted by broader mandates to protect vulnerable populations irrespective of the source of threats, as seen in the Democratic Republic of the Congo's (DRC) MONUSCO mission and South Sudan's UNMISS. This gave peacekeepers, at least in principle, a duty to protect civilians from the armed forces of their own government. Meanwhile, PoC mandates have become increasingly robust. Peacekeepers are now routinely authorised to use 'all necessary means' to protect civilians, and some missions are given specific protection tasks requiring the use of force. For example, MONUSCO's Force Intervention Brigade was mandated to 'neutralise' non-state armed groups, specifically the March 23 Movement (M23). In Mali, MINUSMA was authorised to use force 'in active defence' of the mandate and instructed that its PoC obligations should be understood as including a duty to protect non-combatants from asymmetric threats such as terrorism.[13] UNSCR 2295 (2016) called on the mission to 'anticipate, deter, and counter threats, including asymmetric threats, and to take robust and active steps to protect civilians, including through active and effective patrolling in areas where civilians are at risk, and to prevent the return of armed elements to those areas'.[14] In some instances, notably MINUSMA, the rules of engagement issued to individual missions – often given as a reason why peacekeepers could not use force in support of their mandate – have been adjusted to permit a more proactive and offensive approach to the use of force for PoC purposes.

Yet despite the steady proliferation and widening of PoC mandates, the elaboration of what this might mean in practice has been slow and hesitant. Consistent with peacekeeping's tendency towards the ad hoc, different missions have approached the question of using force to protect civilians in different ways. This has reached the point where most, if not all, other areas of peacekeeping activity are being retrofitted to align with PoC. As John Karlsrud has noted, a 'shift in priorities has occurred where the protection of civilians (PoC) has replaced liberal peacebuilding as the main rationale for UN peacekeeping operations, where institution building and other peacebuilding activities have been subsumed into one of the three pillars of the UN PoC doctrine'.[15] General questions about how UN peacekeepers ought to go about protecting civilians, and especially about the place of force within that agenda, have remained unanswered, even as practice itself has evolved. Not until 2010 did the General Assembly's committee responsible for overseeing peacekeeping (the 'C-34') acknowledge the emergence of PoC mandates and the need to think seriously about reconfiguring missions – their doctrine, guidance, training and deployments – to meet this challenge. The committee's engagement triggered a rapid institutionalisation of policy, doctrine and training, culminating in the promulgation of new UN policy on PoC in 2015, updated in 2019. This defined the PoC mandate as 'all necessary means, including, where necessary, the use of force, up to and including deadly force, to protect civilians under threat of physical violence. The Security Council has specified that the mandate to protect civilians applies within the limits of the capabilities of a peacekeeping operation and within its areas of deployment.'[16]

Within this context, implementation remains a challenge. While the use of force has always been available for the implementation of this mandate, in practice force is rarely used. A report of the UN Office of Internal Oversight Services published in 2014 noted a 'persistent pattern of peacekeeping operations not intervening with force when civilians are under attack', and that the use of force was in fact 'routinely avoided as an option'.[17] Part of the reason why missions remain reluctant to employ force to support PoC stems from concerns about its effects on wider mission goals. With so little experience on which to draw, there is a pervasive fear that using force to protect civilians will prove counterproductive.

Protection and force in UN peace operations

There are good reasons for thinking that, overall, the emergence of robust civilian protection in UN peacekeeping has had positive effects. In 2013, Lisa Hultman, Jacob Kathman and Megan Shannon showed that peacekeeping can be an effective way of protecting civilians since, when deployed in sufficient numbers, peacekeeping missions tend to reduce levels of civilian victimisation. Moreover, they found that the greater the number of peacekeepers deployed, the greater the effect on violence against civilians.[18] These effects were found not just at the national level, but also at the subnational level, with later research showing that the reduction of violence against civilians is greatest in the places where UN peacekeepers are deployed in the greatest numbers.[19] Another study confirmed that the presence of peacekeepers had positive local effects, showing that even small deployments could reduce the duration of local conflicts.[20] In 2014, Hultman, Kathman and Shannon demonstrated that when peacekeepers were deployed into situations of ongoing conflict – as many now are – the number of troops deployed was positively related to reduced battlefield deaths.[21] The deployment of peacekeepers is also associated with reduced civilian victimisation after war.[22] Interestingly, this research shows that *who* is deployed matters: armed peacekeepers had a positive effect, whereas the deployment only of unarmed observers had either no effect or a negative effect.

Others have found similar relationships. Eric Melander, for example, provides evidence that peacekeepers deter atrocities against civilians.[23] Peacekeeping has also been found to contribute to civilian protection in indirect ways. For example, peacekeeper deployment significantly reduces the likelihood of a conflict spreading across borders, and the human-rights reporting that missions facilitate can shorten conflicts and promote negotiated settlements.[24] These studies have also helped to identify important problems, perhaps chief among them the fact that UN peacekeepers are much more effective when it comes to protecting civilians from non-state armed groups than they are at protecting them from their own government's forces. Indeed, subnational data suggests that the deployment of peacekeepers makes relatively little difference to levels of government abuse.[25]

There seems little doubt, then, that the deployment of peacekeepers with PoC mandates helps to reduce civilian victimisation. It is not just that civilian victims in conflict-affected countries with peacekeepers fare better than those in countries without peacekeepers, but that regions, towns and villages within conflict zones do better when peacekeepers are present than when they are absent. There are a number of reasons for this, and no general consensus on what they are, but one in particular stands out: the presence of peacekeepers increases the costs associated with civilian victimisation. Potential costs range from the reputational damage associated with being named and shamed, to the increased chance of judicial punishment or sanctions for atrocity crimes when investigations are facilitated by peacekeepers or demanded by the UN, to the more direct costs associated with the heightened potential for armed resistance when peacekeepers are present. In short, it is cheaper and easier to abuse civilians when peacekeepers are absent than when they are present. Peacekeepers also manage and restrict the cross-border flows of people and arms that can facilitate atrocities, reinforce social norms against civilian victimisation and increase the likelihood of more coercive Security Council responses.

Discussion of the doctrinal frameworks for the use of force in peace operations, something that was historically taboo because peacekeepers were assumed to be in the business of using only minimal force in self-defence, has become more transparent.[26] According to the January 2017 guidelines issued by the UN's departments of Peacekeeping Operations and Field Support on the use of force by military components in UN peacekeeping operations, '"force" is defined as the use of, or threat to use, physical means to impose one's will'.[27] The guidance also states that 'the objective of the use of force in peacekeeping operations is to influence and deter, not necessarily to defeat threats seeking to threaten or harm United Nations personnel or associated personnel or the civilian population'. The document goes on to caution that any use of force must be 'consistent with the principles of gradation, necessity, proportionality, legality, distinction, precaution, humanity and accountability', as well as 'limited in its intensity and duration to what is necessary to achieve the authorized objective and, commensurate with the threat'.[28]

The guidelines also describe different levels of graduated force along a use-of-force continuum (see Figure 1).[29] Firstly, 'authoritative presence' refers to a show of force or the 'physical presence of a contingent with the credible capacity to use appropriate force through for example foot, vehicle or air patrols'.[30] This authoritative presence by UN peacekeepers comprises actions characterised by 'cooperative control', such as physical appearance, verbal command, search techniques and apprehension tactics. Secondly, 'non-deadly force', including unarmed force, is the degree of force 'necessary to compel compliance or dissuade aggressors that is neither intended nor likely to cause death or serious bodily injury'.[31] Escalation to non-deadly force by UN peacekeepers could include 'defensive tactics' such as the use of riot-control equipment (shields, water cannons, soft kinetic projectiles); 'compliance techniques' such as the use of chemical irritants, riot-control agents and shows of force including aviation; and the use of

Figure 1: **Continuum for the use of force in UN peace operations**

Core Objective Safety and security of UN military/police and those being protected as well as the rights and well being of the aggressors during a legitimate peacekeeping operation	**Use of Force Continuum**	
	Important! The specific details in this chart are for illustrative purpose only. Military units must tailor the details of their mission-specific requirements, equipment and level of training.	
Level of Force	**Threat Actions**	**UN Action/Reaction**
DEADLY FORCE	**ASSAULTIVE (SERIOUS/FATAL ACTION)** • Threat uses weapons, undertakes life threatening weaponless assault, and/or disarms a military/police	**LETHAL** • Use of firearm and strike to vital areas
NON-DEADLY FORCE	**ASSAULTIVE (NON LIFE THREATENING)** • Threat conducts non-life threatening activities but has the potential to cause physical harm to peacekeepers/civilians, e.g.: stone throwing, use of incendiary devices, sabotage. **RESISTANT (ACTIVE)** • Threat wrestles/pushes military/police or pulls away **RESISTANT (PASSIVE)** • Threat is unresponsive (refuses to move dead weight) or exhibits danger cues	**DEFENSIVE TACTICS** • Use riot control equipment including shield, water cannon, soft kinetic projectiles, etc. **COMPLIANCE TECHNIQUES** • Use chemical irritant application, riot control agents/barricades/cordon/show of forces including aviation. **CONTACT CONTROLS** • Takedowns, handcuffs, threat of using force.
AUTHORITATIVE PRESENCE	**COMPLIANT** • Threat shows positive or cooperative behaviour	**COOPERATIVE CONTROL** • Physical appearance, verbal command, search techniques and apprehension tactics

Source: United Nations Department of Peacekeeping Operations/Department of Field Support, 'Guidelines: Use of Force by Military Components in United Nations Peacekeeping Operations', Ref. 2016.24, January 2017, p. 5, https://info.publicintelligence.net/UN-PeacekeepingForces-2017.pdf.

'contact controls' such as handcuffing detainees or threatening to use force. Thirdly, the guidelines describe 'deadly force' – 'the ultimate degree of force' – as 'the level of force which is intended, or is likely to cause death, regardless of whether death actually results'.[32] Recourse to the use of lethal force, including armed force, is a last resort in peacekeeping, reserved for circumstances where there is believed to be sufficient aggression and intent to kill or exact grievous bodily harm. Although the use of deadly force is carefully circumscribed in the mission rules of engagement (for military) or directives on the use of force (for police), the guidelines insist that 'reluctance to use deadly force when warranted by the situation may lead [to] greater damage, may put the reputation of the United Nations at risk, or may lead to mission failure'.[33] This is particularly true in the realm of protecting civilians. By stipulating that it is authorising missions to protect civilians under Chapter VII of the UN Charter, the Security Council provides uniformed peacekeepers sufficient coercive leverage, up to and including the use of lethal armed force, to implement and defend this mandate.

The UN approach to PoC operations

The 2019 policy issued by the United Nations Department of Peace Operations on PoC articulates a three-tiered operational concept for realising PoC mandates on the ground. Tier I concerns protection through dialogue and engagement; Tier II is about the provision of physical protection; and Tier III is concerned with efforts to support the establishment of a protective environment.[34] While uniformed peacekeepers play roles in all three tiers, they have particular responsibilities and play critical roles in Tier II, aimed at prevention and the assurance of robust intent to protect civilians.

Four phases

The policy lays out four clear phases for operational activities and PoC tasks: 1) assurance and prevention, 2) pre-emption, 3) response and 4) consolidation.[35] The use of coercive measures may be required and is permissible in all four phases. Phase 1 (assurance and prevention) includes efforts to project mission presence. This manifests primarily through 'routine and passive measures', such as high-profile patrols and other force deployments, in order to demonstrate to local communities the mission's intent to protect them from physical violence.[36] However, this can also involve engaging with local security forces and non-state actors to improve situational awareness, risk assessment and early warning. These types of activities and engagements are the routine practices of military PoC efforts in most UN peace operations.

When heightened risks are identified and efforts to prevent and assure have proven, or are likely to prove, inadequate, phase 2 (pre-emption) involves proactive efforts to intercept, neutralise or defuse situations before hostile acts can be carried out. These can include lethal as well as non-lethal actions. For example, a number of mission strategies developed to implement PoC mandates now include directives to take positive steps to support protection. MINUSMA's PoC strategy, for example, stipulates that 'the protection of civilians mandate embodies an active duty to protect; missions do not engage in protection only in reaction to an attack'.[37] Activities in this phase focus on imposing an authoritative presence sufficient to deter attacks through the application of non-deadly force. Specific activities comprise the defence of key installations and sites, as well as preventive force deployment and posture. The latter could encompass increased high-visibility patrolling (including joint patrols with human-rights and other civilian components); closer liaison with government/non-government armed actors and potential parties to the conflict; and the use of intervening forces. Quick-reaction forces, special forces or reserves may be deployed to create buffer zones and deter or prevent incidents. Unilateral operations, such as those conducted by the Force Integration Brigade in the DRC, and joint operations conducted with host-government forces, as in the DRC, Mali and Central African Republic, to degrade and sometimes 'neutralise' non-state armed groups that display clear hostile intent towards civilians can also be understood as pre-emptive action that employs the use of lethal force.

Where pre-emption has failed to de-escalate tensions and violence erupts, more forceful measures are warranted in phase 3 (response). A range of reactive measures, including the provision of physical protection to civilians around UN bases and compounds – and potentially even the defence of protected areas such as refugee camps, safe corridors and safe areas – may be implemented. Phase 3 can also involve the rapid interpositioning of troops and direct military operations up to and including the deadly use of force.[38] Attack helicopters and quick-reaction forces may be used to prevent, limit or stop harm to civilians.[39] Though this use of lethal force for PoC purposes is uncommon, and peacekeepers typically make headlines in this regard for inaction rather than action,[40] it is nevertheless entirely consistent with the majority of mission mandates, their legal authority and, increasingly, the expectations of vulnerable civilians. It is also possible that parallel forces, such as the French-led operations *Barkhane* in Mali and *Sangaris* in Central African Republic, could be called upon to provide airstrike assistance and reinforcements, though the legalities, expectations and ramifications associated with this are less clear.[41]

Once the violence has subsided, phase 4 (consolidation) is less likely to involve coercive measures. Nevertheless, the need for continued reassurance and protection demands a robust presence, and often the establishment of defence positions by uniformed personnel.[42] The more common role for military and police peacekeepers in this phase is to maintain a secure environment to enable others, including human-rights officers, PoC advisers, child-protection officers, women's-protection advisers and gender advisers, to perform PoC work, such as providing medical assistance to victims, conducting investigations into and collecting evidence of human-rights violations, and pursuing accountability.

From this, it is important to understand that the use of force for PoC can involve a range of proactive, reactive and deterrent activities that – in theory – ought to be calibrated on a sliding scale depending on the specific phase of a PoC threat or incident.

The police role

While the military is the principal actor with respect to the use of force, UN police are also understood to have an active duty to protect.[43] Guidelines promulgated in 2017 on the role of UN police in the protection of civilians state that 'Security Council resolutions authorizing the use of "all necessary means" to protect civilians are applicable to UN police, even if the resolutions do not set out the specific role intended for UN police'.[44] The guidelines also lay out the roles and responsibilities of police in contributing to PoC efforts under all three tiers of the operational concept outlined earlier. Though they have more involvement in tiers I and III than the military component, the police component is also expected to contribute to the direct physical protection envisaged under tier II, and in some circumstances is expected to use force to support civilian protection.

UN police activities to provide physical protection are undertaken primarily by Formed Police Units (FPUs), which provide a response to threats to public order or violence against civilians. The UN's policy on FPUs points out that PoC is envisaged as one of three core functions.[45] This is important given that where there is no military weaponry present or any large-scale or sustained use of firearms, FPUs have primacy over the military component in providing a response on behalf of UN peace operations.[46] The use of force by UN police is governed by directives on the use of force. As the UN's individual police officers are often unarmed, these directives are predominantly relevant to the FPUs that make up a significant proportion of the overall police numbers deployed.

UN police work to analyse threats; prevent, pre-empt and respond to violence against civilians; establish a presence in areas under greatest threat; and assume a credible deterrent posture in accordance with the applicable directives. Being armed, FPUs can carry out preventive, high-visibility patrols and provide protection to unarmed patrols or escorts for convoys. This presents difficult challenges where UN police are expected to contribute to PoC in situations involving political violence, for example by providing riot control at elections-related demonstrations. Not only do such situations carry significant operational challenges, they also stretch PoC beyond instances of armed conflict and tie it to the forcible protection of human rights.

Reflecting on experience and practice

While it seems clear that the deployment of peacekeepers with robust mandates for civilian protection produces positive effects, the reasons why this is the case – and why these effects are more apparent in some places than in others – remain unclear. The positive effects of peacekeeping seem to occur almost irrespective of what peacekeepers actually *do.* Studies have identified a relationship between an operation's size and its effect (the bigger the better), and between the type of peacekeepers deployed and their impact on civilian victimisation (soldiers being better than observers), but research has yet to uncover a relationship between what peacekeepers do and the level of civilian insecurity. Do contingents that conduct robust patrols produce better results than those less likely to use force? Are proactive postures more effective than reactive ones? Investigations into the effectiveness of specific civilian-protection actions at the tactical level – rather than the overall impact of peacekeepers' deployment compared to situations in which no peacekeepers, or only observers, are deployed – yield quite different results. On the one hand, as the UN Office of Internal Oversight Services found,[47] there are very few instances of classic interposition operations, in which peacekeepers literally interpose themselves between civilians and their armed tormentors. Rarely, if ever, do peacekeepers intervene with force to stop ongoing attacks on civilians. On the other hand, there are many examples of missions in which different types of force have been used in keeping with UN guidelines. Using a dataset of 188 such cases, Stian Kjeksrud found that the tactical use of force was 'mostly successful' more often than it was 'mostly unsuccessful', but that the margin between these outcomes was not large (69 compared to 50), and that in a significant number of cases (61) the outcomes were uncertain.[48]

The use of force has had mixed results

The conclusion supported by this data – that the use of force to support protection has had mixed results thus far – is also supported by a quick survey of recent experience. Arguably the most impressive results were achieved in West Africa. With significant British assistance, UNAMSIL helped establish a viable government in Freetown and supported offensive operations that resulted in the military defeat of the Revolutionary United Front, a group responsible for widespread atrocity crimes, and the end of Sierra Leone's civil war. UNAMSIL was withdrawn at the end of 2005, having largely fulfilled its mandate. Force also played a significant role in Côte d'Ivoire, where, during an eruption of violence after the disputed 2010–11 elections, UNOCI troops operated alongside French *Licorne* forces to engineer the quick departure of the defeated incumbent, Laurent Gbagbo, and resolve the crisis.[49] The effect on the protection of civilians was profound. Côte d'Ivoire is not without problems, and there are significant questions about the sustainability of the gains it has made, but progress has been significant and the role played by peacekeepers' use of force is relatively clear.

The UN's mission in South Sudan (UNMISS) was initially deployed to support the new state there. When the country descended into a civil war in late 2013 led by President Salva Kiir Mayardit and his former deputy Riek Machar, the Security Council demonstrated its new commitment to civilian protection by paring back the mission's objectives to just two – civilian protection (and human-rights monitoring) and securing the delivery of humanitarian aid – while simultaneously increasing its size.[50] This, as Craig Murphy has argued, represented a significant change of strategy for the council, away from traditional peacekeeping and towards civilian protection as the *primary* mission goal.[51]

Facing an acute protection crisis, UNMISS adopted important innovations. Learning the lessons of Srebrenica, it opened the gates at UN bases to allow imperilled civilians to seek protection, rather than keeping them shut. Initially the idea of local staff as an ad hoc response to a serious crisis, 'open doors' became UN policy, giving rise to a strategy of establishing and maintaining 'PoC sites' for the provision of direct protection and humanitarian aid when needed.[52] At other times, UNMISS provided information to civilians about impending threats and advice about when and where to flee. One of its more ambitious innovations was *Operation Unity* II, featuring aerial patrols designed to enhance deterrence through presence and to make peacekeepers more responsive to emerging threats. But although these and other protection measures undoubtedly saved lives, the mission also experienced significant problems. PoC sites inadvertently encouraged displacement and created tensions; some contingents refused to leave their barracks when called upon to protect civilians; and technical problems and government opposition meant that *Unity* II largely failed. Underlying these problems was the fact that the UN and the African Union failed to craft a political strategy for the peacekeepers to support. Discord within the Security Council – and in particular, China's support for Juba – meant that proposals for a more coercive political approach involving the disarming, demobilisation and reintegration of combatants from both sides did not get far.[53] As a result, South Sudan's crisis persisted.

The UN's inability to usher conflict-affected countries out of a crisis is equally well exemplified by its experience in the DRC. Exasperated by a decade of halting peace punctuated by extreme violence, much of it against civilians, the Security Council took the innovative step, in 2013, of establishing the Force Intervention Brigade (UNSCR 2098).[54] Comprising units drawn from within MONUSCO, the brigade, as noted, was mandated to undertake offensive operations against M23. It did so with considerable success, though the brigade, and MONUSCO more generally, struggled to achieve similar success against other armed groups, such as the Democratic Forces for the Liberation of Rwanda (FDLR), the Lord's Resistance Army and the Allied Democratic Forces. As such, islands of stability in the DRC found themselves surrounded by seas of instability. The UN as a whole has also struggled to protect civilians from abuses committed by the DRC's own armed forces, and its criticism of those abuses has pushed the government to continually threaten to withdraw its consent for and cooperation with the UN mission. The Force Intervention Brigade's role also gave rise to concerns about the blurring of the lines between peacekeeping and peace enforcement, and the relationship between the brigade and the principle of impartiality.[55]

The UN has had a similar experience in Central African Republic. Although MINUSCA has not succeeded in resolving the country's protection crisis, the situation since 2016 would have been 'immeasurably worse', according to observers, had it not been deployed.[56] In that country, the government lacked the capacity, and sometimes the will, to protect civilians; more than a dozen armed groups were fighting each other and preying on civilians; and attacks on humanitarian workers were more common than in Afghanistan, Iraq or Somalia. Thus, UN peacekeepers had to assume responsibility for maintaining order in several parts of the country. In Bambari, for example, MINUSCA adopted a robust posture, conducting armed patrols to provide reassurance and deter attacks, especially by criminal gangs and the so-called ex-Séléka (an alliance of militia groups), while also conducting robust operations that included the use of attack helicopters to prevent and limit the movement of non-state armed groups. Peacekeepers were also reinforced periodically when tensions were high in order to prevent attacks. Still, on several occasions the mission failed to prevent or respond effectively to attacks on civilians. For example, in October 2016 it failed to respond to an attack on a camp for internally displaced people in Kaga Bandoro, which left dozens of civilians dead and forced thousands to flee to UN installations for protection. Shortly afterwards, peacekeepers in Bria abandoned their posts protecting a hospital when they came under attack and, as in South Sudan, remained in their bases as violence escalated.[57] The mission has also been plagued by accusations of sexual abuse and exploitation by its own soldiers and civilian staff, to which it has not always responded well.

As in South Sudan, there was until very recently no viable political process in Central African Republic. The situation is further complicated by the absence of a viable government and essentially non-existent state authorities – more than two-thirds of the country lies outside even the formal control of the state. As such, the UN's strategy is limited to providing what protection it can. Indeed, the UN has tended to avoid involvement in mediation at the national level because the prospects were so poor and the dangers of alienating parties and complicating protection so high.[58] Instead, it focused on negotiating a web of local peace agreements, drawing on the leadership shown by community groups, religious leaders, women's organisations, local government, elders and trusted international agencies.[59] It has also employed an innovation first developed in Haiti to good effect: community violence-reduction projects. Developed in specific communities with significant local input and funding from the World Bank, Canada and the European Union, community violence-reduction projects target the most volatile communities and aim to prevent young people from joining armed groups by creating employment through public-works schemes and supporting new businesses.[60] Still, the mission lacks the capacity to provide consistent physical protection across the country, and struggles at times to protect civilians even from itself.

The UN mission in Mali (MINUSMA) was deployed to stabilise the country following an insurgency in the north that was hijacked by extremist groups. Its mandate demanded the prioritisation of PoC, and was unprecedented in directing peacekeepers to 'anticipate, deter, and counter threats, including asymmetric threats, and to take robust and active steps to protect civilians, including through active and effective patrolling in areas where civilians are at risk, and to prevent the return of armed elements to those areas'.[61]

In the absence of Malian defence and security forces, the interposition of MINUSMA troops at crisis points in the main northern cities of Timbuktu and Kidal may have had deterrent effects with PoC benefits. However, since being deployed, MINUSMA has rarely, if ever, used force expressly for PoC purposes.[62] The UN has proven ineffective in ensuring the protection of civilians more generally, partly because it has not really been mandated to tackle the most prevalent threats. The predation of bandits and criminal groups throughout the lawless northern regions, as well as the dangers posed by increasingly militarised intra- and inter-communal conflict in Mali's central regions, are the main threats to civilians.[63] However, the mission and its PoC strategy focused instead on conventional armed groups and extremist groups that are generally careful not to target the civilian populations they depend on for support and legitimacy.

MINUSMA does not conduct military counter-terrorism operations. However, the mission's relationships with the host government and parallel forces such as the G5 Sahel and the French operation *Barkhane*, which explicitly do engage in counter-insurgency, have arguably caused MINUSMA to creep into a counter-terrorism role. This has helped to make PoC more difficult. Firstly, the UN has become a target for extremist groups, and consequently as much as 90% of MINUSMA's resources have been dedicated to force protection, leaving little for civilian protection.[64] Secondly, the politics of this positioning mean that UN forces struggle to 'do no harm'. Frequent attacks on mission patrols and convoys mean that the presence of peacekeepers among populations can imperil rather than protect civilians. Furthermore, the mission's close alignment with national security forces that have at times been abusive (anti-terrorist operations, for example, have involved the persecution of the Fula people) means the UN can appear to be aiding or abetting such behaviour, and thereby indirectly contributing to civilian insecurity. Thus, MINUSMA has struggled to protect itself, let alone civilian populations vulnerable to shifting conflict dynamics and everyday instability.

If the positive effects of peacekeeping on civilian victimisation have been achieved in conditions where, as Kjeksrud shows, less than 40% of actions involving the use of force could be judged 'mostly successful', then it seems fair to assume that improvements to how force is actually employed could yield improved results overall. In other words, Kjeksrud's finding suggests that the UN has not yet realised the full potential of what could be achieved through the use of force to protect civilians. This conclusion seems to be supported by our overview of some ongoing PoC missions. Notwithstanding the risk of unintended consequences,[65] it seems clear that UN peacekeepers do make a positive difference to civilian protection, but that their capacity to do so is inhibited by two sets of factors. The first are familiar operational considerations. Though UN peacekeeping provides significant indirect protection through presence, UN missions still lack sufficient numbers of mobile, trained, equipped and motivated peacekeepers to enable them to consistently protect civilians from direct attacks. In each of the missions reviewed, we found evidence of peacekeepers improving protection outcomes, but also proving themselves unable and sometimes unwilling to act to halt attacks on civilians.

The second set of factors are strategic and political. In Central African Republic and South Sudan, and to an extent in the DRC, UN peacekeepers do what they can to protect civilians in the absence of a viable political process. In Mali, the Security Council's strategy of supporting one of the combatants (Mali's government) pushes peacekeepers towards the role of combatants and inhibits their capacity for impartiality. In each of these cases, peacekeepers have found it difficult to translate the immediate short-term goals achieved through robust protection into sustained gains. In practice, the creation of islands of stability, or more protective environments in particular locales, has often failed to produce the hoped-for changes at the national level, in part because the host government has proven unable or unwilling to assume responsibility for protection, and in part because the absence of a viable political process or positive national political leadership means there are few incentives for armed groups to change their behaviour – much less to disarm and disband.

UN peacekeepers do make a difference

Learning lessons

There are four main lessons that might be learned from these experiences.[66] Firstly, the relationship between protection and politics is fraught. Analysts and officials agree that protection must be built around a political framework that tackles the causes as well as the consequences of armed violence against civilians.[67] In practice, however, that is not always possible.

Viable political frameworks cannot be conjured from thin air in places where national political leaders exhibit little interest in compromise or reform. General trends observed in one case or aggregated from several yield relatively little in terms of specific advice for particular missions. Nor does the UN have the luxury of sending peacekeepers only to those places where the local parties are committed to the kind of security-sector reform and disarmament initiatives necessary to allow peacekeepers to gradually hand over to national authorities. In such cases, it is not enough to assert the 'primacy of politics' or insist on the centrality of security-sector reform – though both of these are important. Attention needs to be paid to how peacekeepers protect in the absence of a political framework, how local gains can be sustained and expanded geographically in such circumstances, and what peacekeepers themselves can do to create 'ripeness' – conditions that encourage actors to engage in meaningful political processes.

Secondly, protection must be a core priority, not an optional extra. The record of practice thus far suggests that a deliberate, conscious and concerted focus on civilian protection throughout a mission tends to produce the best effects. The success of the Force Intervention Brigade against M23 and the initial 'open doors' strategy in South Sudan were achieved thanks to concerted efforts focused on the protection of civilians. Where PoC has figured alongside other priorities, the outcomes have been more mixed, as in Mali and with the MONUSCO experience more generally. The most significant failures have been seen in cases where PoC was considered, if at all, as subsidiary to other goals, as in Rwanda and Bosnia, where the UN prioritised peace processes – such as they were.

Thirdly, the use of force should be treated as an element of overall strategy, not as an addendum to it. Peace operations are predominantly military operations, and the use of force to deter, coerce or compel is a necessary element. Indeed, where missions are authorised under Chapter VII of the UN Charter, they are explicitly called upon to use 'all necessary means' to protect civilians. The planners of peacekeeping operations need to think about how force – and its threat – can be used to create the conditions needed to facilitate political or protection goals, and to incorporate this into mission planning.

Finally, missions must align capabilities and goals – an observation that has been made many times but warrants repeating. To achieve their mandates, missions must be capable of escalating and sustaining the use of force. Yet in Central African Republic and South Sudan, UN peacekeepers lacked the capabilities needed to consistently fulfil their protection mandates. Three particular capability shortfalls were evident. Firstly, there were not enough peacekeepers. Violations against civilians occur mainly when peacekeepers are absent; increasing their numbers can therefore be expected to improve protection. Secondly, peacekeepers are too often reluctant to leave their bases when confronted by threats to civilians. Thirdly, even when present, willing and able, peacekeepers often lack the capacity to use overwhelming force due to inadequate mobility and equipment.

Military force can be employed to induce 'ripeness' in situations where national political leaders stymie peace efforts. Since the mid-1990s, the UN has been of the view that this is a role for multinational operations, not UN peacekeepers. However, with peacekeepers increasingly deployed to situations of ongoing armed conflict, they are commonly faced with this scenario. If they are to avoid being trapped in unending operations, then fresh thinking about the applications and use of force may be required.

Building effectiveness

These lessons point to a number of areas, both operational and political, that, if strengthened, could enhance the effectiveness of the use of force for PoC. These include:

Whole-of-mission PoC. The first step is to ensure that protection of civilians is a priority for the whole of the mission – that its strategy is geared towards protection and its senior leadership and personnel-contributing countries understand that they will be judged first and foremost on their performance with respect to protection. Despite missions having developed mission-wide PoC strategies, it is often the case that protection is seen as the remit of a mission's uniformed components, or of a PoC unit close to the mission's leadership but with very little capacity. It is also clear that different contingents have different perspectives on the importance of PoC relative to other mission goals, as well as to force protection. Consequently, there is still a great deal of room for improvement in the extent to which PoC planning and response are conducted in a whole-of-mission fashion.

Sensitisation and training. While guidance and doctrine for PoC has proliferated in recent years, personnel are not always sensitised to it or trained for it. Military, police and civilian peacekeepers could all benefit from predeployment training that seeks to provide a basic understanding of PoC in UN peacekeeping. In-mission training that is tailored to the needs of particular missions, and a greater awareness among missions' senior leadership of PoC as a priority mandate, would also improve the chances that force is deployed effectively. This should include sensitisation on the roles and responsibilities, division of labour and inter-operability between military and police, and between uniformed and civilian components. Regular, scenario-based desktop exercises based on local conflict dynamics and exigencies would also be an important component of such training.

Early warning and threat analysis. Despite some recent progress in identifying protection needs, missions require more nuanced analysis capabilities if they are to better understand the nature of threats to civilian populations. In particular, there is a need to get beyond the binary categorisations of 'state' and 'non-state' – and to avoid generic labels such as 'terrorist' or 'criminal' – to more clearly identify the sources of threats, how they are related to each other and how they affect civilian insecurity. In the absence of this more relational understanding, threats may be missed, and the use of force may exacerbate rather than alleviate civilian vulnerability in the longer term.[68] Ultimately, better analysis informing more tailored responses to threat profiles will improve the design and implementation of strategies for PoC.

Force enablers. In order for peacekeepers to better leverage forceful means of protecting civilians, they require additional specialised capabilities in quantities far greater than currently provided. Assets such as intelligence, surveillance and reconnaissance, strategic and tactical airlift, and medical facilities are currently lacking, but could make active protection more possible (by helping forces to reach locations of civilian insecurity) and more likely (by helping to overcome the risk aversion of personnel). Similarly, decisions on the use of force as a last resort could clearly benefit from missions' non-uniformed elements, which make significant contributions to prevention and early warning of civilian insecurity. Additional capabilities relating to gender, women and child protection would also be helpful.

Strategic communications. In order to better manage expectations of local populations, missions need to develop ways to better engage with communities, disseminate information and more clearly explain PoC mandates. When peacekeepers use force against certain spoilers and come to be perceived as partial, the need for information operations is even more acute. Building on the public-information components of missions (such as radio stations and social-media platforms), as well as developing more strategic communications, would offer opportunities to create an environment more conducive to the effective use of force.

Accountability frameworks. Any recourse to coercive measures will be better governed if frameworks that hold peacekeepers accountable for their performance are implemented.[69] This means that, rather than focusing on delivering activities and other 'outputs' (such as patrols), there is some responsibility placed on mission leaders and contingent commanders for the outcomes and effects of their undertakings. This is likely to work best if such responsibility is integrated into an incentive structure that values and rewards PoC action, and holds accountable those who favour indefensible inaction. The use of performance data in subsequent planning also has the potential to improve the fulfilment of PoC mandates. By extension, accountability frameworks that deter misconduct, and that take action against abuse and malfeasance by both uniformed and civilian personnel, are likely to increase the credibility of the UN in the eyes of locals, and to add to perceptions of peacekeepers as protectors who 'do no harm' and use their superior strength in defence of civilian well-being.

Prioritise protection. Traditionally, peacekeeping was primarily concerned with monitoring or managing peace agreements. Now that PoC has emerged as a key priority, these goals can sometimes be in tension. For instance, missions are often sent to assist host governments to implement peace agreements, but PoC mandates can place missions in direct confrontation with the host governments they are sent to assist. This was the dilemma experienced by UNMISS in South Sudan and MONUSCO in the DRC. More needs to be done to foreground PoC thinking in conflict analysis, decision-making and mission activities to realise this operational imperative.

Align PoC efforts with political strategies and find better ways of coping in the absence of a viable political process. While it is commonly acknowledged that a political strategy is the *sine qua non* for contemporary peace operations, how to achieve such a strategy is less clear. They are often equated with support for a political process among elites at the national level, but such processes are not always in place. Furthermore, strategic links to politics at the local level are usually less well developed. This is partly because Security Council mandates rarely articulate a political strategy as such.

The uncertainty surrounding missions' political goals makes it difficult to anchor and align protection measures to political strategies. Further clarity on the meaning and significance of political strategies is clearly necessary to guide and delimit PoC efforts. In addition, more needs to be done to identify the ways that force can be aligned to political strategies that do not undermine other UN or peacekeeping goals. Otherwise, there is a risk that PoC will be directed by military, rather than political, considerations.[70] This is a problem because in places where military thinking has directed the political strategy, peacekeeping has found itself in quagmires. Security Council members need to broaden their understanding of how political considerations affect PoC and show greater willingness to apply pressure as necessary on conflict parties, including host governments, through diplomatic means (including sanctions) to deliver mission aims and to impose accountability for attacks on civilians and peacekeepers. Missions must also be allowed to act on their mandates and to incentivise bold leadership and brave service.

Renewed commitment. There is a need for the major personnel-contributing countries to commit to avoiding caveats that present hurdles to implementing mandates, and that limit command and control. While it is not feasible to eradicate all caveats, a system that makes these clear to senior mission leaders should be a minimum requirement. There is also a need for greater communication between the Security Council, the UN Secretariat and personnel-contributing countries to ensure that all stakeholders are committed to the same goals. Initiatives such as the 'Kigali Principles' and

Action for Peacekeeping, which advocate for meaningful PoC, offer a way of building this constituency and harnessing political will for action.[71]

* * *

Peacekeepers can and do make a positive contribution to civilian protection, yet there are grounds for thinking that they could do even more. Doctrinal and operational thinking has begun to take shape, but this has been slow regarding the use of force, and there are lessons still to be learned from the field. The practice of PoC without clear, viable and inclusive political processes might sometimes undermine the capacity of peacekeepers to fulfil their tasks, but peacekeepers are often confronted with precisely that situation. In addition to closing some of the technical and operational gaps that peacekeepers confront, more attention needs to be paid to questions of how peacekeepers themselves can be used to shape political conditions, and how missions might protect civilians in the absence of a viable political process. Withdrawal in such circumstances is not an option.

Acknowledgements

This research was supported by the Australian Research Council through Discovery Project grant [DP1601022429] and DECRA fellowship [DE170100138].

Notes

1   United Nations General Assembly, 'Report of the Secretary General Pursuant to General Assembly Resolution 53/35: The Fall of Srebrenica', A/54/549, 15 November 1999, p. 106, para. 496 and p. 108, para. 503.

2   Ibid., p. 108, para. 506.

3   Ibid., p. 106, para. 495.

4   Ibid., p. 107, paras 500, 497 and 499, respectively.

5   Ibid., p. 108, para. 505.

6   Ibid., p. 108, para. 502. See also para. 504.

7   See Alex J. Bellamy and Edward C. Luck, The Responsibility to Protect: Promise to Practice (Cambridge: Polity, 2018), chapter one.

8   UN Security Council, UNSCR 1265, 'The Protection of Civilians in Armed Conflict', 17 September 1999, http://unscr.com/en/resolutions/1265.

9   UN Security Council, UNSCR 1289, 'The Situation in Sierra Leone', 7 February 2000, para. 10(e), http://unscr.com/en/resolutions/1289.

10 See Siobhan Wills, Protecting

Civilians (Oxford: Oxford University Press, 2009).

11 United Nations, 'Report of the High-level Independent Panel on Peace Operations on Uniting Our Strengths for Peace: Politics, Partnership and People', A/70/95, S/2015/4462015, p. 11.

12 UN Security Council, UNSCR 2364, 'The Situation in Mali', 29 June 2017, http://unscr.com/en/resolutions/2364.

13 UN Security Council, UNSCR 2295, 'The Situation in Mali', 29 June 2016, para. 19(d), http://unscr.com/en/resolutions/2295.

14 *Ibid.*, para. 19(c)(ii).

15 John Karlsrud, 'From Liberal Peacebuilding to Stabilization and Counterterrorism', *International Peacekeeping*, vol. 26, no. 1, 2019, p. 3, doi: 10.1080/13533312.2018.1502040.

16 United Nations Department of Peace Operations, 'The Protection of Civilians in United Nations Peacekeeping', Ref. 2019.17, 1 November 2019, p. 5, para. 16. See also United Nations Department of Peacekeeping Operations/Department of Field Support, 'Protection of Civilians: Implementing Guidelines for Military Components of United Nations Peacekeeping Missions', Ref. 2015.02, February 2015, p. 5, para. 13.

17 United Nations General Assembly, 'Evaluation of the Implementation and Results of Protection of Civilians Mandates in United Nations Peacekeeping Operations: Report of the Office of Internal Oversight Services', A/68/787, 7 March 2014, p. 1.

18 Lisa Hultman, Jacob Kathman and Megan Shannon, 'United Nations Peacekeeping and Civilian Protection in Civil War', *American Journal of Political Science*, vol. 57, no. 4, 2013, pp. 875–91.

19 Hanna Fjelde, Lisa Hultman and Desirée Nilsson, 'Protection Through Presence: UN Peacekeeping and the Costs of Targeting Civilians', *International Organization*, vol. 73, no. 1, 2019, pp. 103–31. Stefano Costalli found no such subnational effect in Bosnia, though it is important to remember the idiosyncrasies of that case, including the presence of large numbers of peacekeepers in besieged Sarajevo, the lack of a protection man-date and the safe-areas problem. See Stefano Costalli, 'Does Peacekeeping Work? A Disaggregated Analysis of Deployment and Violence Reduction in the Bosnian War', *British Journal of Political Science*, vol. 44, no. 2, 2017, pp. 357–80.

20 Andrea Ruggeri, Han Dorussen and Theodora-Ismene Gizelis, 'Winning the Peace Locally: UN Peacekeeping and Local Conflict', *International Organization*, vol. 71, no. 1, 2017, pp. 163–85.

21 Lisa Hultman, Jacob Kathman and Megan Shannon, 'Beyond Keeping Peace: United Nations Effectiveness in the Midst of Fighting', *American Political Science Review*, vol. 108, no. 4, 2014, pp. 737–53.

22 See Jacob Kathman and Reed Wood, 'Stopping the Killing During the "Peace": Peacekeeping and the Severity of Postconflict Civilian Victimization', *Foreign Policy Analysis*, vol. 12, no. 2, 2016, pp. 149–69.

23 Erik Melander, 'Selected to Go Where Murderers Lurk? The Preventive Effect of Peacekeeping on Mass Killings of Civilians', *Conflict*

Management and Peace Science, vol. 26, no. 4, 2009, pp. 389–406.

24 See Kyle Beardsley, 'Peacekeeping and the Contagion of Armed Conflict', *Journal of Politics*, vol. 73, no. 4, 2011, pp. 1,051–64; Kyle Beardsley and Kristian Skrede Gleditsch, 'Peacekeeping as Conflict Containment', *International Studies Review*, vol. 17, no. 1, 2015, pp. 67–89; and Brian Burgoon et al., 'From Media Attention to Negotiated Peace: Human Rights Reporting and Civil War Duration', *International Interactions*, vol. 41, no. 2, 2015, pp. 226–55.

25 See Fjelde, Hultman and Nilsson, 'Protection Through Presence'.

26 See, for example, United Nations Department of Peacekeeping Operations/Department of Field Support, 'DPKO/DFS Guidelines: Use of Force by Military Components in United Nations Peacekeeping Operations', Ref. 2016.24, January 2017.

27 *Ibid.*, p. 3, para. 6.

28 *Ibid.*, p. 4, para. 8.

29 *Ibid.*, p. 6, para. 12(a).

30 *Ibid.*

31 *Ibid.*, p. 6, para. 12(b).

32 *Ibid.*, p. 6, para. 12(c).

33 *Ibid.*, p. 6.

34 United Nations Department of Peace Operations, 'The Protection of Civilians in United Nations Peacekeeping', p. 9, para. 40.

35 *Ibid.*, pp. 9–17. See also United Nations Department of Peacekeeping Operations/Department of Field Support, 'Protection of Civilians'.

36 United Nations Department of Peacekeeping Operations/Department of Field Support, 'UN Infantry Battalion Manual', vol. 1, 2012, p. 100.

37 This is from MINUSMA's PoC strategy, but similar accounts appear in PoC strategies for MONUSCO and UNMISS. 'Protection of Civilians' strategies for MINUSMA, MONUSCO and UNMISS, on file with authors.

38 Examples of phase-3 operations include the Standing Combat Deployments (SCDs) that underpinned MONUSCO's 'Protection Through Projection' concept.

39 See United Nations Department of Peacekeeping Operations/Department of Field Support, 'Protection of Civilians', pp. 18–20.

40 Failures to prevent attacks on civilians in PoC sites have recently occurred in South Sudan and nearby bases in the DRC and the Central African Republic.

41 See Lisa Sharland and Alexandra Novosseloff, 'Partners and Competitors: Forces Operating in Parallel to UN Peace Operations', International Peace Institute, 2019; and Shannon Zimmerman, 'Parallel Lines in the Sand: The Impact of Bi-lateral Interventions on UN Peace Operations in Mali and the Central African Republic', *Global Governance*, forthcoming in 2021.

42 Personnel might, for example, protectively accompany civilians carrying out certain tasks, such as conducting firewood patrols with women around camps for internally displaced people, as in Darfur and South Sudan.

43 See Charles T. Hunt, 'Protection Through Policing: The Protective Role of UN Police in Peace Operations', International Peace Institute, 2020, p. 6.

44 United Nations Department of Peacekeeping Operations/Department of Field Support, 'The Role of United

Nations Police in the Protection of Civilians', 2017, p. 9, para. 32. See also Charles T. Hunt, 'Rhetoric Versus Reality in the Rise of Policing in UN Peace Operations: "More Blue, Less Green"?', *Australian Journal of International Affairs*, vol. 73, no. 6, 2019, pp. 609–27.

45 United Nations Department of Peacekeeping Operations/Department of Field Support, 'Policy (Revised): Formed Police Units in United Nations Peacekeeping Operations', Ref. 2016.10, 2017, para. 13.

46 *Ibid.*, para. 51.

47 See UN Office of Internal Oversight Services, 'Evaluation of the Implementation and Results of Protection of Civilians Mandates in United Nations Peacekeeping Operations'; and UN Office of Internal Oversight Services, Inspection and Evaluation Department, 'Inspection of the Performance of Missions' Operational Responses to Protection of Civilians (POC) Related Incidents', 2018.

48 Stian Kjeksrud, 'The Utility of Force for Protecting Civilians', in Haidi Willmot et al. (eds), *Protection of Civilians* (Oxford: Oxford University Press, 2016), pp. 329–49.

49 See Charles T. Hunt, 'Côte d'Ivoire', in Alex Bellamy and Tim Dunne (eds), *The Oxford Handbook of the Responsibility to Protect* (Oxford: Oxford University Press, 2016), pp. 693–716.

50 See UN Security Council, UNSCR 2155, 'Reports of the Secretary-General on the Sudan and South Sudan', 27 May 2014, http://unscr.com/en/resolutions/2155; and Mark Malan and Charles T. Hunt, 'Between a Rock and a Hard Place: The UN and the Protection of Civilians in South Sudan', Institute for Security Studies, ISS Paper 275, November 2014.

51 Craig Murphy, 'The United Nations Mission in South Sudan and the Protection of Civilians', *Journal of Conflict and Security Law*, vol. 22, no. 3, 2017, pp. 367–94.

52 See Walt Kilroy, 'The Evolution of Civilian Protection in Peacekeeping Mandates: The Reality of UNMISS Operations in South Sudan', *Irish Studies in International Affairs*, vol. 29, 2018, pp. 133–43.

53 See Charles T. Hunt, 'Waiting for Peace: A Review of UNMISS' Political Strategy in South Sudan', United Nations University, 2020.

54 UN Security Council, UNSCR 2098, 'The Situation in Democratic Republic of the Congo', 28 March 2013, http://unscr.com/en/resolutions/2098.

55 See Lars Muller, 'The Force Intervention Brigade: United Nations Forces Beyond the Fine Line Between Peacekeeping and Peace Enforcement', *Journal of Conflict and Security Law*, vol. 20, no. 3, 2015, pp. 359–80; and Emily Paddon Rhoads, *Taking Sides in Peacekeeping: Impartiality and the Future of the United Nations* (Oxford: Oxford University Press, 2016).

56 This was one of the principal findings of the Center for Civilians in Conflict's 2017 report, 'The Primacy of Protection: Delivering on the MINUSCA Mandate in the Central African Republic'.

57 See *ibid.*

58 See Marie-Joëlle Zahar and Delphine Mechoulan, 'Peace by Pieces: Local Mediation Initiatives and Sustainable

Peace in the Central African Republic', International Peace Institute, November 2017.

59 See Robert Muggah, 'The UN Can't Bring Peace to the Central African Republic: But It Can Help Solve Local Conflicts. Here's How', *Foreign Policy*, 16 August 2018.

60 See *ibid.*

61 UN Security Council, UNSCR 2295, para. 19(c)(ii).

62 One possible use of force may have been in the Tabankort incident, in which an attack helicopter was used against MNLA fighters during a skirmish later justified partly for PoC reasons, but arguably more a case of force protection intended to rescue and defend an entrapped Bangladeshi contingent caught in the crossfire.

63 See United Nations, 'MINUSMA Strategy on the Protection of Civilians in Mali', 22 March 2017.

64 Lieutenant General (Retd) Carlos Alberto dos Santos Cruz, 'Improving Security of United Nations Peacekeepers: We Need to Change the Way We Are Doing Business', 19 December 2017, p. 16, https:// peacekeeping.un.org/sites/default/ files/improving_security_of_united_ nations_peacekeepers_report.pdf.

65 See Charles T. Hunt, 'All Necessary Means to What Ends? The Unintended Consequences of the "Robust Turn" in UN Peace Operations', *International Peacekeeping*, vol. 24, no. 1, 2017, pp. 108–31.

66 This discussion draws on, but amends somewhat, the lessons outlined by Alan Doss in 'Great Expectations: UN Peacekeeping, Civilian Protection, and the Use of Force', Geneva Centre for Security Policy, 2011, https:// www.gcsp.ch/News-Knowledge/ Publications/Great-Expectations-UN- Peacekeeping-Civilian-Protection-and- the-Use-of-Force.

67 See Ralph Mamiya, 'Protection of Civilians and Political Strategies', International Peace Institute, 2018; and Adam Day et al., 'The Political Practice of Peacekeeping: How Strategies for Peace Operations Are Developed and Implemented', United Nations University, 2020.

68 See Adam C. Day and Charles T. Hunt, 'UN Stabilisation Operations and the Problem of Non-linear Change: A Relational Approach to Intervening in Governance Ecosystems', *Stability: International Journal of Security and Development*, vol. 9, no. 1, 2020, doi: 10.5334/sta.727.

69 See, for example, the proposal by Patrick Cammaert in the South Sudan inquiry that he led: 'Executive Summary of the Independent Special Investigation into the Violence in Juba in 2016 and the Response by the United Nations Mission in South Sudan', United Nations Security Council, S/2016/924, 1 November 2016, p. 9.

70 See Mamiya, 'Protection of Civilians and Political Strategies', p. 2.

71 See International Conference on the Protection of Civilians, 'Kigali Principles on Protection of Civilians in Peace Operations', 28–29 May 2015, http://civilianprotection. rw/wp-content/uploads/2015/09/ REPORT_PoC_Short-Version.pdf; and United Nations Peacekeeping, 'Action for Peacekeeping (A4P)', https://peacekeeping.un.org/en/ action-for-peacekeeping-a4p.

Review Essay

The Trouble with Regime Change

Lawrence Freedman

Losing the Long Game: The False Promise of Regime Change in the Middle East
Philip H. Gordon. New York: St. Martin's Press, 2020. £23.99/$29.99. 368 pp.

The one relief that comes after reading this sharp, sobering account of a series of calamitous policy failures resulting from efforts at regime change in the Middle East is the knowledge that the author is back in government advising US Vice President Kamala Harris on national security, and so is in a position to help prevent a new folly. That said, his insights into decisions taken during the Obama administration warn of how competing pressures on policymakers can still produce perverse and unwanted outcomes.

The stories Philip Gordon tells are generally well known, but the cumulative impact of his lucid and analytical retelling, with the occasional insider observation, is salutary. He opens with a coup that was at the time celebrated as a successful masterstroke by the CIA and Britain's Secret Intelligence Service (also known as MI6). In 1953, the shah of Iran's position was restored after Mohammad Mossadegh, the awkward prime minister who wished to nationalise the country's oil assets, was removed in a coup the agencies helped to engineer. Later chapters deal with Soviet-occupied Afghanistan, Taliban-controlled Afghanistan, the aftermath of the 2003 invasion of Iraq and the heady days of the 'Arab Spring' of 2011, as first Hosni Mubarak

Lawrence Freedman is Emeritus Professor of War Studies at King's College London.

Survival | vol. 63 no. 3 | June–July 2021 | pp. 171–180   https://doi.org/10.1080/00396338.2021.1930413

of Egypt and then Muammar Gadhafi of Libya were pushed out, concluding with unsuccessful efforts to mobilise proxy forces to oust Syria's Bashar al-Assad. They make for painful reading, with much 'happy talk' from proponents of decisive action, regular triumphs of hope over experience and a conviction in the face of failure that there was still a way forward, if only the right people could be found, equipped with the right support packages and backed by a determined show of resolve.

The basic lesson is not to set in motion events that are likely to move well beyond your control in situations you do not fully comprehend. Getting rid of an obnoxious or discredited regime may be relatively easy. But the consensus on the need for a change may evaporate when it comes to choosing the replacement. Who makes the choice and what will be needed to ensure

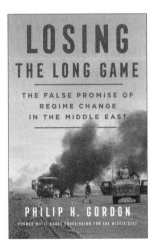

LOSING
THE LONG GAME

THE FALSE PROMISE OF
REGIME CHANGE
IN THE MIDDLE EAST

PHILIP H. GORDON
FORMER WHITE HOUSE COORDINATOR FOR THE MIDDLE EAST

that the new government succeeds? All those whose ambitions have been squashed and agendas ignored under a dictatorship feel that at last their moment has come and seek to move into the vacuum created by the abrupt termination of the old regime. Those whose interests were served by the old regime will not wish to let go of their privileges even as their opponents seek to exclude them.

Instead of a bright new dawn, of an inclusive and accountable government labouring for the collective good, there is likely to be an intense power struggle. In the absence of strong institutions to contain and channel this struggle it may well become violent. Once that happens the consequences for ordinary people may be worse than the crude repression of a tyrannical regime. Attempts by outsiders to hold the ring or impose some sort of political order of their own will be resented. Foreigners will be assumed to be occupying the country for their own purposes, whether to seize vital assets or to encourage a government of compliant puppets. Aware of such charges, even a friendly new leadership will soon need to demonstrate its independence and patriotism. Should it then become subject to the same pressures and temptations as its predecessors, it will be considered something of a disappointment. Yet it will also be hard to disown.

Claims will be made about its promise and effectiveness in order to justify full support and protection. Meanwhile, in the internal jockeying for power, particular factions will look to other regional powers as potential sponsors, making it even harder for the new regime to establish legitimacy and exert influence. In this way the initial disruption at the centre may have ripple effects that soon spread, potentially destabilising neighbouring countries.

A record of frustration

Gordon provides no basis for optimism that the United States can manage these processes successfully. One might think that one of his starker conclusions – 'Americans don't know enough about the Middle East' (p. 257) – could be remedied by encouraging better knowledge and a cadre of individuals with language skills and familiarity with local culture. But shaping a country's politics requires a detailed grasp of its complexities that is unlikely to be acquired other than by having a well-established presence within the country. That is exactly what hostile regimes do their utmost to prevent. Civil wars draw in chancers, grifters, traffickers and charlatans, along with idealists, democrats and patriots. Sorting out the claims of various groups demanding support is apt to lead to error and embarrassment. While there is no reason to suppose that people in the Middle East are less interested in democracy and human rights than anywhere else, economic chaos, divided societies and routine violence do not provide the optimum conditions for them to flourish.

In the short term, a competent autocrat might bring a degree of stability, but once he or she starts to use repressive means to sustain it, then reasonable questions will arise about what has been achieved by all the upheaval. Alternatively, without stability and with continuing chaos, even after a substantial effort, those arguing for patience and perseverance will face different questions about whether vital interests are really at stake and the other priorities that need attention. Local groups and individuals associated with the US will become aware of its waning enthusiasm and conclude that Washington may not be a dependable partner over the long haul. They will start to hedge their bets. 'The iron rule of regime change in the Middle East', concludes Gordon, 'seems to be that its costs will be higher than expected, unintended consequences will emerge, and results will leave much to be desired' (p. 267).

The United States' long engagements with Iraq and Afghanistan give force to this conclusion, and the positive popular response to President Joe Biden's decision to withdraw all forces from Afghanistan suggests that there will be little appetite for repeat performances in the future. There is now a more realistic appreciation of the limits of American power. However noble its intentions – Gordon rules out simple malevolence as an explanation for the policy failures he describes – the US does not have the capacity to take on divided countries that have suffered from years of tyranny and turn them into tolerant democracies.

Toppling regimes, however, is only one part of the story of American policy in the Middle East. An equally high priority during the period covered by this book has been to keep regimes in power. From this perspective, the original cause of instability was not fumbling Western attempts at regime change but more effective efforts by socialist, anti-colonial, anti-Zionist and nationalist radicals. In the 1950s and 1960s they succeeded in toppling a series of pro-Western monarchs, with Gamal Abdel Nasser showing the way forward in Egypt. The new regimes lacked democratic accountability but, at least for a while, did not appear short of popular support. They were also courted by the Soviet Union. Their continued hostility not only to Israel but also to other conservative states meant that resisting their efforts became a Western imperative.

This enterprise did not start well with the chaotic British and French plot to depose Nasser over his nationalisation of the Suez Canal in 1956, and there were many subsequent setbacks. The upheavals in Afghanistan thus began not with the Soviet invasion of 1979, let alone the effort to chase out the Taliban in 2001, but with the overthrow of the monarchy in 1974. Yet the fact that the Gulf monarchies are still in place and, despite long expectations to the contrary, a king still runs Jordan and a new sultan has just taken over in Oman, can be taken as a testament to the eventual if partial success of this policy. It often required more than a light touch. The US and the United Kingdom regularly used force or threats of force for this purpose, most dramatically with Kuwait in 1991. Meanwhile, with little to show for their decades in power, the radicals became weaker as popular discontent grew in response to personality cults, repression and corruption.

The Iran factor

Iran plays a central role in this story. Gordon is correct about the legacy of the 1953 coup in Iran. It would have been better over the long term if a way had been found to work with Mossadegh and accommodate his demands for greater Iranian control over its oil assets. The immediate effect of the coup, however, was to give the shah, who was already in place, more power. His fall at the start of 1979 was not the inevitable result of those events. He allowed his regime to become ever more decadent and oppressive. The extra wealth resulting from the oil price rises of 1973–74 was not matched by any serious effort at economic or political reform. The shah's poor health did not help, especially as revolutionary forces gained momentum in 1978. He dithered between bringing in the army and addressing popular concerns, and so did neither. The revolution led immediately to the hostage crisis with the United States, which doomed president Jimmy Carter's run for a second term; then to a war with Iraq, which prompted Iraq's attempt to annex Kuwait; and subsequently to *Desert Storm* and the American garrison in Saudi Arabia, which infuriated Osama bin Laden, prompting the attacks of 11 September 2001 and the US move into Afghanistan, which was followed, albeit from a tenuous logic, by the US-led intervention in Iraq in 2003. Of course, none of this was inevitable either. My point is only that a failure to prevent regime change was followed by massive state instability, even leaving aside the role of Iran-sponsored groups in Bahrain, Lebanon, Syria and Yemen.

Carter's desire to move away from what he believed to be the cynicism of the Nixon administration and take human rights seriously in foreign policy was one factor unsettling the shah's regime, but Carter also famously described Iran as an 'island of stability', and overall his approach followed that of his predecessors in being governed by Cold War and oil considerations. There was always a pragmatic view that all regimes needed a modicum of popular consent to survive, and some embarrassment at the requirement to lavish praise on absolutist rulers, but after 1979 the Iran example warned of the consequences of allowing friendly regimes to be toppled. Up to Iraq's occupation of Kuwait in August 1990, distaste for Saddam Hussein's tyrannical rule was tempered by the need to contain Iran and the possibility that he might be weaned away from the Soviet camp. And, as Gordon reminds us, even after Kuwait was liberated, then-president George H.W. Bush was advised not to attempt to push on to Baghdad and overthrow Saddam because of the chaos that could result.

The continuing US neuralgia over Iran is reflected in Gordon's opening discussion of Donald Trump's preoccupation with it. Trump abandoned the nuclear deal negotiated by Barack Obama supposedly in pursuit of one that was much improved. To achieve this, he adopted a strategy of 'maximum pressure', cutting off the country's means of economic support. The aim was to coerce Tehran into major concessions, so that it would abandon not only the nuclear project but also attempts to influence regional affairs. But the real hope was that Iran might be brought to economic collapse and popular revolt. Mike Pompeo, Trump's secretary of state, observed that even if Iranian behaviour was not changed by the pressure, 'the people can change the government. What we're trying to do is create space for the Iranian people' (p. 5).

Gordon warns Americans to look at such claims with deep suspicion. Yet the deliberate ambiguity in Trump's strategy also points to the question of what counts as attempted regime change. Intent is not always a good guide to outcomes. He addresses the charge that at times there are no alternatives to regime change, by pointing to more modest options to deal directly with specific issues. For example, relief efforts can address humanitarian distress, or military deployments can deter threatened aggression, or targeted sanctions and diplomatic pressure can seek to discourage proliferation or support for terrorism. But while the demands that might accompany coercive measures might be modest, situations can escalate, as one thing – for example, Iranian threats to disrupt tanker traffic or attacks on Saudi oil facilities – leads to another. When NATO countries intervened in the former Yugoslavia, the aim was to contain, mitigate and eventually reverse the effects of Slobodan Milosevic's policies. The process ended with him being forced out of office and put on trial in the Hague.

The Arab Spring

In some cases, Gordon acknowledges, it is best to do nothing, accepting that it is important not to make a situation worse even if it cannot be made better. But the stories he tells of the Obama administration demonstrate the pressure to 'do something' in the face of obnoxious behaviour, and the difficulty of distinguishing between coercive policies designed to change a regime's behaviour and those designed to bring it down. During the Arab Spring of 2010–11, Obama was unenthusiastic about the idea of regime change. He could see the pitfalls and the difficulty of describing a satisfactory end-state. The US had long since reduced its dependence on Middle Eastern oil. He was not pushing for change. It was being demanded by popular movements whose supporters were articulate, had a good grasp of social media and were difficult to ignore.

The first major test came with the challenge to Egyptian president Mubarak's position. Once Obama concluded that Mubarak was unlikely to be able to hang on for much longer, he sought a peaceful transition. The issue then became one of whether or not it was possible to allow Mubarak to do so on his own terms, for he had worked closely with the US as Egypt's leader, or whether to identify more closely with those demanding immediate change. In the Situation Room, the older hands wanted the former, while younger staffers believed that the president had to embrace the forces of change. Their argument about being on the 'right side of history' prevailed. Whether a more orderly transition was ever possible is debatable but now unknowable. We do know that in the short term the Muslim Brotherhood managed to get into power, until they were displaced by a military coup. Unfortunately, history has neither a right nor a wrong side, a point reinforced by the subsequent events in Libya and Syria.

Syria saw the most catastrophic civil war of the Arab Spring. The regime survived only with the help of Hizbullah, Iran and Russia. Prior to 2011, Obama had sought to repair relations with Assad, with a view to making progress on a peace agreement with Israel. The American president hesitated to align with Syrian protesters when they got going in March, not because he did not want them to succeed but because he did not want them to be discredited as American agents. As Assad sought to crush the opposition,

Obama found it increasingly difficult to hold back from taking diplomatic and economic measures in response. Eventually he sided with the opposition, but despite creating expectations that the full weight of American power would be applied against Assad, what the administration brought to bear was never enough.

There was no good policy on Syria available, but the tension between a desire to seek Assad's exit and the determination to limit American liabilities led to a mess. The administration willed ends but not means. It set 'red lines' on the regime's chemical-weapons use and prepared to act when they were used, but then held back. It armed and trained rebel groups without ever being sure whether they were the right groups, and saw weapons find their way to the more unsavoury militias. And it ended up having to turn its attention away from the Assad regime and towards one such militia – the Islamic State – when it brutally seized territory in Syria and Iraq and declared a caliphate. The Russians can claim victory because Assad remains in power, although Turks and Kurds, and Israel and Iran, have been engaged in their own conflicts on Syrian soil, and no resources are available to reconstruct the country.

*   *   *

All American administrations have struggled to navigate the complex politics of the Middle East. The immediate agenda item for the Biden administration is to work out how to engage with Iran, at a time when hardliners are seeking to consolidate their position in Tehran. Washington's two major regional allies, who encouraged the Trump administration to take on Iran, are wary. The United States will urge Israel to moderate its policies towards the Palestinians and encourage Saudi Arabia to get out of Yemen and return to a path of political reform. Both will warn that, if pushed too hard, risks of instability will increase. The issues of how far to promote democracy and human rights will not, of course, stop with the Middle East. They will continue to influence relations with Russia and China.

Against impossibly high standards of success there can only be failure, yet accepting that little can be done can lead to acquiescing in great evils.

One legacy of the events Gordon describes should be that the administration of which he is now a part knows enough not to exaggerate America's ability to reshape international affairs and reconstruct individual countries according to their preferences. But once the prudent, 'realist' conclusion is reached that irritating, obnoxious and hostile states cannot readily be pushed aside or transformed through decisive action into something more acceptable, the challenges faced in dealing with them may also be vexing and frustrating. Gordon argues that the best alternative to regime change may be what George Kennan advocated for the Soviet Union at the start of the Cold War: 'long-term, patient but firm and vigilant containment' (p. 269). The contemporary Middle East, however, is more fluid and complex than Cold War Europe. Firm and vigilant policies may still feel like attempts at regime change to the targets. More awkwardly questioning the dubious policies of supposedly friendly regimes can still cause instability.

Review Essay

Britain in a Contested World

Mitchell B. Reiss

**Global Britain in a Competitive Age: The Integrated Review
of Security, Defence, Development and Foreign Policy**
Cabinet Office. London: UK Government, 2021. 114 pp.
Available at https://www.gov.uk.

The United Kingdom's referendum vote in June 2016 to leave the European
Union has been described as a long-overdue reassertion of British sovereignty, a spasm of jingoism that will impoverish generations to come and
everything in between, with passions high on all sides. While some politicians have heralded Brexit as an opportunity for Britain to chart a new
future, their views have been largely discounted as partisan posturing, and
as more bluff and bluster than a sober assessment of what challenges might
lie ahead. After all, Remainers and other critics complain, Brexit advocates
never presented a plan or clearly articulated a path that would lead to the
'sunlit uplands' promised by Member of Parliament and leading Brexiteer
Andrea Leadsom.[1]

Now Prime Minister Boris Johnson and his administration have developed such a plan in what may constitute the most comprehensive and
significant rethinking of British foreign and defence policy since the debacle
at Suez more than 60 years ago.

Mitchell B. Reiss is former Director of Policy Planning at the US State Department and Special Advisor to
the Northern Ireland Peace Process with the rank of Ambassador. He currently is an international consultant
advising on higher education and historic sites.

Survival | vol. 63 no. 3 | June–July 2021 | pp. 181–192   https://doi.org/10.1080/00396338.2021.1930415

At that time, Britain's status as a leading post-war imperial power was shattered by a series of foreign-policy setbacks, in particular its ill-planned invasion – alongside France and Israel – of the Suez Canal Zone, which had been nationalised by Egyptian leader Gamal Abdel Nasser. The Eisenhower administration, dealing with a popular uprising in Hungary at the same time, publicly opposed this unilateral use of force. Most devastating to London's ambitions was the pressure the United States applied to the pound. Without US support during the Suez crisis, the UK no longer had the foreign-exchange reserves to purchase the food and energy supplies it needed.[2]

The damage to Britain's imperial confidence arguably stung more than the political, economic and military reversals. Britain's post-war decline had not only been laid bare, but Suez had also exposed the limits of the UK's ability to act independently of the United States. Washington had now assumed London's place in the post-war order, as the Eisenhower administration briskly sided with the cause of Arab nationalism in a bid to stave off Soviet inroads across the Middle East.

A few months later, in March 1957, Britain retreated further with its decision not to join the Treaty of Rome, which created the Common Market, passing up the chance to lead a united Europe. That same month, the new defence minister, Duncan Sandys, issued a defence White Paper that marked a fundamental rethinking of Britain's defence posture and its strategic role in a post-Suez world.[3] In particular, it eliminated national service and emphasised a larger role for nuclear weapons. More broadly, the White Paper tried to reconcile the reality of Britain's declining economic strength with its abiding aspirations to great-power status.

Britain in a post-Brexit world

The run-up to the Brexit referendum was characterised by the lack of any serious advance defence and security planning. While Johnson's approach during the Brexit debate seemed reminiscent of the wilful insouciance captured by the satirical newspaper headline 'Fog in Channel, Continent Cut Off', Theresa May's government stumbled into a post-Brexit world with a this-can't-really-be-happening vertigo. The Johnson government has come a long way since it took office in July 2019. As Britain looks to the world in 2021, it appears unwilling to accept a diminished global status. Instead, it wants to forge an entirely new identity for itself. The centrepiece of this effort is *Global Britain in a Competitive Age: The Integrated Review of Security, Defence, Development and Foreign Policy*. Not just an interdepartmental product by career mandarins, it was driven and guided by foreign-policy experts at Downing Street, most notably the King's College London historian John Bew, who solicited a range of views from external experts and think tanks, including the Center for a New American Security in Washington DC, Australia's Lowy Institute, France's Institut Montaigne and Britain's Policy Exchange.

The government has also generated an array of other initiatives that collectively aim to reset the country's strategic course in a competitive world, and to counter technological disruption, environmental degradation, pandemic diseases and the erosion of democratic norms. No longer bound by the EU's rules, Johnson and his team have realised that trade policy can now be leveraged as another tool of foreign policy. In July 2020, the UK established its first autonomous sanctions regime for human-rights violations. Two months later, the Foreign and Commonwealth Office was merged with the Department for International Development, substantially transforming both institutions. The resulting Foreign, Commonwealth and Development Office (FCDO) now allows London to align its development efforts more closely with its diplomacy to further promote foreign-policy goals.

The Ministry of Defence has kept pace. Within the last year, it has issued three major reports: one removing barriers between operations and war fighting; a second pushing for a full-spectrum, integrated approach to threats; and a third that examines the resilience of its supply chains and identifies those elements of its core industrial base that are needed to support these efforts.[4] Within the last year, the government has also established a new National Cyber Force and announced funding for a new Counter Terrorism

Operations Centre. New strategies for cyber security, artificial-intelligence defence, and integrating military and civilian space policy will all be published in 2021.

The new thinking reflects the prime minister's ambition, audacity and, above all, urgency. As noted in *Global Britain*: 'A defence of the status quo is no longer sufficient for the decade ahead' (p. 11). Despite having written a biography of Winston Churchill, Johnson has chosen not to adopt the famous Churchillian concept of three interlinking circles comprising the Commonwealth, the English-speaking world – especially the United States – and Europe, with Britain occupying the 'very point of junction' between them.[5] Rather, the integrated review, along with the other defence and security papers, suggests a more realistic vision for Britain in a world where threats from Russia are growing, China's power and global influence are increasing, and European security remains essential.

Revised strategic outlook

Global Britain drew attention upon its initial release primarily for its intent to expand the UK's nuclear deterrent from 225 to 260 warheads. This marked a policy reversal after three decades of reductions and the publication of the 2015 security review, which had pledged to reduce the stockpile to a maximum of 180 warheads – a number that was deemed sufficient at the time 'to ensure that our deterrent is not vulnerable to pre-emptive action by potential adversaries'.[6] *Global Britain* cites a rising risk from unnamed states, widely assumed to mean Russia above all, that are 'investing in novel nuclear technologies and developing new "warfighting" nuclear systems … to seek to coerce others' (p. 76).

This argument did not impress arms-control advocates, who contended that the UK's warhead increase would sabotage non-proliferation efforts, notably the Non-Proliferation Treaty (NPT) Review Conference this coming August. If the conference fails, however, it will do so for other reasons. The purported causal relationship between vertical and horizontal proliferation is unproven. For example, at the end of the Cold War, the nuclear arsenals of the United States and the Soviet Union/Russia were massively reduced (as was, to a lesser degree, the UK's). During the same period, however,

India, Pakistan and North Korea all greatly enhanced their nuclear-weapons capabilities. As nuclear analyst Heather Williams has observed, the UK 'perceives the security environment to have become so much worse that it chose to increase its nuclear stockpile amidst growing pressures to disarm'.[7]

Accompanying the increase in warhead numbers are two other changes to the country's nuclear strategy. The first is a shift to strategic ambiguity. *Global Britain* argues that greater ambiguity would enhance deterrence by increasing uncertainty in the calculations of adversaries, producing greater strategic stability – adopting reasoning similar to Russia's and China's. Consequently, Britain will 'no longer give public figures for our operational stockpile, deployed warhead or deployed missile numbers' (p. 77).

The second doctrinal change is in the circumstances under which the UK could employ nuclear weapons. The paper reiterates Britain's traditional policy of not using, or threatening to use, nuclear weapons against any member in good standing of the NPT, but also lays out some potential exceptions. Britain will now reserve the right to abandon the assurance of no first use if it is attacked with other weapons of mass destruction, 'or emerging technologies that could have a comparable impact' (p. 77). Thus, the UK might retaliate with nuclear weapons in response to certain kinds of non-nuclear aggression, such the use of hypersonic weapons or even a devastating cyber attack. This change significantly lowers the threshold for the possible first use of nuclear weapons.

Against a background of a more volatile security environment and higher risks of conflict, *Global Britain* identifies four strategic objectives for the next five years. The first is to sustain and increase its comparative advantages in science and technology. It notes that the UK is ranked fourth in the latest Global Innovation Index and attracts venture capital at a level that exceeds that of France, Germany and Sweden combined. *Global Britain* commits the government to increasing research-and-development spending in science and technology by 2.4% of GDP by 2027; a complementary initiative to attract global talent to work in the country has already been established by adjusting the country's immigration regulations.

The UK also aspires to shape the liberal international order, whose laws, rules and norms are increasingly under assault from China. Within these institutions, Britain will emphasise the importance of protecting and pro-moting open societies and democratic values from external manipulation, work to shape the global digital environment to favour 'digital freedom' over 'digital authoritarianism', and help develop nascent frameworks that will manage the future frontiers of genetic engineering, cyberspace, artificial intelligence and space.

In addition, *Global Britain* aims to defend the homeland and its interests overseas from the full spectrum of threats – especially those originating from Russia, which the document says 'remains the most acute threat to our security' (p. 18). It also plans for greater resilience in countering cyber threats and for effective strategic warning of any future pandemics. Finally, it calls for preparation for displacement caused by climate change, consistent with the prime minister's declaration to make climate change his top international priority and his pledge – the first by a leader of a major industrial economy – to meet a target of net-zero greenhouse-gas emissions in the UK by 2050.

Continuity and change

Global Britain echoes earlier documents in many ways. The UK will continue to rely on the United States as 'the UK's most important strategic ally' and on NATO for collective security (p. 26). Britain will remain the largest European NATO defence spender, committing 2.2% of GDP. It will also continue to invest in counter-terrorism capabilities and promote human rights and sustainable development. But it is the policy changes that distinguish the integrated review. These include the largest defence-budget increase since the end of the Cold War. While *Global Britain* incorporates the economically realistic expectation of a 4% decrease in military personnel by 2025, it envisions forces that will be better trained and equipped, with enhanced readiness. Greater resources will be allocated to drones and cyber warfare. The goal is to build a smaller but more capable and potent force that can meet the most likely future threats.

In addition to the modernisation and bolstering of UK security and defence, *Global Britain* outlines a new 'tilt' towards the Indo-Pacific region. Indeed, the shadow of China looms over Britain's entire rethink. According to a senior Whitehall official, 'the whole Integrated Review is really about China. The emphasis on S&T [science and technology]. Shaping the international order. Changes to defence, cyber and space. They were all done with China in mind.'[8] London brings important assets to this fight, especially in terms of trade, human rights and soft power. The Indo-Pacific already accounts for more than one-sixth of all UK global trade, and over the past few years Britain has signed new trade deals with Australia, Japan, New Zealand, Singapore and Vietnam, and agreed to an Enhanced Trade Partnership with India as a precursor to a formal trade agreement. On human rights, Johnson offered British overseas nationals and family members in Hong Kong the right to live and work in the UK, with a path to British citizenship, after China violated its bilateral agreement and imposed a repressive national-security law. It has also been outspoken about the egregious human-rights violations in Xinjiang province. London appointed an ambassador to the Association of Southeast Asian Nations in 2019 and, the following year, created a new director-general position at the FCDO dedicated to the Indo-Pacific. The BBC and the British Council remain highly effective soft-power assets for waging the intensifying ideological competition in the region against China's brand of state-directed authoritarianism.

Although there is no doubt that the United States would welcome a significant UK military presence in the Indo-Pacific to help defend the rules-based order and counter China, it is unclear how effective and robust the UK's role would be in an 'away game'. *Global Britain* concedes that the Euro-Atlantic region is 'where the bulk of the UK's security focus will remain' (p. 14). A close reading of the review also indicates that its geostrategic approach is selective, with special attention given to East Africa, the Gulf region and the Indian Ocean because of historic ties and present interests.

What could go wrong?

Whether Britain will realise its aspiration to play a more significant role independently and globally depends on whether the UK can afford to do so. The prime minister and authors of *Global Britain* obviously think so and have designed their initiatives accordingly. Like Sandys's Defence White Paper, it recognises the limits of Britain's ability to underwrite the costs of global engagement. The paper emphasises integration, new partnerships and a general rationalisation effort, all designed to be more efficient and less expensive, the merged FCDO being a prime example. It also recognises difficult trade-offs, most notably in the armed forces. Will this be enough? Perhaps, but it is not an encouraging sign that the government will be cutting its foreign-aid budget this year from 0.7% to 0.5% of gross national income.[9] A better indicator will be the outcome of the multi-year Spending Review in autumn 2021. Defence spending has already been allocated for the next four years. It remains to be seen if the Spending Review will match resources with the ambitions of *Global Britain*.

Another question is whether this strategy can win sufficient bipartisan support to ensure it is sustainable should there be a change in government. This appears possible. Although Keir Starmer, the Labour Party leader, has criticised *Global Britain*, his qualms concern mainly the increase in nuclear warheads and the possibility of further reductions in the armed forces, rather than the country's general strategic direction.[10]

What about the United States?

Global Britain is based on a fundamental assumption that the United States will play an active role in the world, providing security; supporting free trade, global health and progress on climate change; and promoting human rights and democratic governance. (The paper might have turned out differently had Donald Trump been re-elected.) Specifically, the document banks on the United States' return to global leadership and a reinvigoration of the alliance system. It acknowledges that 'the United States will remain our most important bilateral relationship, essential to key alliances and groups such as NATO and the Five Eyes, and our largest bilateral trading partner and inward investor' (p. 20). The review reinforces the distinctiveness of the transatlantic relationship, partly because the UK is more comfortable than other European partners with the United States' re-establishment as a committed NATO member. Recall, for example, that it was French President Emmanuel Macron who spoke favourably of Europe's 'strategic independence' during the Trump years. Another factor is the UK's willingness to share not just the burdens but also the risks of deploying to conflict zones and actually fighting. Without ever using the term, *Global Britain* clearly foresees a new type of 'special relationship' between a more capable and self-confident UK and the US.

It helps that the two countries share a similar assessment of the strategic environment. The short-term threats identified in *Global Britain* closely match those articulated by the US Office of the Director of National Intelligence in its 2021 'Annual Threat Assessment of the U.S. Intelligence Community'.[11] China, Iran, North Korea, Russia, the COVID-19 pandemic, terrorism and climate change are all priorities. Furthermore, the longer-term trends cited in *Global Britain* broadly track those identified in the US intelligence community's quadrennial product, 'Global Trends 2040: A More Contested World'.[12]

The Biden administration already seems to be responding to the challenges *Global Britain* highlights by reshaping American institutions. President Joe Biden has established new positions at the National Security Council (NSC) for global health, democracy and human rights, and cyber and emerging technologies. Russia once again has its own NSC senior director and is not subsumed under the European and Eurasian Affairs directorate. There is also a new tsar in charge of the Indo-Pacific region. And former secretary of state John Kerry has been appointed special presidential envoy for climate.

Will Britain succeed?

Brexit was really a wager that a UK freed from an unwieldy EU and its abundance of procedures, rules and regulations could be more agile, respected, secure and prosperous; Britain could then successfully navigate its own way in the world as it had previously done for centuries. It is still too soon to collect any winnings; the next five years will determine whether the UK's bet was sound.

Global Britain provides a basis for cautious optimism. It articulates first principles and a framework by which the UK will be able not merely to survive in an uncertain world, but to thrive in it. It takes a broader conception of national security than its American counterparts have done – at least up to now – and one that seems well suited to the interconnectedness of the twenty-first century. Yet it is the tone more than the substance of the review that is most striking: it is less apologetic and complacent about decline, and far more ambitious, forward-thinking and positive about what Britain can achieve than comparable documents issued by predecessor governments have been.

Margaret Thatcher, who first entered Parliament in 1959, complained of a 'Suez syndrome' that affected the political classes, who seemed more willing to accept and manage the country's gradual decay than to reimagine and re-engineer Britain's greatness.[13] *Global Britain* suffers from no such infirmity in setting out its bold course for the UK in a post-Brexit world.

Notes

1 '"I Want to Guide Britain to the Sunlit Uplands" – Full Text of Andrea Leadsom's Leadership Speech', *Spectator*, 4 July 2016, https://www.spectator.co.uk/article/-i-want-to-guide-britain-to-the-sunlit-uplands---full-text-of-andrea-leadsom-s-leadership-speech.

2 Much has been written about Suez. For a critical insider analysis of the crisis, see Anthony Nutting, *No End of a Lesson: Story of Suez* (London: Constable, 1967).

3 UK Government, 'Defence: Outline of Future Policy', March 1957, http://filestore.nationalarchives.gov.uk/pdfs/small/cab-129-86-c-57-84-34.pdf.

4 UK Ministry of Defence, 'Introducing the Integrated Operating Concept', 21 October 2020, https://assets.publishing.service.gov.uk/government/uploads/system/uploads/attachment_data/file/922969/20200930_-_Introducing_the_Integrated_Operating_Concept.pdf; Claire Mills, 'Integrated Review 2021: Emerging Defence Technologies', House of Commons Library, Briefing Paper No. 9,184, 25 March 2021, https://researchbriefings.files.parliament.uk/documents/CBP-9184/CBP-9184.pdf; and UK Government, 'Defence and Security Industrial Strategy', March 2021, https://assets.publishing.service.gov.uk/government/uploads/system/uploads/attachment_data/file/971983/Defence_and_Security_Industrial_Strategy_-_FINAL.pdf. See also UK Ministry of Defence, 'Defence in a Competitive Age', March 2021, https://assets.publishing.service.gov.uk/government/uploads/system/uploads/attachment_data/file/974661/CP411_-Defence_Command_Plan.pdf.

5 See Richard Davis, 'WSC's Three Majestic Circles', International Churchill Society, *Finest Hour*, no. 160, Autumn 2013, https://winstonchurchill.org/publications/finest-hour/finest-hour-160/articles-wsc-s-three-majestic-circles/.

6 See UK Government, 'National Security Strategy and Strategic Defence and Security Review 2015: A Secure and Prosperous

United Kingdom', November 2015, https://www.gov.uk/government/publications/national-security-strategy-and-strategic-defence-and-security-review-2015.

7 Heather Williams, 'UK Nuclear Weapons: Beyond the Numbers', *War on the Rocks*, 6 April 2021, https://warontherocks.com/2021/04/u-k-nuclear-weapons-beyond-the-numbers/. This article provides a thoughtful examination of the new UK nuclear policy.

8 Personal conversation, April 2021. One commentator who immediately grasped that *Global Britain* was designed to meet the challenges posed by China is Charles Moore. See Charles Moore, 'Britain Does Not Want a New Cold War – But We Have To Be Ready for One', *Daily Telegraph*, 19 March 2021, https://www.telegraph.co.uk/news/2021/03/19/britain-does-not-want-new-cold-war-have-ready-one/.

9 The UK is the only member of the G7 to meet the UN Sustainable Development Goals; it has ranked first among G7 members in terms of percentage of Official Development Assistance funding for the past ten years. The cuts this year will place the UK behind only Germany, which will contribute 0.67%.

10 See Sienna Rodgers, 'Starmer: Integrated Review Breaks Goal of Reducing Our Nuclear Stockpile', *Labour List*, 16 March 2021, https://labourlist.org/2021/03/starmer-integrated-review-breaks-goal-of-reducing-our-nuclear-stockpile/; and '"Real Risk" Armed Forces "Will Be Stripped Back Even Further" – Sir Keir Starmer', *American Global News*, 16 March 2021, https://americanglobalnews.com/2021/03/real-risk-armed-forces-will-be-stripped-back-even-further-sir-keir-starmer/.

11 Office of the Director of National Intelligence, 'Annual Threat Assessment of the U.S. Intelligence Community', 9 April 2021, https://www.dni.gov/files/ODNI/documents/assessments/ATA-2021-Unclassified-Report.pdf.

12 National Intelligence Council, 'Global Trends 2040: A More Contested World, Office of the Director of National Intelligence', March 2021, https://www.dni.gov/files/ODNI/documents/assessments/GlobalTrends_2040.pdf.

13 See Margaret Thatcher, *The Path to Power* (New York: HarperCollins, 1995), p. 91.

Book Reviews

Europe
Erik Jones

Workaway: The Human Costs of Europe's Common Labour Market
Jonathon W. Moses. Bristol: Bristol University Press, 2021.
£30.00. 264 pp.

People often combine work and travel as a source of adventure – think 'gap year'. That kind of work–travel experience is not, however, what 'freedom of movement' in Europe's common labour market is about. There is travel within Europe and, with any luck, there is employment. Some people who seek work in Europe may find extraordinary opportunities there, but for most people the goal is something closer to survival than adventure.

In his powerful new book, Jonathon Moses uses the term 'workaway' to capture the perilous nature of European economic migration. The term comes from his experience as an able-bodied seaman plying the North Atlantic at the end of the 1980s. A workaway is a sailor who agrees to work without pay to get from one port to another in the hope of better opportunities. Surrendering one's passport to an unknown ship's captain to toil without pay is probably more 'adventure' than most gap-year travellers would accept, yet for many this is all that Europe has to offer.

Moses's story raises two questions: who participates in Europe's 'free movement of labour', and what did the founders of the European Union want from labour-market integration in the first place? Moses points out that most economic migrants in Europe come from outside the EU. Many are hoping to escape from hardship and poverty; many are also fleeing violence and oppression. Intra-European economic migrants come mostly from a small number

Survival | vol. 63 no. 3 | June–July 2021 | pp. 193–200   https://doi.org/10.1080/00396338.2021.1930416

of countries such as Greece, Italy, Poland and Romania. Frequently, the two groups overlap as workers from outside the EU come to fill the gaps left by those who travel to work within Europe.

None of this looks like a reasonable – or desirable – European 'project'. It is hard to imagine that anyone working to build the Union in the 1950s (or 1990s) was dreaming of the day when Moldovans could fill the gaps left by Romanians who have departed to care for Italians whose children have gone to work in London or Paris. This sounds more like the mass movements that followed the Second World War, and that the economic community was created to mitigate.

So how did the EU end up in this situation? Moses points to two intermediate projects that have framed Europe's common labour market. One is the embrace of 'market efficiency' as the primary instrument for macroeconomic adjustment. The other is the construction of the euro as a common currency. Both have worked to undermine trade unions and the welfare state in ways that have imposed large social, political and economic costs on Europeans everywhere.

The two projects are obviously connected. The creation of a common market only makes sense if one believes that markets are 'common' – meaning that a market for goods is much the same as a market for labour or capital, and that any of these markets is potentially much the same in one country as it is in the next. It is a short step from that commitment to believe that the best measure for market performance is 'efficiency', and the best way to enhance efficiency is to build a common currency. The freedom of movement we have today is an unintended consequence of those commitments.

The solution, Moses argues, is to reimagine European societies as places where workers have value beyond the labour they contribute, where that value may be different from one place to the next, and where, crucially, efficiency is only one goal among many. This Europe will not have unified institutions and will not offer so much freedom of movement. Its members may well reclaim their national currencies too, if necessary. But Moses believes it will be a more stable and prosperous place than the EU is today. Not everyone will agree with this prescription, but it is a serious argument that no European can afford to ignore.

The Everyday Nationalism of Workers: A Social History of Modern Belgium
Maarten Van Ginderachter. Stanford, CA: Stanford University Press, 2019. $30.00. 265 pp.

Nationalism is hard work. Elites can dream up songs and symbols. They can celebrate special dates. They can teach history, language and values in schools. They can even use the institutions of the state to invoke fear, purpose, solidarity and admiration. But none of that will prevent ordinary citizens from embracing identities based on their own lived experience. When they do embrace 'imagined communities', there is no telling whose imagination they will find most compelling.

Maarten Van Ginderachter's brilliant social history of Belgium illustrates the challenge. Admittedly, the Belgian state never made huge efforts at nation-building. The country was rich, industrialised and urbanised in the nineteenth century, particularly in relation to other parts of continental Europe. But the state was anaemic, the army was underfunded and inequitable, the monarchy was unloved, schools were ineffective, and the working class was underpaid and largely illiterate. This juxtaposition of features is unusual. Modernist theorists of nationalism have argued that developing the nation as an 'imagined community' is necessary to support the complex division of labour that an industrialised capitalist economy represents. Apparently, Belgium's liberal and Catholic elites disagreed. Instead, they sought to keep the state out of industry and the workers in the pews.

The liberals and Catholics were uneasy bedfellows for a host of reasons, including control over education. But that is not Van Ginderachter's main concern. Rather, his aim is to underscore the role that the socialist Belgian Workers' Party played in the acceptance of Belgian statehood, and in the fostering of separatist Walloon and Flemish linguistic and geographic identities. That point is significant because nineteenth-century socialist parties rejected both the state and the nation, and the Workers' Party was no different. Hence, it is surprising that Belgian patriotism and linguistic competition emerged alongside – and to a large extent from – the evolution of Belgian socialism.

The story is complicated, because Belgium is divided by ideology, language and geography, in addition to class. All three divisions were important for Belgian elites, for whom being liberal, Catholic or socialist was a matter of personal commitment; speaking French was either a symbol of status or an imposition; and geographic location provided the human and physical resources that could be used to create wealth and power. For members of the working class, however, those divisions lacked the same salience, because they were taken for granted. In ideological terms, few if any workers were liberal; Catholicism and socialism were important, but only in an abstract sense, because the communities rarely mixed. Similarly, language and geography are a package, and so can be taken for granted; if anything, poor Flemish workers aspired to learn French so that they could move to seek jobs in Walloon factories.

The expansion of suffrage and the gradual shift from single-member districts through plural voting to proportional elections at the end of the nineteenth century and the start of the twentieth upset the balance of power among elites. The Belgian Workers' Party was particularly frustrated. Voting expansion was the party's long-term objective. It purchased those reforms by becoming loyal to the state, and hence encouraging Belgian workers to become more patriotic (or at least not to push back against expressions of patriotism). And yet this resulted in many rural workers voting Catholic, particularly in Flanders. As the socialists criticised Flemish workers for failing to support the movement, they inadvertently reinforced the elite competition between language groups and geographic communities – both over political identity and in relation to the state. The result does not point directly to the sharp divisions over identity politics we see in Belgium today; the experience of two world wars was also important. But Van Ginderachter makes a powerful case that 'identification is a context-dependent process' (p. 161) for most people, a process that is hard for political elites to control.

Partnering with Extremists: Coalitions Between Mainstream and Far-right Parties in Western Europe
Kimberly A. Twist. Ann Arbor, MI: University of Michigan Press, 2020. $75.00. 226 pp.

European governments have a long history with right-wing extremism. They also have a history of promoting multiculturalism. This explains much of the mainstream aversion to right-wing political movements that take a strong stand against immigration and in defence of the nation. That aversion is less powerful than analysts may think, however. When faced with the choice between getting into power and staying outside, mainstream centre-right parties are often willing to 'partner with extremists'.

Kimberly Twist has a very clear and compelling explanation for this pattern. Centre-right politicians see the chance to enter government as the only way to accomplish their policy agendas. Mainstream politicians realise that far-right political movements tend to be flexible on issues unconnected with immigration. If tightening the rules on migrants is the price to be paid for tackling other political priorities, then even an unpleasant partnership is worth the effort.

Twist supports her analysis through a broad overview of the scholarly literature on coalition formation and a tighter focus on the recent experience of Austria and the Netherlands. These countries are interesting because they reveal moments when the centre-right was willing to embrace a coalition of extremes, and moments when they looked for other options. Twist also explores how the mainstream parties try to co-opt immigration as an issue for campaigning and – by widening her analysis to include France and the United Kingdom – how much the choice between proportional elections and first-past-the-post contests can influence their behaviour, and that of their supporters.

Twist concludes that the choice to partner with the extremes is much like any other coalition bargain – it is hardly unique to the centre-right. The centre-left faced similar dilemmas in dealing with the communists, and for similar reasons. This is not to deny that the far right has an important place in European history; rather, it is to suggest that any decision about working with right-wing, anti-immigrant parties today is unlikely to be overly influenced by that legacy.

Twist's argument is compelling, but it also raises questions about what is captured by the left–right spectrum, whether the choice politicians face is positive or negative, and what might disqualify a political party as a potential coalition partner. The left–right issue is central to Twist's argument. The literature on right-wing parties is enormous; to position herself, the author has to offer a precise definition of the term. She chooses to define 'far right' as a party that privileges defence of the nation and national integration (p. 5). That definition implies that the left–right spectrum ranges from cosmopolitanism to nationalism.

Hers is a clear choice, but that may not be how politicians see it. Instead, they may see left and right through the more traditional lens of labour and capital. If so, they are likely to care more about ideological proximity than policy issues (p. 32). In doing so, they might make a negative choice and refuse to join forces with a party from the other side of the labour–capital spectrum, even if this means giving ground on an issue such as immigration. They might even make that choice when the only available coalition partner is obviously incompetent, which is what may have happened in the Netherlands in 2002.

Then again, there may be some disqualifying consideration that prevents political parties from working together. Personal animosity is one possibility, as between two far-right Austrian parties after 2002 (p. 79). The weight of past experience may also be relevant. If the Netherlands' Christian Democrats were reluctant to partner with the Labour Party in early 2002, that is probably because they had been ousted from power by a previous coalition. Past experience of grand coalition also weighed on the Austrian People's Party in 2000, only the memory was fresher. Coalition choices are rarely a straightforward matter.

The Truth Society: Science, Disinformation, and Politics in Berlusconi's Italy
Noelle Molé Liston. Ithaca, NY: Cornell University Press, 2020.
$25.95. 240 pp.

The truth about most subjects is not something that we find out ourselves through personal experience. Rather, it is delivered to us as more or less passive recipients. The messenger may be deemed trustworthy because of institutional affiliations, personal characteristics or both. When the message fits nicely with other truths that we have received, or expectations that we have, the delivery is easier. When we hear what we expect (or want) to hear from voices that we trust, the 'truth' becomes almost self-evident.

This notion of truth lies at the heart of Noelle Molé Liston's inquiry into recent developments in Italian politics and society. The story she tells might have been about any country, but Liston chose Italy because the people there seem to have lost faith in the truth as an objective notion that can be grounded in empirical reality. They embrace superstition, promote conspiracy theories and – literally – put scientists on trial. The courts even prosecuted a group of seismologists for manslaughter because they failed to predict an earthquake.

Liston does not have a causal explanation for this state of affairs, but she theorises that it has something to do with the overlap between politics, technology and media. Her theory starts with Silvio Berlusconi, the media mogul who emerged as a populist in the early 1990s and then went on to dominate Italian politics for the next three decades. Her argument is that Berlusconi used the media so aggressively and so cynically to promote himself that he broke the bonds that connect television to truth. In that vacuum, satire emerged as the most popular form of entertainment. This helped to restore the truth to public conversation, but it also underscored the reason for cynicism.

Beppe Grillo's Five Star Movement emerged as a response to this media environment. Grillo rejected television, not least because television disowned him. In its place, Grillo promoted new digital forms of communication. This offered the promise of truth, but in different packaging and without institutional manipulation. The problem, as Liston points out, is that the digital universe is also manipulative. More important, the algorithms that shape the message are an essential feature and not a bug: the programmers design them to meet expectations by conforming to whatever prior truth we have accessed or received. Worse, the algorithms can shape the messenger as well as the message. Liston points to suspicions that Five Star Movement leader Luigi Di Maio is the first 'algorithmic' populist, perfectly chosen to represent those features that people disenchanted with traditional elites want to see in their elected representatives.

Such deep manipulation of the truth has profound consequences. When we cannot trust the messenger, the medium, the message or our own expectations, then nothing connects us to reality apart from lived experience. Liston follows a group around Italy that convinces people to spill salt to prove that doing so will not cause something bad to happen; this is the group's strategy for debunking superstition and restoring confidence in science. Setting up a stand in a crowded square to convince random people to spill salt is also a perfect metaphor for their desperation.

Liston's musings are brilliantly provocative. It is impossible to read this book without making comparisons. Italy may be an extreme case, but no place is immune to cynicism. The book's main flaw is that someone has done a poor job fact-checking it. Matteo Salvini is leader of the Lega, not the Five Star Movement (p. 87); 'Walter Bersani' is not a politician (p. 77); and Enrico Letta was not 'elected prime minister' (p. 20). These mistakes are irrelevant to Liston's argument, but they undermine her credibility. Then again, perhaps someone is trying to send us a message.

Bowling for Communism: Urban Ingenuity at the End of East Germany
Andrew Demshuk. Ithaca, NY: Cornell University Press, 2020.
$39.95. 272 pp.

Most analyses of the end of the Cold War, and of what happened in its aftermath, focus on revolutionaries and reactionaries. But most people who experienced those events fell somewhere in between. They were not happy with communism but had few illusions they could reform it, and did not expect to overthrow it either. Instead, they sought to make the best of a bad situation. They learned to work around the system when they could not work within it. They faced powerful opposition and ran important risks. They also managed to make their world a better place. Their contributions might not have been dramatic, but they remain historically significant.

Indeed, the efforts made by individuals from across communist societies – party functionaries, skilled professionals, ordinary citizens – not only had a positive impact on daily life, but also laid the foundations for what came after. If you look closely enough, you can see evidence of such efforts across East Germany. Perhaps the most striking evidence can be found in the urban landscape. Andrew Demshuk uses Leipzig to illustrate the 'urban ingenuity' of local officials and residents during the Cold War era. Their adversary was Berlin as much as it was communist central planning. And if Leipzig was somehow 'saved' after communism, it was thanks in large measure to their plans and ambitions.

Demshuk's argument is a powerful reminder that politics is only a small part of the wider context that shapes how people live. Buildings, neighbourhoods, recreational facilities, churches and monuments are more immediate; they are also more important. Such structures separate the private from the public, shape how people interact and provide the symbols for local identification. The communist authorities clearly understood this relationship between identity and urban planning. That is why they focused so much attention on reshaping the urban landscape; it is also why they placed so much emphasis on creating standard, affordable housing.

What those authorities failed to understand is that communities thrive on difference. Communities also take pride in aesthetics. The more communist authorities replaced historic buildings with prefabricated or standardised apartment blocks, the more they took away from everyday lived experience. Demshuk marvels that so many analyses of the fall of communism make the same mistake. They place too much emphasis on citizens' frustration with politics and not enough on their desperation over the destruction of urban spaces.

Demshuk's argument is revealing insofar as he demonstrates how much effort people invested in improving local conditions. They rebuilt churches, restored houses and even created shared recreational facilities like the bowling alley in the book's title. Moreover, they did this with support from local bureaucrats who focused on resources, not politics. The people donated their time; the bureaucrats found the money and materials.

It was not enough. The people of Leipzig could improve things on the margins, but the damage was too widespread. Images of the city's decay became a metaphor for life under communism. People across the country could identify with the plight of that city and the helplessness of its residents. In turn, the country's leadership quickly realised how this identification could fuel popular protest.

When communism fell and capitalism replaced it, it was not immediately obvious how this might affect the urban environment. Some investors came with plans to restore urban monuments; others came to raze them to profit from the value of the location. The 'market' was not indifferent to these motives – but it certainly did not channel rewards based on good intentions, and neither did it encourage coherence. Escaping from communism created a different context in which the people of Leipzig sought to improve their daily lives. It also gave them a new set of challenges.

Culture and Society
Jeffrey Mazo

Doom: The Politics of Catastrophe
Niall Ferguson. London: Allen Lane, 2021. £25.00. 496 pp.

Failures of State: The Inside Story of Britain's Battle with Coronavirus
Jonathan Calvert and George Arbuthnott. London: Mudlark, 2021. £20.00. 432 pp.

COVID-19: The Great Reset
Klaus Schwab and Thierry Malleret. Geneva: Forum Publishing, 2020. $19.99. 282 pp.

By the beginning of May 2021, a year and a half after the first case of COVID-19 probably appeared in China, there had been nearly 150 million total cases and more than three million deaths worldwide. Nor is there an end in sight; some countries responded quickly and are doing relatively well, others dithered and are only now beginning to get things under control, and still others are facing the worst as a second or third wave strikes. With things in flux, it might be thought too soon to write even the first draft of history, yet dozens of books on the causes, cures and consequences of the pandemic have already appeared, some within a few months of the outbreak. Three such books – *Doom*, *Failures of State* and *The Great Reset* – stand out from the crowd by virtue of their detailed research, analytical depth or scope. *Doom*, published in April, covers up to late January 2021. *The Great Reset*, putting the pandemic in its historical context, appeared in May 2021 but was essentially finished in September–October 2020, before the second wave. *Failures of State* was published in April, and traces the course of the pandemic response in the United Kingdom up to late January 2021. *The Great Reset* was finished in June 2020 and came out in July, but is less about COVID per se than about 'future histories' in the pandemic's aftermath. Even if, as seems likely (and in some respects has already occurred), these various assessments will be overtaken by events, each of the three will be in its own way of enduring value for the policymakers and historians of the post-COVID world.

In *Doom: The Politics of Catastrophe*, conservative British historian Niall Ferguson acknowledges that it is impossible 'to write the history of a disaster that is not yet over' (p. 285). His book is not, however, a history of COVID, but, as he says at the outset, 'a general history of catastrophe … from the geological to the geopolitical, from the biological to the technological'. Key concepts include the classification of disasters into 'black swans' (completely unexpected), 'grey rhinos' (inevitable but uncertain) and 'dragon kings' (so extreme they stand outside the expected distribution, and are associated with tipping points or phase transitions); and the importance of network theory to understanding how disaster turns to contagion, both literally and metaphorically. 'If there ever was a grey rhino', Ferguson writes, 'COVID-19 was it' (p. 245).

The broad synthesis of history, economics, political science and network theory that makes up the bulk of *Doom* is on a par with Ferguson's previous influential work on empires, financial history and social networks. The final three chapters on the current pandemic, however, are the weakest part of the book; Ferguson lets his conservative world view colour his interpretations. He blames the unchecked spread of the virus on a systemic failure of government (in particular, in Latin America, the UK and the United States). This was not, he argues, the fault of populist leaders, but a failure of the administrative state. In arguing that individual leaders such as US president Donald Trump, UK Prime Minister Boris Johnson and Brazilian President Jair Bolsonaro do not bear primary responsibility, he overcorrects. If civil servants and department and agency heads bear much of the blame, as he argues, they were acting under or appointed by leaders who did not just abdicate leadership, but were ideologically opposed to and took active measures to undermine the administrative state itself. The leaders and the led were operating at cross purposes. He argues that lockdowns were, in retrospect, an overly indiscriminate response (p. 330), yet also (and more correctly) concludes that the way they were lifted was 'dumb'. His claim that lockdowns were superfluous has not stood the test of time. Elsewhere, he disingenuously accuses the *Washington Post* of publishing and having to correct fake news about Trump's cuts to pandemic prevention (p. 315), yet his citations show that the paper was correcting someone else's misconstruction of a pre-pandemic article about planned, not completed cuts. Similar perhaps minor but unnecessary and contentious errors scattered throughout distract from the larger number of valid insights.

In *Failures of State: The Inside Story of Britain's Battle with Coronavirus*, an in-depth chronological look by two *Sunday Times* investigative journalists, Jonathan Calvert and George Arbuthnott, at Britain's response to COVID-19 offers a case study of failed leadership and ideological blindness. On paper, the UK was once one of the best-prepared countries in the world for a disease outbreak such as COVID. It had a detailed pandemic plan in place, but years of austerity after the global financial crisis had led to the depletion of equipment stockpiles and training. The authors detail how the distraction of Brexit, Johnson's libertarian impulses and a large dollop of complacency led to this decline before the outbreak, and then to inconsistent policies and belated implementation as the crisis loomed. There is little that will be new to UK readers who lived the events – in fact, much of the book is based on the authors' newspaper articles over the course of the pandemic – but bringing it all together in one place makes their case starkly clear. Calvert and Arbuthnott pull no punches, placing the blame for Britain's relative failure to cope with the crisis firmly at the foot of the prime minister. If even half of what they describe is correct (and there is no reason to doubt it), it is a damning indictment.

Much of the key detail for the critical weeks between 24 January 2020 (when the UK's cross-government emergency committee COBRA first met to discuss the virus) and the imposition of lockdown on 23 March comes, to be sure, from a single unnamed Downing Street adviser, whose reliability and motives the reader has no way to assess. Yet the picture painted by this source is consistent with and sometimes corroborated by documents, and by named individuals in a position to know. A stronger critique is that *Failures of State* has a lingering air of what Americans would call 'Monday morning quarterbacking', or 20/20 hindsight. A case could be made that, at least until March, Johnson and his government were doing the best they could with limited information. Indeed, in January 2021 the prime minister accused critics of his pandemic policies of viewing them through a 'retrospectoscope'. Yet the fact remains that from the start the policies were wrong, belated and inconsistent, whether the failure was ideological, intellectual or personality based, and that even if it could be for-given in retrospect the first time, Johnson repeated his mistakes not once but twice. This inability to learn from errors extended to the failures (and successes) of other countries hit by the pandemic.

Besides the condemnation of the UK's pandemic response in real time, the key insight of *Failures of State* is that the choice between protecting lives and protecting jobs and the economy – the root of the government's belated action and premature relaxation – is a false one. It is impossible to protect or reopen the economy without first bringing the virus under control, since widespread contagion itself damages the economy as workers and consumers fall ill or take matters into their own hands through self-imposed lockdowns. In fact, as the authors point out, Johnson's decision to impose lockdown on 23 March was the act of a follower rather than a leader. This insight should have been obvious from the start, as it was to governments that coped better (particularly in Asia), as well as to advocates of lockdown in Europe, the UK and the US. Yet even an economic historian like Ferguson was still arguing in autumn 2020 that keeping the economy open (while isolating older and more vulnerable people, and enforcing social distancing and mask-wearing) would have been 'a more rational strategy' (p. 342). On the other hand, Klaus Schwab (founder and executive chair of the World Economic Forum) and Thierry Malleret (senior director of the forum's Global Risk Network) conclude in *COVID-19: The Great Reset* that 'the myth of having to choose between public health and a hit to GDP growth can easily be debunked' (p. 42).

Whereas Ferguson only touches lightly on the broader future consequences of the pandemic in *Doom*, making sweeping geopolitical claims premised on his conservative world view and a particular view of US–China rivalry, Schwab and Malleret explore historical precedent but focus on the future. They argue, without using the term, that the COVID pandemic is truly a 'dragon king'. The best historical model is not the 1918 flu pandemic or the Great Depression, but rather the Second World War, 'the quintessential transformational war, triggering not only fundamental changes to the global order and the global economy, but also entailing radical shifts in social attitudes and beliefs that eventually paved the way for radically new policies and social contract provisions' (p. 15). COVID, they argue, will be similarly transformational one way or the other, and we should do what we can to ensure that the change will be as positive as it can be.

Although Schwab and Malleret agree with Ferguson that the pandemic is not a 'black swan' event, they argue that it will 'provoke many black-swan events through second-, third-, fourth- and more-order effects' (p. 34). Since today's world is an interconnected and complex set of subsystems, predicting these effects is nigh impossible, and is even harder if specialists stay in their silos, as they are wont to do. This is why, the authors say, 'addressing complex trade-offs, such as containing the progression of the pandemic versus reopening the economy, is so fiendishly difficult' (p. 26). Their goal instead is to conjecture about 'what the post-pandemic world might, and perhaps should, look like' (p. 19).

This they do by looking at the problem across scales from the 'macro' to the personal. At the macro level, they explore, discuss and synthesise areas such as growth and employment, fiscal and monetary policy, inequality, social unrest, big government vs market-based solutions, the social contract, globalisation and nationalism, global governance, US–China rivalry, fragile and failing states, the environment and climate change, and the digital revolution. This is an ambitious and necessarily abstract undertaking, but is closely argued and supported by examples. On the US–China relationship, for example, they are much more nuanced than Ferguson on the nature and even existence of a new cold war, the underlying causes of the rivalry and the potential or possible outcomes.

At the micro level, Schwab and Malleret discuss how these macro trends may affect particular industries and sectors, the nature of business organisations, supply chains and resilience, stakeholder capitalism and environmental, social and governance (ESG) considerations, among other topics. At the individual level, they explore social relations, moral choices, mental health and well-being, work–life balance and conspicuous consumption. All three levels are intertwined, as are the trends and tensions at each level. They conclude that many of the trends suggest that the new world will be less open and cooperative, but there is an opportunity to replace 'failed ideas, institutions, processes and rules with new ones better suited to current and future needs' (p. 248). This is the 'Great Reset'.

One unfortunate derivative effect of the pandemic is, ironically, *The Great Reset* itself. The 'Great Reset' was the theme of the World Economic Forum's 50th anniversary meeting in June 2020, and will be the theme of the 2021 Davos meeting. From the start, conspiracy-theory movements such as QAnon latched on to the term, as they had the United Nations' Agenda 21 before it, as a nefarious agenda of global elites, this time tied up with COVID-19 denialism and vaccine conspiracy theories. A glance at the Amazon page for the book, for example, shows an unusual and perhaps unique pattern in its reviews: about 50% are five-star reviews, but 25% are one-stars. Reading the latter is a case study in delusional thinking. As Naomi Klein (herself a vocal critic of the World Economic Forum) put it, the Great Reset 'has turned into a viral conspiracy theory purporting to expose something no one ever attempted to hide, most of which is not really happening anyway, some of which actually should'.

In 1963, Bob Dylan called on writers and critics to document and project a very different cultural shift: 'keep your eyes wide; the chance won't come again'. The authors of *Doom*, *Failures of State* and *The Great Reset* have all taken the chance, ignoring Dylan's further advice ('don't speak too soon / for the wheel's still in spin'). If, as seems likely, our times are truly a-changin', these three books read together represent a good first draft of the history, present and future of this transformation.

The Uncounted
Alex Cobham. Cambridge: Polity Press, 2020. £14.99. 200 pp.

Sound public policy – whether dealing with a pandemic, promoting economic development or devising an equitable tax system – relies on data. Yet raw numbers and statistics can be misleading or incomplete due to obstacles, accidents or political interference in how they are gathered and processed. In *The Uncounted*, economist and tax-policy expert Alex Cobham argues that the representative, distributive and compulsive features of states – 'who decides', 'what people get' and 'what people are required to do' – all rely ultimately on counting people. How this counting is done may appear to be a technical issue, but is in fact 'powerfully political' (p. 2) and creates a systematic bias towards needlessly high inequality.

Cobham uses the term 'uncounted' to describe 'a politically motivated failure to count'. There are two sides to this coin. Marginalised groups, such as ethnic minorities, women and the poor, are further marginalised if they are not sufficiently represented in the data that informs policy priorities. At the other end of the spectrum, those with power can be further empowered if, for example, they can keep wealth and income from being accurately counted. These are, as Cobham puts it, 'the Unpeople Hidden at the Bottom' (Part I) and 'the Unmoney Hiding at the Top' (Part II). Both are, by definition, impossible to quantify exactly, but the uncounted at the bottom comprise at least 5% of the global population, and perhaps run into the billions. There are many fewer at the top, but Cobham estimates revenue loss from uncounted assets to be £500–800 billion worldwide, or about 2–4% of total government revenue.

People can be uncounted because they are disproportionately difficult to reach, because they avoid being counted out of concerns over government attention or because they have been deliberately overlooked. This can have enormous repercussions for political power and the allocation of economic resources, in rich as well as less rich countries. Problems also arise not just because people go uncounted, but because of the ways the numbers we do have are used. The common metrics of gross domestic product or the Gini coefficient of inequality are, for example, deeply flawed. Cobham shows that even though the UN's Sustainable Development Goals (2015–30) represent moves away from such flawed metrics, they can still create perverse incentives for data collection and analysis.

This includes not just those goals intended to directly improve the lot of the poor, but also those that do so indirectly through an equitable tax system (Sustainable Development Goal 17) and through reducing illicit financial flows stemming from corruption, money laundering and tax evasion (Goal 16, especially 16.4). It is this aspect Cobham focuses on in Part III, 'The Uncounted Manifesto'. His solution to the uncounted at the bottom is institutional: a UN commission on data quality, collection and interpretation, with parallel national and local-government or civil-society bodies. His solution for the uncounted at the top includes a similar UN institution, but also a financial-transparency convention, a global asset registry and a radical reform of international taxation. This focus reflects Cobham's background and expertise in tax policy. Yet the uncounted at the top matter mainly because they affect our ability to leave none of those at the bottom behind. The key message of *The Uncounted* is that those who aren't counted don't count, and who does the counting matters. At the very least, if we can't count accurately, how we count should be laid bare for all to see.

Deepfakes: The Coming Infocalypse
Nina Schick. New York: Twelve, 2020. $22.00. 224 pp.

In Robert Heinlein's classic 1966 novel *The Moon Is a Harsh Mistress*, the leader of a successful lunar rebellion never appears in person, only on live video. This is because he is actually an artificial intelligence (AI) which has to create a fake but realistic on-screen image to communicate to the public. In 2021, while lunar colonies and true AI are still science fiction, synthetic people on video are fast becoming reality. Nina Schick's *Deepfakes* assesses the state of the art, the threat it poses in the context of the information ecosystem and how it can be addressed.

The term 'deepfake' (from 'deep learning' and 'fake') was coined in 2017 to denote the use of recently developed AI technology to create synthetic audio and visual media; in her book, Schick adds the qualification that this must be done maliciously or with the intent to deceive. Synthetic audio and still photography are already indistinguishable from the real thing; video is less convincing, but Schick argues conservatively that perfection is only five to seven years away. Misinformation and disinformation, including synthetic people such as 'The Man Who Never Was' created by British intelligence as part of a deception operation in the Second World War, are not new, but the emerging technology, Schick suggests, will make them easier to produce by orders of magnitude. As a distinct and particularly persuasive form of fake news, deepfakes can use and extend well-established fake-news avenues to create a 'fucked-up dystopia', in the words of a deepfaked Barack Obama (bit.ly/3dI51u0) created as a public warning about the threat. There are also second-order effects of deepfakes, where the simple existence of the technology gives a boost to conspiracy theories that real media are in fact synthetic.

Only a small part of *Deepfakes* is devoted to the technology itself; the rest is context. Schick covers well-trodden ground on, for example, Russian disinformation campaigns, fake news in political campaigns in the West and elsewhere, financial scams and COVID-19 conspiracy theories. Ironically for a book that is essentially about whether we can believe what we see, in the case of Russian efforts to meddle in the 2016 US presidential election, she relies entirely on US government reports; the interested reader would be better served going straight to the horse's mouth. On the other hand, her four predictions about the role of a corrupted information ecosystem in the 2020 election (the book was published in August 2020) appear to have been spot on.

Schick's solutions for, or at least defences against, the 'infocalypse' include a more widespread and constant recognition of the problem institutionally, culturally and individually; assured availability of identifiably accurate information and vetting of online information; and actively fighting back. She adduces the example of Estonia, which over the last decade and a half has used the first two solutions to develop multilayer defences against concerted disinformation campaigns.

Even if Schick has exaggerated the threat of deepfakes and the infocalypse, the implications of the new technology are still chilling. *Deepfakes* is a fascinating, compelling and ultimately disturbing exploration of a future information environment in which bad information and faked media will exceed the ability of individuals or society to cope.

Latin America
Russell Crandall and Britta Crandall

State of War: MS-13 and El Salvador's World of Violence
William Wheeler. New York: Columbia Global Reports, 2020.
$15.99. 167 pp.

The origin story of the infamous Mara Salvatrucha (MS-13) street gang has many twists and turns, as well as inconsistencies. As security analyst William Wheeler writes in this concise, unsettling book, MS-13 came into the world in the early 1980s, just as the Salvadoran civil war was raging and hundreds of thousands of the country's citizens were fleeing north, particularly to Washington DC and Los Angeles, among other North American destinations. The 'ecology' of Los Angeles's 'fierce gang warfare' was to exert a powerful influence on these war-rattled Salvadorans, who, in barrios such as MacArthur Park, started their own American-style gangs, much like their Chicano (US-born Latinos) and African-American predecessors had done (p. 28).

This might have remained a 'Made in the USA' phenomenon had Bill Clinton's White House, in response to domestic unease about illegal immigration from south of the border, not started deporting foreigners with criminal records. That fateful move ensured that members of MS-13 and its arch-rival Barrio 18, both *sui generis* LA gangs, were also deported, along with their iconography, their clandestine networks and, most infamously, their barbaric practices, such as collecting bribes, hazing inductees and murdering traitors. As Wheeler puts it: 'In the Hobbesian landscape of a region [the so-called 'Northern Triangle' comprising Honduras, El Salvador and Guatemala] reeling from endemic poverty, wars, and political violence, the struggle for survival and dominance of these Americanized gangsters produced a sociological phenomenon' (p. 25). Today, in El Salvador, upwards of 60,000 residents are involved in MS-13, with an estimated ten times as many people involved in some sort of informal collaboration with it, out of a total population of only six million.

Wheeler wants his readers to see that the rise of MS-13 is indisputably a legacy of El Salvador's civil war and the 'underlying inequality that had precipitated it but was nonetheless never resolved by its outcome' (p. 26). The author believes that the United States made matters worse by backing the country's 'right-wing government' against a motley assortment of incipient Marxist guerrilla groups in the late 1970s (p. 30). Yet, contrary to the author's premise, the historical record shows that successive US administrations also backed democratically elected governments, including that of Christian Democrat José

 https://doi.org/10.1080/00396338.2021.1930419

Napoleón Duarte. This certainly does not absolve the US for its role in creating the problem, but it does complicate the tale.

State of War features a host of interviews that provide invaluable insights into the evolution and instincts of a fearsome criminal enterprise. The author finishes the book by speculating on how MS-13, its rivals and its variants – in the US, the Northern Triangle and elsewhere – might evolve. Seeing as how MS-13 is now known to be receiving the cooperation of police forces in Honduras, this path will continue to alarm us.

**No Option but North: The Migrant World and the Perilous
Path Across the Border**
Kelsey Freeman. New York: Ig Publishing, 2020. $17.95. 280 pp.

'When Mexico sends its people, they're not sending their best … They're bringing drugs. They're bringing crime. They're rapists.' Real-estate tycoon Donald Trump uttered these inflammatory words in June 2015, when he announced his candidacy for the Republican nomination for the presidency. If he had ever expressed an interest in gaining a more accurate and nuanced understanding of undocumented immigration across the US–Mexico border, idealistic author Kelsey Freeman might have recommended that he spend a year in a Mexican migrant shelter listening to harrowing stories of rape, robbery and even death told by individuals and families making their way to *el norte*.

Freeman could credibly make such a suggestion because this is exactly what she did after graduating from college. Having received a prestigious Fulbright scholarship, she headed to the industrial centre of Celaya, in Mexico's Guanajuato state, to teach English for a year. That posting in itself would have afforded a lifetime's worth of adventures for most recently minted American undergraduates, but Freeman ended up engaging in much more than language instruction. Within a couple of weeks of arriving in Celaya, the compassionate young *gabacha* (as Mexicans call *gringas*, or female foreigners) started talking with migrants at a local half-way house, aptly named *El Refugio*. Freeman then spent close to a year conducting interviews, although very deliberately not accompanying the migrants on the rest of their journeys, as an embedded reporter might do. The author quickly came to understand that just about all of her interviewees were caught up in a migration web comprising drug cartels, both corrupt and honest police, coyotes (traffickers), and even the security staff of private train and bus companies. 'What I found in these migrant stories', she writes, 'was far beyond anything I could have possibly anticipated, a dark world deep beneath the surface of life in Mexico filled with kidnapping, and assault, cartels and police, rape and unbelievable brutality' (p. 13).

El Refugio housed a large but variable share of the migrants leaving behind the gang warfare and climate-change woes of the Northern Triangle. Seemingly everyone had an awful story: 'Abraham had been kidnapped by the infamous Zetas [Mexican cartel], beaten, and barely escaped. Jacqui, an eight-months pregnant woman traveling with her two toddlers, risked everything whenever she hauled her kids atop the freight train' (p. 14). These migrants were only about half-way to the US–Mexico border.

Freeman laments that stereotypes about brown immigrants pouring over America's borders – the very imagery Trump demagogued in his speech – 'are breeding a hatred that stomps out the humanity' of the kind of people she met in Mexico (p. 252). 'If we can change the racist narrative aimed at those who cross the southern border,' she writes, 'the web of policies that dehumanizes migrants can also shift' (p. 15). One might be tempted to ask whether, leaving Trump-style nativism aside, it is possible to support the deportation of undocumented immigrants without being racist. President Barack Obama comes to mind, whom critics called the 'Deporter-in-Chief' for the number of unauthorised immigrants repatriated during his two-term presidency. Obama might have responded that as president of the United States, he had a duty to enforce the law. Regardless of where one stands on the issue, it is difficult to read Freeman's book without being dismayed by the suffering of *El Refugio*'s residents.

Fair Trade Rebels: Coffee Production and Struggles for Autonomy in Chiapas
Lindsay Naylor. Minneapolis, MN: University of Minnesota Press, 2019. $27.00. 280 pp.

On 1 January 1994 the North American Free Trade Agreement (NAFTA) came into effect – and ski-mask-wearing, rifle-toting, media-savvy Zapatista insurgents in Mexico's poverty-stricken Chiapas state launched their anti-neoliberal, pro-indigenous rebellion. Reams of books and studies have subsequently examined the who, what and why of the once-vaunted Zapatista movement, particularly its mysterious leader, Subcomandante Marcos, who reached celebrity status in Mexico and throughout the world.

In this ethnography, US-based geographer Lindsay Naylor focuses on the underlying issues that drove the movement, deliberately choosing to research not the Zapatistas themselves, but rather the experiences of small coffee farmers in self-proclaimed autonomous zones. Naylor exposes and unpacks a fascinating paradox: even as these 'Chiapaneco' coffee-growing rebels protested the system, many simultaneously engaged with it through the fair-trade coffee business. Fair trade is certainly better than unfair trade, but Naylor is understandably unconvinced that the fair-trade seal of approval – no matter how much it allays the guilt of millions of java imbibers across the developed world – is sufficient to address the myriad social, economic and political injustices in Chiapas. In the end, Naylor concludes, the rebels wanted only dignity and autonomy, even though their involvement in the coffee trade meant they were participants in a global corporate agricultural chain. As is so often the case with this sort of intensive, well-crafted study, Naylor tells a story that is far more nuanced than we might have assumed – like a *café con leche*, it is a blend of black and white.

US Hegemony and the Americas: Power and Economic
Statecraft in International Relations
Arturo Santa-Cruz. Abingdon: Routledge, 2019. £39.99.
237 pp.

Arturo Santa-Cruz, a Cornell-trained scholar of international relations and political economy at Mexico's University of Guadalajara, is the author of a pro-digious number of books and articles on North America. In *US Hegemony and the Americas*, an impressive and original work, Santa-Cruz sets out to chronicle the ebb and flow of Uncle Sam's hegemony in the western hemisphere by examin-ing Washington's economic statecraft, from the 1970s to the present. The author characterises Latin America as a subordinate power, arguing that Washington established hegemony over Latin America via its economic policy, a conclusion that could also apply to other developing regions of the world. His analysis focuses on the years 1971–89 and 1990–2000, the hiccups and heartache of which he scrutinises in detail, including Latin America's so-called 'lost decade' in the 1980s and the controversial yet ultimately successful IMF- and US Treasury-led debt-relief plan.

Santa-Cruz's analysis is bolstered by a discussion of Canada's economic ties with the US, the details of which reveal that Ottawa did not always have as 'special' a relationship with Washington as both sides liked to proclaim. The author also explains at length what he means by key terms including 'hegem-ony', 'power' and 'authority' in regional orders, and how they apply to the western hemisphere. For students and even scholars of international relations, *US Hegemony and the Americas* will be an excellent refresher course.

Marijuana Boom: The Rise and Fall of Colombia's First Drug Paradise
Lina Britto. Oakland, CA: University of California Press, 2020.
$29.95. 352 pp.

Colombia is known for coffee, cocaine, FARC guerrillas and, more recently, a massive influx of Venezuelan refugees. Often overlooked but no less historically significant was the explosion of the marijuana industry in the 1970s, which occupied a liminal period between the banana and cotton cultivation of the mid-twentieth century and the rise of the cartels. Lina Britto seeks to raise awareness of this forgotten chapter of Colombian history in *Marijuana Boom: The Rise and Fall of Colombia's First Drug Paradise*. Based on extensive research and numerous oral histories, *Marijuana Boom* centres on Colombia's vast Greater Magdalena region. It traces the emergence of cannabis cultivation, its brief golden age, and its rapid decline at the hands of counter-narcotics programmes, tensions among industry players and the cocaine industry.

The stage was set for marijuana cultivation in Colombia by the banana boom of the 1920s, when the United Fruit Company moved into the district, built infrastructure and contracted local planters. In the following decade, commodity production in the area shifted somewhat to leather as the area's growing German community and *criollo* smugglers began to supply hides and tanning materials to Nazi Germany. But the same infrastructure that had been used for banana cultivation could be repurposed for another, far more odoriferous crop: cannabis.

At its peak in the 1970s, Colombia supplied a staggering 70% of the United States' marijuana, making it the largest marijuana exporter in the world. The resulting influx of foreign exchange gave a massive boost to the local economy and helped to influence the development of Colombian culture. In one particularly entertaining chapter, Britto describes the ways in which folk music and parties called *parrandas* helped the *marimberos* (drug traffickers) to define their identity as representatives of an industry that was 'socially legitimate yet illegal' (p. 117). The music and ostentatious parties reinvented and mythologised *marimbero* culture while serving as an outlet to release tension between the traffickers. The marijuana trade was to come crashing down around 1978, however, as the US and Colombian governments began an aggressive interdiction campaign. With national and international forces working against the *marimberos*, a culture of cooperation gave way to one of desperation and violence.

As drug use entered the cultural mainstream in the US, the idea that the 'war on drugs' should be taken to the source gained credence in policy circles. Thus, as *Marijuana Boom* points out, a domestic problem (the failure to curtail

Americans' drug use) became a foreign-policy issue. Richard Nixon created the Drug Enforcement Administration in 1973, which promptly set up a large operation in Colombia. This renewed emphasis on combatting marijuana traffickers helped to militarise the campaign, which Bogotá conceptualised as a counter-insurgency operation – a type of warfare in which it had gained significant experience.

Marijuana Boom is a rich addition to the historiography of the Colombian drug trade, and Britto skilfully avoids the dangers that can arise when an argument incorporates oral histories. The passage of time can produce distortions, which is why archival research tends to dominate in the academic world. *Marijuana Boom* demonstrates the value in supplementing thorough archival research with the collection and analysis of oral histories.

With Frederick Richardson

Closing Argument

The Life and Times of Michael Elleman, 1958–2021

Mark Fitzpatrick

I

Michael S. Elleman knew missiles inside and out, forward and backward. During the trajectory of his career, he worked to make them more lethal, then, developing misgivings, to limit them. In the words of journalist David E. Hoffman – author of *The Dead Hand*, about the dangerous legacy of the Cold War arms race[1] – 'Michael Elleman was a pioneer, determined to make the world safer. He pursued that goal as an engineer, a government contractor, a UN inspector, and lastly as a think tank expert.'

Science was in Elleman's blood. At the University of California at Berkeley, he obtained bachelor's and master's degrees in physics, a field of study that was influenced by his father. Daniel D. Elleman was a renowned physicist at NASA's Jet Propulsion Laboratory, who trained to be an astronaut and whose research laid the grounds for magnetic resonance imaging technology. A friend, the legendary physicist and 1965 Nobel physics laureate Richard Feynman, taught Mike about astronomy and the lasting importance of mentoring.

Elleman's first professional mission was to improve America's ability to wreak nuclear destruction. After finishing graduate school in 1981, he

Mark Fitzpatrick is an IISS associate fellow, was executive director of IISS–Americas from 2015 through 2018, and headed the IISS Non-Proliferation and Nuclear Policy Programme for 13 years. He had a 26-year career in the US Department of State, including as deputy assistant secretary of state for non-proliferation. This article draws on the author's two previous obituaries for Elleman that appeared on the Survival Editors' Blog on 24 February 2021 and in *Arms Control Today* (April 2021).

Survival | vol. 63 no. 3 | June–July 2021 | pp. 215–220   https://doi.org/10.1080/00396338.2021.1930420

joined Lockheed Martin Research and Development Laboratories in Palo Alto, helping to develop propulsion systems for a number of ballistic missiles, including the submarine-launched *Trident* D5. Nuclear deterrence was the name of the game for the superpowers, and neither side could get enough of it. Before the end of the Cold War in 1991, the US and the Soviet Union together possessed over 60,000 nuclear weapons, many times more than needed to, as Winston Churchill put it, 'make the rubble bounce'.[2]

Elleman worked at Lockheed Martin for two decades. Along the way, he decided it would be better to control than to create these dangerous weapons. His research focus on missile propellants and detonation mechanics began to skew towards weapons-dismantlement technologies. A two-and-a-half-year stint as a science fellow at Stanford University's Center for International Security and Arms Control (CISAC)[3] fanned an interest in non-proliferation and honed the research and writing skills that would become hallmarks of his ensuing scholarship.

At Lockheed Martin, Elleman helped develop technologies to enable the US Navy to destroy solid-propellant rocket motors in a safe and environmentally sound way. Working with the NATO Science Committee, he shared these technologies with the former Soviet states in an effort to dismantle long-range missiles through the US-funded Cooperative Threat Reduction programme. Elleman's ex-Soviet hosts resisted discarding products they considered to have great value. Officials in Ukraine wanted to convert 17,000 tons of volatile and dangerous rocket fuel for some civil purpose. They wondered whether they could process it into shampoo, rust inhibitor or perhaps a chemical to help preserve fruit. According to Hoffman's interview notes for *The Dead Hand*, Elleman worked with Soviet officials to establish factories and engineering processes that could be used to eliminate weapons without hurting the environment.

II

In the late 1990s, Mike joined several visits to Iraq by the United Nations Special Commission (UNSCOM), which was disbanded in 1999 amid allegations that the United States had used it to spy on the Iraqi military. Replacing UNSCOM was the United Nations Monitoring, Verification and

Inspection Commission (UNMOVIC), charged with managing inspections of Iraq's missile infrastructure and headed by former Swedish foreign minister Hans Blix. In 2002, Mike was recruited to join UNMOVIC. Although Blix and his team were making progress in their mission to verify the elimination of Iraq's weapons of mass destruction (WMD), the United States under president George W. Bush, with support from British prime minister Tony Blair, was nevertheless determined to invade Iraq. No WMD were found in Iraq during or after the war. The experience taught Mike about policy failure and the potential of multilateral diplomacy.

What he had learned working in the former Soviet states paid great dividends in Iraq. In his first inspection, he noticed that *Volga* missiles' engines – which Iraq claimed had been indigenously produced – were in fact made in Russia. As at other steps in his career, he picked up life-long lessons and friends at UNMOVIC. Former fellow inspector Charles Duelfer has characterised Elleman 'as one of the fraternity of arms control experts and practitioners who really understood the relationship between ideals, technology, and practicalities of verification'.

After the US-led invasion obviated the UN mission in Iraq, Elleman resumed his focus on the dismantlement of obsolete Soviet arms. With the Washington-based consulting firm Booz Allen Hamilton, he carried out Cooperative Threat Reduction projects in Azerbaijan, Georgia, Kazakhstan and Russia, and for strategic-arms elimination, biological safety and security, and proliferation prevention.

After WMD were deemed absent from Iraq, Iran became America's new bête noire due to its development of nuclear-weapons-related technologies and the missiles to carry any such weapons. In 2009, I commissioned Elleman to contribute a chapter on missiles to an updated IISS strategic dossier about Iran's proliferation challenges. Putting his all into the task, he produced not one chapter but five, enough for an entire book on its own.[4]

The IISS then hired Mike outright to serve in its new office in Bahrain, where he provided ballast to the operation and mentorship to a mostly young staff. In addition to continuing his focus on Iran, he helped me produce a book about North Korea's security challenges.[5] This time, though, limited funding meant that we had to keep the missile section to a single long chapter. Mike typically had an overabundance of knowledge to contribute to the task at hand.

The proliferation challenges of Iran and North Korea became Mike's preoccupation during the last 12 years of his career. At the IISS, most recently as director of the Non-Proliferation and Nuclear Policy programme, he co-authored four books and wrote a hundred or so articles, op-eds and other analytical works on how to manage the risks posed by the spread of nuclear and missile technology.

Among Mike's significant contributions to the non-proliferation field was his 2017 investigation into why North Korea was able to achieve success in its first-ever test launches of intercontinental ballistic missiles. After detailed analysis of the data and interviewing former Soviet engineers, Mike concluded that North Korea had obtained cast-off Soviet-era RD-250 rocket engines, probably from the Yuzhmash missile factory in Dnipro, Ukraine, bordering the breakaway Donbas region. He found corroborating evidence about a Ukraine connection, but did not rule out the alternative possibility the leftover engines had simply been stored in Russian warehouses before North Korea acquired them. Mike's thesis, written up in a leading *New York Times* story, became an international cause célèbre.[6] Internet trolls attacked him mercilessly, going after his family as well, to the point that he found it prudent to quit social media. He never abandoned his hypothesis, however, or his intellectual integrity.

III

Without seeing Mike regularly, and usually even then, one would not have known of his health problems. The man was a three-time All-American swimmer at Berkeley in the late 1970s, and twice on the National Collegiate Athletic Association championship team. His high-school coach has called his inspired 200-metre freestyle win against a heavily favoured opponent, in which Mike clocked the fastest time in the event of the entire year and the second-fastest in history among US high-school swimmers, 'one of the greatest gifts in my lifetime'.[7] Mike retained a handsome vitality set off by an ever-present smile. Laps under the California sun, however, may have triggered the melanoma that struck him a few years ago. He defeated the cancer once, earning a clean bill of health from his doctors just last year. But the killer returned before Christmas, creating painful tumours throughout his body. Yet he kept working full time, up until early February, when he took sick leave for what he thought would be a few weeks. He passed away on 20 February at the age of 62, survived by his wife Tatyana (Tanya), ten-year-old son Nikita, mother Irene and brothers Daniel Jr (Hiromi) and Bruce.

The news prompted an overwhelming outpouring of tributes, praising his intelligence and expertise, his humour and humility, and his passion for work and family. Journalists referred to his willingness to share his knowledge and his knack for doing so in understandable terms. Foreign missions in Washington, to which he provided deeply informed insights to advance international understanding, were equally appreciative. Younger colleagues cherished his gift of mentorship. Treating everyone as his equal and intent on helping them grow professionally, he made junior staff feel respected and valued in whatever endeavour. Målfrid Braut-Hegghammer, a physicist at the University of Oslo, wrote that 'for a new generation of analysts, he made sure we had a seat at the table. We are bereft.'

Former NATO deputy secretary-general Rose Gottemoeller called Elleman 'a national treasure in his deep knowledge of missile programmes across the world and a heck of a nice guy'. Siegfried Hecker, senior fellow emeritus at Stanford University, noted that 'Mike was discerning and collegial, unfailingly gracious and generous, and always friendly and unpretentious, and I would add he was the consummate professional. One could always rely on Mike for the unvarnished truth.' Former Ambassador to Russia Michael McFaul, also at Stanford, called Elleman 'a dedicated patriot, but also a citizen of the world, who truly believed in the mission of making our planet a safer place'.

Scott Sagan of CISAC offered a closing memory: 'Mike was a man with many interests and great knowledge about all of them. I recall one evening when we went to a San Francisco Giants baseball game together, and in between innings, he explained to me how to assess Iraqi missile accuracy, the differences between left bank and right bank Bordeaux blends, and the qualities of a beautiful Heriz carpet. When he left the seats to go get something to eat, a neighbouring fan who must have been listening in to our conversation, tapped me on the shoulder and asked, "Who is that guy?" I just said, "My friend, Mike Elleman".'

For someone with such refined tastes, he had little interest in the aesthetics of his office space. Adorning the walls was always something to get around to later. But a few months before his death, he proudly mounted a black and white photo of the inside of a main booster engine for the *Saturn* V – the tallest, heaviest and most powerful rocket in history, used by NASA for all of the *Apollo* manned space launches. To quote from an email he sent to the photographer: 'it illustrates quite dramatically two of the most important technology developments that advanced American rocketry: the use of cooling tubes to construct the combustion chamber and exit nozzle rather than a double-walled metal shell; and, the insertion of baffles on the injector plate to disrupt and attenuate the effects of combustion instabilities that impact all large, liquid-fuel rocket engines.' As his business card once simply stated, Mike Elleman was a 'rocket scientist'. Missiles were his life.

Notes

[1] David E. Hoffman, *The Dead Hand: The Untold Story of the Cold War Arms Race and Its Dangerous Legacy* (New York: Doubleday, 2009).

[2] See, for example, America's National Churchill Museum, 'Winston Churchill and the Cold War', https://www. nationalchurchillmuseum.org/winston-churchill-and-the-cold-war.html.

[3] CISAC's full name changed to Center for International Security and Cooperation in 1998.

[4] See IISS, *Iran's Ballistic Missile Capabilities: A Net Assessment* (London: International Institute for Strategic Studies, 2010).

[5] IISS, *North Korean Security Challenges: A Net Assessment* (London: International Institute for Strategic Studies, 2011).

[6] William J. Broad and David E. Sanger, 'North Korea's Missile Success Is Linked to Ukrainian Plant, Investigators Say', *New York Times*, 14 August 2017, https://www.nytimes. com/2017/08/14/world/asia/north-korea-missiles-ukraine-factory.html.

[7] See Burt Kanner, 'The Big Swim', Burt Kanner's Memories, 18 May 2017, https://burtsmemories. com/2017/05/18/the-big-swim/.

Correction

Article title: Rebel with a Cause
Author: Russell Crandall
Journal: *Survival*
Bibliometrics: Volume 63, Number 2, pages 171–180
DOI: https://doi.org/10.1080/00396338.2021.1906002

When this article was first published online, the fifth sentence of the third full paragraph on page 172 read as follows:

Adam Clayton – one of just two African Americans serving in the US House of Representatives – arrived in Cuba in early 1959 and joined Castro at a massive rally in Havana, where the congressman sang the praises of El Comandante's new policies.

This has now been corrected to read:

Adam Clayton Powell, Jr – one of just two African Americans serving in the US House of Representatives – arrived in Cuba in early 1959 and joined Castro at a massive rally in Havana, where the congressman sang the praises of El Comandante's new policies.

This correction has been made to the online article.

Printed and bound by CPI Group (UK) Ltd, Croydon, CR0 4YY

13/11/2024

01788266-0007